A MYSTICISM OF KINDNESS

THE BIOGRAPHY OF
"LUCIE CHRISTINE"

A Mysticism of Kindness

The Biography of "Lucie Christine"

Astrid M. O'Brien

University of Scranton Press

Scranton and London

Library of Congress Cataloging-in-Publication Data

O'Brien, Astrid M.
 A mysticism of kindness : the Lucie Christine story / Astrid M. O'Brien.
    p. cm.
 Includes bibliographical references (p.   ).
 ISBN 978-1-58966-206-3 (pbk.)
 1. Lucie Christine, 1844-1908. 2. Catholic women--France--Biography.
3. Women mystics--France--Biography. 4. Catholics--France--Biography.
5. Mystics--France--Biography. I. Title.
 BX4705.L7957O27 2010
 282.092--dc22
 [B]

                                                                2010044692

Distribution:
University of Scranton Press
Chicago Distribution Center
11030 S. Langley
Chicago, IL 60628

PRINTED IN THE UNITED STATES OF AMERICA

J'ai cherché comment faire mieux aimer Dieu aux âmes. Comment les porter à lui, les persuader qu'Il est au-dessus de tout bien, comment leur laisser transparaître cette Suavité, cette Douceur, cette Paix inénarrable, ce mystère, ce Tout qui se révèle à l'âme sans qu'elle le puisse dire ; comment obéir à l'Esprit Saint, à ce feu que je sens dans mon âme et qui veut se donner, se répandre. Comment le communiquer à toutes les âmes que touche mon âme; et je n'ai pas trouvé d'autre moyen, de plus puissant que la bonté.

I have sought how to make souls love God better. How to bring them to him, persuade them that he is above any good, how to illuminate for them this sweetness, this wondrous peace, this mystery, this all which reveals itself to the soul without the soul being able to say how; how to obey the Holy Spirit, this fire that I feel in my soul and which wishes to give of itself, to extend itself. How to communicate this to all those souls that touch my soul; and I have found no other means more powerful than kindness.

Mathilde Boutle

CONTENTS

Preface: Janet Ruffing, RSM — ix

Acknowledgments — xv

Note on the Translation — xvii

Chronology: Contemporaneous French History — xix
    and Mathilde's Life

Introduction — 1

Chapter One: A Parisian Childhood, 1844–1865 — 3

Chapter Two: A Woman of Her Times, 1865–1873 — 17

Chapter Three: A New Life, 1873–1879 — 25

Chapter Four: A Wise Guide, 1879 — 35

Chapter Five: Adoration Réparatrice, Founded in 1854 — 53

Chapter Six: Divine Education, 1881–1882 — 67

Chapter Seven: A Veiled Ostensorium, 1882–1884 — 89

Chapter Eight: A Battered Wife, 1885 — 111

Chapter Nine: Illness and Death of Thomas, 1885–1887 — 125

Chapter Ten: The Harvest Years, 1888–1894 — 151

Chapter Eleven: From Darkness to Light, 1894–1908 — 175

Afterword   193

Notes   199

Bibliography   225

Index   231

PREFACE

ithin the history of Roman Catholicism, for rather complex reasons, we are only now, a hundred or more years after the fact, slowly learning about the development of lay spirituality, especially for married women, that preceded and led up to Vatican II. During the nineteenth century in France, and (I would assume) elsewhere in Europe, there remain the untold stories of countless married women who, through the ordinary sacramental life of the Church and various religious movements supporting the development of women's spiritual lives, discovered through their mystical experiences a profoundly transformative life. This was despite the sexist civil and ecclesial institution of marriage and the limits placed on female education that circumscribed their choices and defined the context of their lives. Astrid O'Brien begins to fill this historical lacuna with her biography of Mathilde Boutle, whom some English-speaking and French readers met through Jesuit Auguste Poulain's publication of her spiritual journal—under the pseudonym of Lucie Christine—in the first decade of the twentieth century in French, and by 1915 in English.

Poulain had, of course, been involved at that time in the scholarly debates about whether or not mystical experience was for the very few or for the many—including laity—who led lives of prayer. He secured the permission of Mathilde's family to publish excerpts from her handwritten journals under the title, *Journal spirituel de Lucie Christine* (Light of Christ). His choice of passages aptly served to illustrate his descriptions of the mystic state as it progressed from the prayer of quiet to full transforming mystical union. Because so many family members were alive at the time, no details about Mathilde's life were given, and hence, the context for interpreting her many mystical experiences, including visionary ones, was missing. In the end, Vatican II endorsed Poulain's position in the 1960s— namely, that among people who prayed, laity as well as religious, many could be expected to experience the "presence of God," the defining character of contemplative prayer and mysticism. That surely means there are many more untold stories of lay women's spiritual lives of which

ix

Mathilde's is one, as was Elisabeth Leseur's, another French laywoman who was born twenty-two years later and also left a hidden journal that was published in French in the second decade of the twentieth century—and whose husband wrote her biography.

Astrid O'Brien has ably contributed to filling that void by telling Mathilde Boutle's story and contextualizing it in relationship to the dramatic changes going on in French civil and church culture with the rise of the very anticlerical political pressure of the Third Republic and the Church's response to it which shaped many of the spiritual influences related to reparation to the Sacred Heart for the godlessness of the new regime. Sacré-Coeur was built as a result of this fervor during Mathilde's lifetime, and we can see the influences on her of prayer before the Blessed Sacrament in reparation for the sins of the nation.

This biography, however, draws a more intimate portrait of Mathilde's particular challenges: an arranged marriage to a husband orphaned as a young child who never managed to separate emotionally from his foster mother, her mother-in-law's constant criticism, the demands of raising five children with great creativity, and her surviving a marriage that became increasingly verbally and physically abusive because of her husband's addiction to absinthe. Mathilde's upper-middle-class status also offered her some advantages. She managed a complicated intergenerational household with the help of servants, and she demonstrated great creativity in the way she personally cared for her own children. She supervised their education and planned elaborate entertainments, travel, and other enriching experiences during the summer holidays, writing and producing plays with them. Her social position required an active social life in the community. In short, her life was full of activities, responsibilities, and harsh challenge. When she had the first mystical experience she describes in her journal, she already had a habit of meditation and frequently participated in the Eucharist. Evelyn Underhill uses Lucie Christine's account as an illustration of a mystical awakening that effects a conversion to a whole new way of life; Lucie was shown by God how she could live in the world and belong entirely to God alone. With this vision, God was also giving her the means for carrying it out.[1] This deepening of an already devout life into a mystical life had to be possible whether or not she knew the current theories; God was clearly showing her the way. All the suffering from illness, loss of her sight, the verbal and physical abuse—all became means in God's hands for her growth and transformation. Unable to change her circumstances, she responded with great courage and became one with the God whose presence she felt and whose love supported and strengthened her. As writers like Wendy Wright have made clear in the twentieth century, family life can be a profound path of holiness. Today, a woman suffering the particular kinds of domestic abuse that Mathilde experienced would be encouraged by spiritual directors, clergy, and social workers to leave the marriage; Mathilde could not. Although such suffering can be and usually is traumatizing and destructive, in Mathilde's case, God used it to draw her closer to God's self.

Although this volume proposes to be a biography, in many ways it is also a spiritual biography—in French, often titled *Une Vie Spirituelle* (an account of a spiritual life)—because there are more concrete details available about Mathilde's spiritual life through her notebooks than about the rest of her day-to-day life in all its particulars. As a specialist in spirituality, I longed to read more details of Mathilde's visionary experiences. Journals are by nature, often repetitious, especially when written for a spiritual director who most likely already knows the details of daily life and the cast of characters. The visionary material cited shows a loving God who comforts, who embraces, who calls, who prepares, who perhaps repairs some of the psychological damage inflicted on Mathilde from her husband, her mother-in-law, and even from perhaps a form of piety that could lead to harsh self-judgments. And yet, we can see Mathilde's own responses through her graced life lead her back to kindness. She chooses to live a hidden life with God, within her family, attracting them to a kind of fullness of life that included the beauty and serenity of nature, the arts of music and drama, and a loving God full of kindness that she mediated within her family.

Finally, Mathilde's consecration as an *agrégée*—a secular member—of the Adoration Réparatrice Community ably demonstrates the mutual support that religious sisters and lay women can offer one another. An innovation in its own day, we have seen such formal associations of lay women and religious women flourish in the late twentieth and early twenty-first century to the advantage of both. The spiritual program laid out for the *agrégées* was extremely flexible, taking into account the responsibilities and circumstances of family life and envisioning the kind of adaptability required by mothers and wives. At the same time, the monthly retreat days provided safe female space and companionship for Mathilde that supported her growing life in God in deep and profound ways. In addition, Mathilde made use of classical spiritual direction with her parish priest to whom we owe the very existence of Mathilde's spiritual journal. Her story is relevant to lay women today who also seek out spiritual directors, make retreats, and join with religious women as associates or oblates as they forge a path of holiness as married women.

Mathilde's life seemed to be so active that except for slipping away in the early morning to daily Mass whenever possible, or throughout the day turning inwardly to God dwelling within her, or glancing at a church tower and "adoring him in the Blessed Sacrament", she had little time for reading classical mystical texts. Thus, the language she uses to describe her experience is often relatively unaffected by the mystical texts or the technical language of French mysticism. It is only through conversations with her spiritual director that she learns there are names for the experiences she is already having. Thus, her accounts of her mystical life are inviting and accessible. Although few of her visions are cited, the "words" she hears, and her felt sense of God usually seem to strengthen her and support her, encouraging her to turn toward God and not be overly distressed by the extremely distressful treatment she received.

Evelyn Underhill again draws on a few quotations from Lucie Christine to illustrate features of the Dark Night of the Soul as described by John of the Cross. She talks about this dark-night experience as a time of "things having gone wrong" for a mystic who has previously enjoyed the consoling and uplifting experience of God. Ian Matthew, in his brilliant descriptions of John of the Cross's teaching on the Dark Night, asserts that any pain that comes into a person's life can be used by God to make room for a deeper gift of God's self to the person. Mathilde's own words show this over and over again. Despite her many profound mystical experiences, her world continues to unravel through her husband's abuse and final illness, through her own failing eyesight that deprives her of the beauty that so drew her to God, and through the events of inner confusion or turmoil. Matthew says, "That is what turns pain into night: grieve, address what can be addressed, do not condone the sin that may be causing the situation, but trust that the Father holds this situation in his hands and will turn it to blessing."[2] These are movements we see over and over again in Mathilde's suffering—caused either by her family circle or from bereavement, loss, and illness. These adversities can all become grace when responded to in such a way that opens more and more room for God to transform the self and fill her with God's self. The great gift of this volume is the glimpse it offers into the depths of Mathilde's experiences of God, both the consoling, life-changing illuminations and the periods of darkness and suffering—all of which take place within the context of marriage, children, business affairs, and all the other normal experiences of illness and bereavement that are part of life.

Janet K. Ruffing, RSM
Professor in the Practice of Spirituality
and Ministerial Leadership
Yale University Divinity School

ACKNOWLEDGMENTS

When one has been working on a manuscript for ten years, the list of those who have aided in the research may be very long indeed. My debt, first of all, is to Mathilde Boutle herself, for her fidelity in keeping her journal, and for the inspiration I have found in it. No less do I owe to her daughter, Melanie Boutle Le Touzé, for having preserved her mother's journal and delivered it to L'Institute de L'Adoration Réparatrice (the official title of the community in Paris of which Mathilde had become a secular member), as well as to the community itself for having recognized its value, given Auguste Poulain, S.J., access to it, and permitted me, almost ninety years later, to photograph it in its entirety in order to write her story. My gratitude to Alain Le Touzé I have expressed in the dedication; his assistance was inestimable, and some of the photographs included here were due to his having taken me to see the places important in his great-grandmother's life.

There are two others, however, who from the beginning both encouraged me and aided me in my research: Rev. Philip Sandstrom and Sister Cecilia, A.R. Dr. Sandstrom made the first contacts with Adoration Réparatrice for me, introduced me to Paris, and made many helpful suggestions for research. Sister Cecilia not only helped me gain the trust of the community and arranged for me to meet Mathilde's great-grandson, but searched the archives for relevant material, including letters not available elsewhere.

Dr. Rosemary Wakeman, of Fordham's History Department, was most generous in suggesting background material on the cultural, political, social, and religious history of France in the nineteenth century, and Dr. Susan Ray, of Fordham's Department of Modern Languages, provided me with a beautifully readable translation of Rev. Romano Guardini's introduction to his German translation of Poulain's edition of Lucie Christine's Spiritual Journal. Dr. Marie Paula Holdman, S.C., of the College of Mount St. Vincent did the same with J. Zahn's appreciative description of it in *Theologische Revue.*

A research grant from Fordham University allowed me to spend a summer at the monastery in Paris photographing the journal, and Rev. Nicholas Lombardi, S.J., took time to explain the technological equipment I would need. A faculty fellowship for the academic year 2006–2007 and a bequest from the estate of Jacqueline Aron gave me the opportunity to devote myself to writing. The research librarians at Fordham's Quinn and Walsh libraries aided my work by locating articles in obscure journals and obtaining out of print books through interlibrary loan with consummate skill and patience. Kevin Burns, an editor based in Canada with a particular interest in works of this type, gave me some very good advice by email early in the writing process, and Dr. Thomas Nevin of John Carroll University emailed me strong support when I was discouraged by rejections from publishers who feared to lose money on a book about an unknown mystic by an even more unknown author. Jo Anne Fordham, Medical and Scientific Writer, Mississippi Medical Center in Jackson and consultant at Boston Medical Center, as well as a dear friend, read every word of the manuscript, making sure that I was not presuming too much on my prospective readers' background knowledge of either nineteenth-century France, or mystical experience. Thanks to her insight, what I meant to communicate is much clearer.

Jeffrey Gainey, Director of the University of Scranton Press, was willing to risk publishing a book on an almost unknown mystic, and provided guidance during the writing process; I am deeply grateful for his interest in bringing the witness of Mathilde's life to a wider public. John Hunckler, the manuscript editor, provided astute comments which greatly improved the narrative. My colleagues, Professors Laura Greeney and Robert Wasserman, gave me greatly appreciated last-minute help in reformulating the citations and the bibliography. Lindsay Karp, Instructional Technologist at Fordham, assisted in the preparation of the data DVD and photographs with generosity and patience.

What sustained me during the long writing process was the love and encouragement of my husband, Dr. Robert C. O'Brien. His belief in me, and his patience and willingness to assist me in every way he could inspired me to approach one publisher after another. To him, especially, my deepest thanks.

A NOTE ON THE TRANSLATION

Translating from French into English is a challenge; this is especially true of Mathilde's French, which is so expressive and filled with illuminative comparisons. The English translation of Poulain's French edition has not always been helpful to me. It was completed in 1915 and sounds stilted to us today. Mathilde and the three divine persons used the second-person singular in addressing each other. We no longer use the English corresponding to this form (*thee, thou, thy,* and *thine*), so I have not used them. Nor have I capitalized the personal pronouns referring to God as Mathilde did; Téqui's 1999 edition of her spiritual journal doesn't do so either. Mathilde uses *âme* (literally, soul) very frequently, in accord with the language of her time; I have tried to avoid the dualism this could suggest by translating it as "spirit' or "person," depending on the context. Where a literal translation did not seem to convey her meaning, I have tried to capture the sense of her words, even when this involved using English words not found in her French.

The best available source is the Téqui edition mentioned above. Her original notebooks have never been transcribed or published, nor have any of the materials regarding Mathilde in the archives of the Institute of Adoration Réparatrice. The family's personal records have never been published.

Almost all the articles written on Lucie Christine, in both French and English, are based on Poulain's edition of her journal, thus they add no new information. The two exceptions are my own article, written after reading Alain Le Touzé's "Little Family Chronicle," and that of Rev. Bernhard Grom, S.J., who accessed my brief article, "Lucie Christine: Nineteenth-Century Wife, Mother, and Mystic"[1] in writing his "'Ich sprach zu Dir, ohn' alle Worte': Die Mystikerin Lucie Christine (1844–1908)."[2] Rev. Grom, who holds a PhD in the Psychology of Religion, found the spiritual development of "Lucie Christine" and her lucid account of it inspiring. His main concern was to show that her mystical experience was not due to being bipolar or any other psychological abnormality. Those interested in this aspect would do well to consult his fine article. There are a few minor discrepancies between his account and mine, due to his having had access only to Dr. Romano Guardini's 1921 German translation of her journal, which lacked the explanatory footnotes of the original French.[3]

Finally, logical but questionable determinations often arise in the reading and analysis of translations, commentaries, and interpretations of a mystic's writings. This caveat applies as well to the effort now before you. It is my hope that this biography will arouse the interest of specialists better qualified than I to investigate and evaluate Mathilde Boutle's contribution to mystical literature.

CHRONOLOGY:
CONTEMPORANEOUS FRENCH HISTORY AND MATHILDE'S LIFE

	CONTEMPORANEOUS FRENCH HISTORY*	MATHILDE'S LIFE (AND INFLUENCES)
1809		Birth of Théodelinde Dubouché
1814	Louis XVIII returns to power	
1815	Defeat of Napoleon at Waterloo	
1824	Charles X becomes king	
1830	Louis-Philippe becomes king	
1833		Dubouché family moves to Paris
1838		Marriage of Melanie Thévenin and Etienne Bellanger
		Marriage of Sara and James Boutle
1844		Birth of Mathilde Bertrand
1848	Revolt in Paris: Second Republic	Jesus asks Théo to found a new religious order
1849	Cholera epidemic	Deaths of Sara and James Boutle, leaving five orphans
1852	Napoleon III: Second Empire	
1859		Ordination of Eugène Grieu
1863		Death of Mother Marie-Thérèse, Théodelinde Dubouché
1865		Marriage of Mathilde Bertrand and Thomas Boutle, February 1
1866		Birth of Melanie Boutle
1868		Birth of Albert Boutle
1869		Boutle family moves to Gisors
1870	Napoleon III declares war on Prussia	Birth of Adolphe Boutle
	Franco–Prussian War, July 15	
	Napoleon III surrenders, September 1	
	The Third Republic is declared	

Contemporaneous French History*		Mathilde's Life (and Influences)
Siege of Paris, September 20 Surrender of Paris, January Revolt in Paris—the Commune, March 26 Defeat of the Commune, May 28	1871	
The Wallon Amendment, January Law permits Catholic universities	1873	Birth of Eugène Boutle Mathilde's first mystical experience, April 25
Republican election victories	1874	The Boutle family moves to Vernon Rev. Eugène Grieu appointed pastor at Vernon
Election of Pope Leo XIII	1875	Birth of Elisabeth Boutle
Encyclical *Aeterni Patris*	1876	
	1878	
	1879	Mathilde first consults Fr. Grieu Melanie Boutle confirmed
Expulsion of Jesuits Expulsion of religious congregations Law providing secondary education for girls Law providing free primary education Law providing compulsory, "lay" primary education	1880	Albert Boutle confirmed
	1881	Mathilde's first eye surgery
	1882	Fr. Grieu asks Mathilde to keep a journal Mathilde becomes an *agrégée*, December 8
Divorce legalized in France	1883	Eugène's First Communion Summer family tour in France; Albert ill in Paris
	1884	Melanie Bellanger buys house, Le Tréport Melanie Bellanger, Thomas, Albert, and Adolphe summer in London

Contemporaneous French History*		Mathilde's Life (and Influences)
Legislative elections, conservative gains		Mathilde and Melanie Boutle, with Mme. Bertrand go on pilgrimage to Lourdes, August 22–25
	1885	Thomas goes on pilgrimage to the Holy Land, March 13
		Death of Melanie Bellanger, March 28
		Thomas begins to drink heavily
		Thomas's first health crisis, August
Law to laicize the teaching profession	1886	Elisabeth's First Communion
First Catholic trade union	1887	Felix Bertrand hospitalized, July
		Death of Thomas, December 27
	1888	Mathilde vows perpetual chastity
		Mathilde moves to Paris with her mother to be near her father
Executive tries to reassure Catholics	1889	Death of Felix Bertrand, March
Leo XIII and Archbishop of Paris discuss conciliatory policies towards the State: the "Ralliement"		Paris Exposition
		Death of Elisabeth, November 27
	1890	Mathilde's twenty-fifth wedding anniversary, February 1
	1891	Marriage of Melanie and Léon Le Touzé, July
Encyclical *Rerum novarum* on social problems		Birth and Death of Elisabeth Le Touzé
	1892	Birth of Charles Le Touzé
Arrest of Dreyfus	1893	Le Touzé family "Grand Tour": France, Germany, and Italy

CONTEMPORANEOUS FRENCH HISTORY*

Year	Contemporaneous French History*	Mathilde's Life (and Influences)
1896	Ministry of Méline; tolerance toward the Church affirmed	Marriages of Eugène and Adolphe; Birth of Jacques, Eugène's son
1897		Birth of Yvonne, Adolphe's daughter
1898	Fall of Méline	Mathilde and Cecile's second pilgrimage to Lourdes
1899	Dreyfus pardoned	
1900		Mathilde began typing her journal
1901	Law on Associations: all religious orders to be authorized by parliament	Birth and death of William, Eugène's second son
1902	Legislative elections; victory of anticlericals; Parliamentary commission to examine proposals for separation of Church and State	
1903	Rejection of congregations' request for authorization	
1904	End of diplomatic relations between France and the Vatican	
1905	Promulgation of the Law of Separation of Church and State	
1906	Dreyfus declared innocent	
1907	Encyclical *Pascendi* against "Modernism"	Death of Mathilde's mother; Mathilde moves in with Melanie and Léon Le Touzé; Alexandrine Boutle sues for divorce
1908	Law on repairs to church buildings	Death of Eugéne Grieu, March 15; Death of Mathilde, April 17

* The French history here cited is based on McManners, *Church and State in France, 1870-1914.*

INTRODUCTION

T he time: April 13, 1908, Monday of Holy Week. The place: an upper-middle-class residence in Paris. The occasion: a family party. Yvonne Boutle has made her First Communion in the morning; it is also her eleventh birthday. The only one missing from the celebration is her beloved paternal grandmother. Mémé is not feeling well enough to join the rest of the family at the table.[1] At dessert time, the maid tells Yvonne that unfortunately the cake has not arrived; perhaps she could go to Mémé and ask what to do. The child does as suggested, and there on the bed is the "missing" cake, aglow with candles. Unable to come to the dinner, Yvonne's grandmother wanted at least to light the candles herself.[2]

This is a touching story—even more so when we learn that Mémé died only four days later. It is no wonder that Yvonne and the family remembered it. But surely nothing unusual; do not many families treasure such stories? But why should the life of a woman who died a hundred years ago, long before the information revolution, matter at all to us today? There are, I think, several reasons. On the surface, she seemed a very ordinary woman: a devoted wife, mother of five children, involved in the cultural and social activities common to women of her class, and affected by the political and religious conflicts raging in France during that time.

But in fact, she was not ordinary at all. She reached transforming union, the highest level of mystical prayer, not as a cloistered nun, but as a laywoman living in a conjugal relationship with her husband. Furthermore, she endured patiently much psychological abuse from both her husband and his foster mother, as well as physical abuse from her husband later while he drank himself into insanity and death. Contemporary studies of spousal abuse have underscored the emotional consequences suffered by abused women. And today no spiritual director would advise a woman to remain in such a destructive environment. She would be referred to a counselor, perhaps to a battered woman's shelter, she might even be asked to consider a divorce. She, however, had none of these options. Even divorce,

1

legalized in the Napoleonic Code,[3] then eliminated under Louis XVIII in 1816,[4] and not allowed by law again until 1884,[5] was not an alternative for this devoutly Catholic woman.

How was it that this woman manifested none of these long-term scars?

How did she come through such a marriage with so much courage and fidelity?

She continued to take care of her family, prevented her husband from bankrupting them (no easy thing at a time when Frenchwomen had no legal standing), and stayed sane. It is in her journal that we learn what, with two exceptions, none of her contemporaries, not even her family, knew: she was sustained by prayer and her trust in God's grace. (She always insisted that what was given to her was not due to any special merit on her part, and that God's grace is no less available to anyone else who seeks it than it was to her.)

Might her life have something to teach us who also live in a troubled and pressured period, who struggle to integrate our faith and our secular activities, and thus to find an ultimate meaning for our lives? It is this writer's belief that her witness may be a source of inspiration and courage for those today who seek to be responsible and contributing members of both their civil society and their faith communities—whatever their creed—for all believers in a transcendent, provident Absolute Being face a similar challenge today.

CHAPTER ONE:
A PARISIAN CHILDHOOD, 1844–1865

Paris at the beginning of the nineteenth century was a worn, wrecked, and exhausted city, with a serious lack of clean water and periodic flooding from the Seine. Armed robbers roamed the streets at night, inflation was rampant, and the country was bankrupt. It would fall to Napoleon to pull France, and especially Paris, out of the immediate chaos of the Revolution. Even if most of his reforms were motivated primarily by self-interest, they offered a real and lasting benefit to France. The engagement of the French with organized religion, particularly with Catholicism, was similarly fraught. The Revolution had inaugurated a "divorce" between Church and State, and although the French Republic offered its citizens secular festivals and official creeds as an alternative to traditional religious practices, the rift between the religious and the national identity of French people largely deepened throughout the post-Revolution period and the early years of the Napoleonic empire.[1]

Thus it is not surprising that a strong religious revival would soon follow. The Enlightenment had promised to free humans through reason, but rationalism had led, or so many thought, to the excesses of the Reign of Terror—and not least because the irrational forces in human nature had been ignored. Moreover, if reason had failed those who had risked everything in its service, what was left to turn to, but its opposite—faith? Typifying these feelings in 1815, Madame de Staël, famous for her dislike of Napoleon, is quoted as saying, "I do not know exactly what we must believe, but I believe that we must believe. The eighteenth century did nothing but deny. The human spirit lives by its beliefs. Acquire faith through Christianity, or through German philosophy, or merely through enthusiasm, but believe in something!"[2]

Aware of this turning to faith, Napoleon had the synagogues reopened, decreed that churches wrecked during the Revolution should be restored, and signed a Concordat with Pope Pius VII, thus bringing France back into the Roman Catholic fold. He restored the old calendar of twelve months, with all its religious festivals, reestablished the Sorbonne, suppressed during the Revolution because of its clerical orientation,[3] and established state secondary schools for boys.[4] Nevertheless, since "Napoleon regarded girls as 'mere machines to make children' who only needed to learn a sentimental and submissive piety,"[5] well educated women remained rare.

The Parisian infrastructure, in the meantime, continued to benefit from Napoleon's oversight. To alleviate flooding, he ordered the construction of the Quai d'Orsay, completed by1806. In 1808, he issued a decree to continue the quays; by 1812 they had been extended 3,000 meters along the banks of the Seine.[6] It was his idea to add a new wing to the Louvre (though this was only completed in 1852 by Napoleon III), and, beginning in 1803, he established in it Europe's largest art gallery, "to provide a permanent home for the many works of art he had stolen from the countries he had conquered and occupied."[7] It is also to Napoleon that Paris owes its present-day system of house numbering, with odd and even numbers on opposite sides of the street, and every street numbered from its position relative to the Seine.[8]

Of equal note, Napoleon remodeled the Constitution and gave France the Code bearing his name. It was voted through the legislature in 1804 and is still, for the most part, in force—although the section that makes women the property of their husbands, and children the property of their fathers, has been repealed. Under Napoleon, the economic and financial system was regulated, and the Banque de France was established.[9] Scholarship also suggests that, during this period, both peasants and the urban working classes seem to have been better fed than before 1789 or after 1815. This was thanks in part to strict government controls on grain exports and price levels.

For all these reasons, the French came to regard the Napoleonic period as one of relative prosperity and security.[10] With his final defeat in 1815, however, the monarchy was reestablished, and the brother of Louis XVI became king under the name Louis XVIII. This monarchy was a constitutional royalty, as France now had a charter that established a parliamentary regime. Louis was not a popular ruler, but a clever and cautious one, so that great disorders were avoided during his reign. He died in 1824, and was succeeded by his reactionary brother, Charles X, who lacked the prudence of Louis, was personally opposed to a constitutional monarchy, and tried to revoke several important reforms enacted during the Revolution, including freedom of the press.

Dissatisfactions grew until, on a stiflingly hot day in late July, rioting broke out in Paris. The July Revolution of 1830 saw liberal deputies calling for the abdication of Charles X and nominating Louis-Philippe, Duc d'Orléans, to succeed him.[11] Louis-Philippe did so in an era that could be called the reign of the middle class, bringing "to this new regime his business experience, his love of order and gain, a mixture of common sense and self-righteousness, and his pacific tastes."[12]

There were not a few who would have preferred a republic, however, and in February 1848, a new revolution broke out, sparked by two years of poor harvests (among other things). Louis-Phillippe abdicated, and a republic was proclaimed. The conflict between the middle class and the working people was not resolved, however, and in June a more serious riot broke out. Promises made by leaders of the Republic had not been kept, and Paris in the nineteenth century was intolerant of unsatisfactory leaders: "Every French head of state from 1824 to 1877—king, emperor, or president—was either overthrown by revolution or forced out of office."[13] Among those accidentally killed by the revolutionaries was the courageous archbishop, Msgr. Affre, who had been trying to mediate an end to the slaughter.[14] The 1848 revolt was violently suppressed, and 1,435 insurgents were ruthlessly shot by government forces.

As republicans became more and more anticlerical in France, the Church became more and more associated with the monarchy, in a relationship increasingly polemical on both sides. Under the Third Republic, this conflict was settled legally by the separation of Church and State, enacted in 1905. To this day, the relationship has not fully been resolved. Instead, the "division between Catholics and the Revolution remained one of the fundamental divides in French society and politics until well after the Second World War (and in some ways is still present)."[15]

Such was the Paris into which a woman—known only by a pseudonym for nearly a century—was born. Auguste Poulain, S.J., the editor of her spiritual journal, called her Lucie Christine (Light of Christ) because her family had expressly forbidden the publication of any identifying information. Even the existence of this journal was practically unknown to her descendants until 1942, when her son-in-law died. Among his effects, the family found a chest containing family mementos, including a reference to the journal. In the early 1990s, four great-grandsons approached the monastery to which the writer's daughter had given the journal at her mother's death; the men asked the nuns' permission to make use of it in writing a family history. Since, with the passage of so many years, the reasons for maintaining secrecy seemed no longer relevant, the nuns agreed.[16] They were even more generous when this author approached them in 1998; they arranged a meeting with Alain Le Touzé, who graciously provided a copy of the "Little Family History." Both the nuns and the family gave their permission for the writing of a full biography.

Only now can the story of Lucie Christine's bravery, wisdom, love, and holiness be told using her own name, Mathilde Boutle, above her writings. She was born in Paris on February 12, 1844, and, six days later, was baptized Marie Marguerite Mathilde Constance in her parish church, St. Thomas d'Aquin. The family called her Mathilde. Her parents, Felix Louis Joseph Bertrand and Henriette Cécile Alexandrine Delaperche, were of the upper middle class. Her father was a clerk of the civil court of the Seine, and their home was on rue St. Thomas d'Aquin, on the Left Bank, in an area known as St. Germain des Près. Her godmother was her paternal grandmother, Olympe Bertrand, and her godfather, her maternal grandfather, Constant Delaperche.[17] Her maternal grandmother, Alexandrine, was the daughter of Hippolyte Alexandre, a notary and the mayor of La Roche Guyon,[18] a town northwest of Paris, founded in the twelfth century. Mathilde and her numerous cousins spent many happy summers at their great-grandparents' home.

She was four years old in 1848, when rioting broke out in Paris. The barricades and the fighting were in the eastern half of the city, however. The battle raged for three days, but did not spread further. St. Germain des Près was spared. But Mathilde's father's sister (Olympe) and her family were affected. Olympe's husband, Auguste Baudoux, was in the National Guard, and was called up to help restore order. He bid his wife and five little ones goodbye without knowing when, or whether, he would return. Olympe prayed fervently for his safety, and he returned unhurt after a few days.[19] Surely her brother and his wife must have been equally concerned and praying as well, though their two daughters, especially the younger, Elisabeth, who was only a year old, were probably not aware of the danger.

The following year saw a new crisis in Paris: cholera. It raged from March until October, 1849. Even though Olympe was pregnant, she did not hesitate to go out to church to worship God and to place the child she was carrying under the protection of the Blessed Virgin. Meeting her on the street one day, her doctor reproached her for her grave imprudence in thus exposing herself to contagion. She herself was not at all worried, considering such behavior altogether natural for one who lived by faith.[20]

We might well agree with the doctor today, but the spirituality of Olympe's era saw her action as a sign of devotion. In any case, it was in the poorest parts of the city, on the Right Bank of the Seine, that cholera took its greatest toll: what is now the eighth arrondissement lost 836 persons, that is, one out of every 126 inhabitants.[21]

Among those lost were the parents of Mathilde's future husband: Sarah and James Boutle, an English couple who had been married at the British Embassy in 1838. All that is known concerning them is that James was born in London, Sarah in Brighton; he could read and write, but she could not. They had neither wealth nor training. James worked first as a coachman, later as a domestic, Sarah as a domestic, later as a seamstress. According to Mathilde's granddaughter, Yvonne, James was Scottish, the son of a Protestant minister; Sarah was an Irish Catholic. Both had been rejected by their families because they married outside the religion in which they had been brought up.[22] The Boutles had five children: Thomas in 1839, Marie in 1841, Sarah in 1843, Catherine in 1844, and Henriette in 1847. Thus the eldest would have been ten, and the youngest only about eighteen months old, when both parents fell ill and died.[23]

Because the city had insufficient resources to provide for all children orphaned by the epidemic, it was necessary to appeal to charitable persons for assistance. Among those responding was Melanie Bellanger, wife of well-to-do Etienne Louis Victor Bellanger. The couple had been married in the same year as had Sarah and James, but were childless; both immediately assumed responsibility for Henriette, the youngest Boutle orphan. The four older children were to be placed in orphanages and provided with an appropriate education. In 1852, Melanie was widowed, and from then on she assumed greater interest in the older Boutle children as well. She seems to have felt so much affection for Thomas that she considered him her son, although she never legally adopted him. In fact, she was not able to do so. According to the Napoleonic code, adoptive parents had to be childless and fully fifty years old, beyond childbearing; Melanie was only 37 when widowed.[24] Thomas, in turn, regarded with unlimited tenderness and attachment the one whom for the rest of his life he called his mother.[25]

Melanie provided Thomas with an excellent Catholic education; he attended the same school as Charles de Cabanoux, Mathilde's first cousin. This was, technically, a minor seminary. Napoleon had given a monopoly of secondary education for boys to his Université, and the lycées and collèges established by it were mainly anticlerical and atheistic. Minor seminaries were thus the only legal way to establish Catholic secondary education. The Jesuits assumed control of eight of them, using them as a front to provide a high-quality secondary education for Catholic boys who did not necessarily have any intention of becoming priests.[26] Thomas seems to have followed a classical program; he studied rhetoric and Latin, earning high praise from his teachers.[27]

Mathilde, during these years, was living at home in Paris. Her formal education, as was customary for girls, ended in 1855—when she was eleven years old—with her First Communion. Poulain, was able to interview some of her friends, and so gives us a little information about Mathilde as a young girl. He reports that the priest who taught the catechism class in her parish church held her in singular esteem, commenting, "She is highly gifted, she will make her mark."[28] Mathilde's parents and grandparents on both sides were deeply committed, practicing Catholics. She drew in their good example with her first breath. Of her first cousins, eleven would later enter the Church, three priests and eight nuns.[29] Is it too much to suppose that, so influenced, she learned piety as naturally as she learned to speak?

Imbued with the teaching of her mother, she began to practice meditation early. She was only six when it occurred to her, while alone in her bed, to imagine Christ dead and pierced on the cross. She was stirred to anger at the cruel behavior of the centurion, but, on reflection, thinking that her sins had been even crueler than the lance of Longinus, she resolved never to sadden Jesus by a deliberate fault.[30] She had an instinctive tenderness towards the Mother of God, praying earnestly for the proclamation of the dogma of the Immaculate Conception, and rejoicing when her longing was fulfilled in 1854.[31] Reflecting later on her ability to remain recollected in the midst of noise, she recalled that as a child, she had loved saying her rosary silently while walking in the streets of Paris.[32] She had prayed since her childhood that God would do whatever he willed with her, as long as she was pleasing to him.[33]

Such precocious spiritual understanding is, unfortunately, uncommon, but to those who believe, not abnormal. Grace builds on nature, and besides her natural intellectual gifts, she was nurtured in an uncommonly devout environment. Writing about Thérèse of Lisieux, a younger contemporary, Thomas Nevin,[34] observes that Thérèse's "parents had prepared a kind of sacred ground for her by their rigorously pious lives: devout to the church, devoted to the children." The same might be said of Mathilde's parents. Another of her childhood friends wrote to Poulain that Mathilde "was almost the eldest sister of innumerable cousins with whom she was brought up in lively sentiments of faith and fraternal affection. About the year 1856, the year of her First Communion, for which she prepared herself in the most edifying manner, [Mathilde] began to appear quite grown up. . . . The older among us were struck by the astonishing intelligence and fervent piety of their beloved big sister and cousin; they remember it still."[35]

This same friend relates that, thereafter, Mathilde was put in charge of their amusements, because she "knew so well how to amuse us and upon occasion how to give us good advice." Once, during Passiontide, "she spoke to us with such love and tenderness about the sufferings of Our Lord that all her little audience were profoundly moved and burst into tears; [she] had hard work to console them afterwards."[36]

Although we have no autobiographical account of how Mathilde spent her day after leaving school, we do have a letter written by her Aunt Olympe. Given the family's status and the slow change of social customs associated with the upper middle class to which they belonged, it is reasonable to suppose that very little of importance had changed for girls between Olympe's adolescence and that of her niece. In 1828, Olympe responds as follows to a friend's inquiry as to her summer activities:

> You would like, my dear Ambroisne, for me to give you a detailed account of how I occupy myself. I assure you that it will not be very interesting, but I want, above all, to satisfy you. I get up at six o'clock, [and] say my prayers. Next, I go to Mass [;] afterwards I dress [my younger sister] Maria, and give her a reading lesson. The bell for lunch rings at ten o'clock; I have lunch: then I return to my room, and change into street clothes. Weather permitting, we stay outdoors from noon until five o'clock; otherwise we return to our work or I practice my piano [lesson]. At five o'clock, [we have] dinner, after which we visit one of our neighbors. We spend the evening there, or [else] one of them comes to [visit] us.[37]

Mathilde's summers with her many cousins at La Roche Guyon may well have been much livelier, especially since she was so good at planning their activities, but during the rest of the year, when she was with her parents and younger sister in Paris, she probably spent her time pretty much as her aunt had described some two decades earlier. Young ladies were

skilled at "sewing," which meant fine needlework, embroidery, and cro-
cheting, rather than dressmaking, which was done by seamstresses. It is
difficult to imagine that, in this environment, Mathilde would have been
knitting, given that activity's association with lower-class women, notably
the tricoteuses of the Revolution,[38] memorialized by Charles Dickens in *A
Tale of Two Cities*. Despite such secular associations, however, Sister
Solange Marie, A.R., a nun at the monastery in Paris, an older contemporary of Alain Le Touzé, and one born into an upper-middle-class family,
reported to Sister Cecilia, A.R., in 2008 that she remembered her grandmother knitting baby clothes for the poor.[39]

Poulain relates two quite unusual incidents from this period. In
1859, French armies were defending the Papal States against a takeover by
Italy's republicans. Two young men, one a relative and the other the son of
very close friends, were sent to the front. At first, news of them reached
their families regularly, but then a prolonged silence ensued. Of course,
everyone feared the worst. Shortly thereafter, each family received a letter,
"fastened with a pin," and written in pencil informing them that their young
man had escaped all danger and would soon return home. Although the
handwriting was unfamiliar, each bore the signature of the respective soldier. In fact, both did return speedily, but who had written the letters? It
was Mathilde who, having received an intuition of the truth, wished to relieve the family's anxiety, but also to hide her own share in the matter.
While out walking with her mother, she had dropped the letters and, pre-
tending that they had been lost by someone else, picked them up again, and
put them in the mail box. Her mother, however, was not fooled.[40]

An even more dramatic example of her intuition—one might actually call it clairvoyance—occurred a year later in the spring of 1860. The
infant son of a Parisian magistrate had been stolen. He had been taken outdoors by a newly hired nanny. She had been approached by an elegantly
dressed woman, who claimed to be the baby's aunt. The woman asked the
nurse to do an errand for her, saying that she would take care of the child
in the meantime. When the nurse came back, there was no sign of "aunt"
or infant. She returned home at once, thinking that she would find both
there already. But they never appeared. All efforts to discover the baby's
whereabouts ended in failure.

Then a letter appeared under the front door of Mathilde's family's
country house. It stated that the infant was not dead, and described in detail
where it might be found, who would be holding it, and in which wardrobe
the clothes the child had been wearing when stolen were hidden. The letter

was unsigned. Mathilde's family was greatly puzzled, but decided it would be unwise to ignore the letter. Accordingly, it was sent to the distracted parents, with the comment that, since it was not known from whom it came, there was no way to determine its veracity. When the information was investigated, the child was indeed found, exactly as described. Afterwards, Mathilde confided to her mother that, having received this information, she could find no better way to pass it on to the baby's family while keeping her identity a secret.[41]

What are we to make of such occurrences? As we will see, Mathilde was a very warm and loving person, full of concern and compassion for all who were suffering. Such telepathic experiences are known to occur between people who have a strong emotional bond, even apart from any deep spirituality. How much more so if one is committed to selfless service to others out of love for God?

Given this commitment, why, we may wonder, did Mathilde not enter a convent, as did her Aunt Caroline's two daughters, and all five of her Aunt Olympe's daughters? There are two documents in the archives of the monastery in Paris which indicate that she had considered the religious state, and had spoken of it to her confessor. No account as to why this interest was not pursued has been found, nor can we claim to guess one. But we do have the report of an 1829 discussion between Mathilde's maternal aunt, the as yet unmarried Olympe Bertrand, and *her* father.

Although Felix Bertrand had the right, according to the Napoleonic Code, to make whatever arrangements he pleased for his daughter's future, he did not wish to do so without her consent and approval. He set before her the two possibilities, the cloister or the world, and asked her to choose which one she preferred. She replied that she felt no inclination to the cloister and, professing complete respect for and submission to her parents' choice, willingly deferred to their desire that she marry Auguste Baudoux, whom they had selected because he was a member of the Sodality of the Blessed Virgin, the organization to which all the elite young men of the day belonged.[42]

When Mathilde grew up, there were other options. Adoration Réparatrice had been founded in Paris in 1854, and both of Mathilde's aunts, Caroline de Cabanoux and Olympe Baudoux had contact with Mère Marie-Thérèse, its foundress. In fact, Olympe later became an *agrégée* of Adoration Réparatrice herself. It was an order unique for its time. Although the nuns normally remained within the convent, they were not cloistered like the Carmelites. Their mission was perpetual Eucharistic adoration in a spirit of reparation, a mission which they sought to share with others, especially laypersons. The Little Sisters of the Poor had been founded in 1840, and there were others, called congregations, which looked after children, taught girls, and nursed the sick.[43] All of these orders, however, lacked the stability and security of the long established and recognized orders.

Thus, a father might well hesitate to entrust his daughter to such a community, as did Mathilde's uncle, Hector de Cabanoux, when Louise, his eldest daughter, expressed her desire to join Adoration Réparatrice in 1858. He asked that she wait a year, but gave tearful permission when the superior, although acknowledging his authority in deciding his daughter's future, stated that she did not believe that such a delay would be in conformity with the will of God.[44] Nor is it likely that a father would have suggested this community to his daughter as a possible choice. Perhaps the younger Felix Bertrand shared his father's and brother-in-law's hesitation in 1864, when his daughter Mathilde, who was twenty, acquiesced in his wish to see her securely settled financially?

We may shudder today at arranged marriages, but might consider that, in view of its high divorce rate, our own system seems less than perfect. Nineteenth-century French parents who loved their children and were not financially constrained would certainly have done all they could to make wise and prudent choices for them, with inquiries made among extended family and friends regarding suitable spouses. Among those Mathilde's parents consulted was her cousin, Charles de Cabanoux, who was four years older than she, and had been ordained in May 1864.[45] Charles remembered a former classmate, Thomas Boutle, well liked by both the teachers and other students, the foster son of a well-to-do widow highly respected because of her generosity to the poor. Charles's younger sister, Marguerite, later described the young Thomas as handsome, cheerful, intelligent, and witty, a pleasant companion and a practicing Catholic. He even had a good singing voice.[46]

Marriage, in nineteenth-century France, was understood as a social and, for some, a religious institution; the young woman and man need not have known each other at all before their respective parents chose them for each other. Nevin states that, during this period, money mattered far more to the French marriage than did love of any sort. Passion had little to do with domestic economy in those days. Young people of the same class and financially secure enough to afford children were deemed useful to the bourgeois family's interests. These families desired their offspring to be fruitful and multiply, and preferred that there be no differences over religion, for these played a substantial role in marital unhappiness. Among prevalent assumptions were these: "Anticlerical husbands tended to be distant, uncommunicative, bored, and perhaps resentful of a cleric's ascendance over their wives."[47] Physical intimacy was expected, but emotional intimacy was not. In fact, "a distance between husband and wife was scrupulously maintained."[48]

People did fall in love, but social class, family finances, and perhaps shared religious faith outweighed a young couple's feelings for each other. There is a very moving letter, included in the will of Albert Lenfant, the uncle of the young man who would become Mathilde's son-in-law, which demonstrates this very clearly. He had fallen in love with a young woman whom he describes as tenderhearted, simple, and upright, with tastes and aspirations like his own, a woman he loved with his whole heart and soul. She reciprocated his feelings completely. But Adrienne belonged to the working class, had no dowry, and "such are the prejudices of this world, and their power [that he] had the cowardice to fear the welcome she would get from his family if he were to marry her. She herself did not want to become part of his family without being certain of the unreserved affection of the family of her beloved." As Lenfant was reluctant to expose Adrienne to a reception which could cause her a great deal of unhappiness, they decided to postpone their union as long as Albert's sister and brother-in-law were still living. Ten years later, after both of Léon's parents had died, they planned to wed; the date chosen was May 10, 1890. Alas, Adrienne died on May 1.[49]

Contact between Mathilde's parents and Melanie Bellanger was arranged and the marriage agreed upon. It is very likely that neither Mathilde nor Thomas were opposed to it. We have no record concerning their feelings for each other at this point, but no one, themselves included, expected the bride and bridegroom to be in love with each other; this was not considered important. What we do know is that Mathilde came to love Thomas deeply; the evidence regarding Thomas's feelings is unclear. In view of his later behavior, we may suspect that he merely acquiesced in his foster mother's choice. Melanie, on her part, must have been delighted; it was a better match than that to which Thomas's humble birth entitled him. It would confirm beyond all doubt his upper-middle-class status. According to the custom of the time, there were three steps in the marriage process: first, the contract was signed; second, there was a civil ceremony; and finally, a religious ceremony was celebrated.

The contract was signed in the home of Madame Bellanger, 4 de la rue du Cirque, rather than in Mathilde's home, 42 de la rue Barbet de Jouy. Melanie stipulated that she would endow Thomas with the sum of fifty thousand francs in cash (the equivalent of one million francs in 1990). Further, Madame Bellanger had expressed and confirmed the intention of facilitating Thomas's study to become a lawyer; the exact grant would be determined later. This was pure benevolence on her part—a moral commitment, not a legal one.[50]

Besides her trousseau, the bride received from her parents the sum of twenty thousand francs, to be remitted once her husband became a notary or, at the latest, five years after their marriage, if he had not completed his studies. As a matter of fact, Thomas never did become a notary. According to Marguerite, he was bored with the preliminary studies and worked on his foster mother behind the scenes until he got her to agree to his abandoning them. He did not really need a profession; the money she had given him (and that which would come to him after her death) was quite adequate for his needs and those of his future family.[51] Mathilde deplored this decision, but was unable to persuade him to continue; until her mother-in-law's death, it was Mme. Bellanger who had the last word in all of Thomas's decisions.[52]

The civil marriage was celebrated on Tuesday, January 31, 1865, at the town hall of the seventh arrondissement, and the religious ceremony the next day at the Church of the Foreign Missionary Society on the rue du Bac, which then functioned as Mathilde's parish church. Her cousin Charles, ordained only nine months earlier and recently assigned to St. Thomas d'Aquin, was delegated by the pastor to receive the marriage vows of the young couple. It appears that Thomas's four sisters were not present for the religious ceremony, since their signatures were not among the 26 on the marriage certificate, although Henriette, the youngest, was present for the signing of the contract.[53] It would seem that, at least at this point, the girls were not considered fully part of the family.

Photographs taken at the time of their marriage show two young persons who lacked neither good looks nor refinement. Both are dressed according to the fashion of the time. Thomas is seated, wearing a checked vest and trousers, and a dark morning coat. His curly hair and sideburns are neatly combed. He holds his hat in his left hand, which rests on his crossed left knee. His right arm rests on a book lying on a small table beside him, and there is a walking stick in his right hand. His look is direct; his expression alert; he seems about to speak. Mathilde is standing slightly sideways, looking away from the camera. Her dark curly hair is combed back off her face, and appears to be caught in a net. She is wearing a rather elaborate dark dress, with long sleeves and a very full floor-length skirt. Her left arm is bent; her hand rests on a small stand; her right arm is at her side. Her expression is calm, but not especially revealing. What is most noticeable is a sort of inner repose and stillness. And indeed, it is not easy to describe her personality. Her great-grandson says that, because of her exceptional spiritual gifts, she appears as a privileged being, whose reputation [since the publication of Poulain's book] has surpassed her family context, even that of her country.[54] Mathilde's cousin Marguerite, who had known her since their childhood and became Mathilde's confidante and support during her difficult marriage, wrote that Mathilde was, by nature and by temperament, very gentle and calm. She never responded in kind to a harsh word or to rude behavior. Within the family, her gentleness was proverbial. She was not physically strong, and in other circumstances might have been rather weak and passive. Grace, said Marguerite, enabled her to grow strong through what she suffered.[55] Certainly, grace sustained her, but grace builds on nature, and Mathilde's descriptions of both the natural world and her religious experiences show her to have been a very ardent woman, with a deep capacity for love.

Suffering can defeat, even harden and embitter a person. Love, on the other hand, can transform suffering, and mystical experience can strengthen love so much that no amount of suffering can defeat it. With due respect to Marguerite's views, we may still suspect that it was Mathilde's great love, not primarily her suffering, that grace strengthened, enabling her to persevere and ultimately bypass the submissiveness inculcated in her by the male-dominated culture of the period. Over time, she would develop the "manly" courage and self-confidence needed to withstand personal abuse and protect her children while continuing to pray for—and to love—those who caused her so much pain.[56]

In her youth, Mathilde became an accomplished pianist; when grown up, she was often asked to play for her family and friends. The clarity and precision of her prose, especially in the difficult context of describing her mystical experiences, make it clear that Mathilde was highly intelligent. She seems also to have had a lively and creative imagination, as she endlessly devised ways to amuse young audiences and players—first her cousins, and later, her children—with theatrical productions during school vacations. Many years later, Mathilde remembers herself as a young girl and woman:

Everything beautiful fascinated and fired my soul with enthusiasm. The first glimpse of the sea from the cliffs drew tears to
my eyes. I often remained whole hours contemplating [it] without being able to express what I felt, and I was rebuked for my
long silences. Music was a veritable passion with me; reading
even more so, and for them I committed many follies in secret;
neither was I weary of admiring the masterpieces of great
painters although I had no talent for painting myself. I could not
express ardently enough the feeling with which all beauty inflamed my imagination. . . . I gave myself up to [these feelings]
with all the power of my will.[57]

CHAPTER TWO:
A WOMAN OF HER TIMES, 1865–1873

After their marriage, Mathilde and Thomas settled with Melanie in Meulan, a community about thirty kilometers northwest of the center of Paris. In the census of 1866, they were listed as residing with her, along with Thomas's eighteen-year-old sister, Henriette, and three domestics. On October 31, 1866, the Boutle's first child, a daughter, was born. She was named Marie Cécile Melanie and was called, as a sign of respect and affection, Melanie, after Thomas's foster mother, who was also chosen as her godmother. In 1868, Mathilde gave birth to a second child, a boy, whom they named Albert. And a year later, in 1869, the young couple and their two little children moved to Gisors, about sixty kilometers northwest of Paris.

Alain Le Touzé, Mathilde's great-grandson, wonders whether this was motivated by the need for more space (a second son, Adolphe, was born on January 21, 1870), by a desire to distance themselves from Thomas's foster mother's dominating influence, or both.[1] Melanie was indeed dominating; Marguerite describes her as authoritarian and intransigent, even though she doted on Thomas.[2] Marguerite was three years younger than Mathilde. She did not enter Adoration Réparatrice until 1868, when she was twenty-one, so she had at least three years to observe both Melanie and Thomas. It must have been during this period that Marguerite first perceived the behavior she later described as Melanie's habit of criticism and stinging jokes, in which Thomas seems to have joined.[3]

Meanwhile in Paris, trouble was brewing again. In 1851, Louis-Napoleon, Napoleon's nephew, had overthrown the Second Republic and established the Second Empire as Napoleon III.[4] His domestic policy would be credited by many with giving France some of the happiest years in her history. The peasants were helped by large-scale public works and improved credit facilities, the workers, by far-reaching social legislation and public housing. More than any other statesman of his time, Louis-Napoleon realized the importance and implications of modern industrialization and did his best to create conditions favorable to its growth. French railway mileage increased more than fivefold during the 1850s alone. He permitted the formation of "limited liability" companies, which protected stockholders and made investment less risky, and in a series of commercial agreements, abandoned the traditional protectionism of France in favor of moderate free trade. As a result, French exports soon exceeded imports. All of this enriched the middle class.[5]

Moreover, Napoleon III was instrumental in transforming Paris. Under his authority, Haussmann was given the freedom and resources to tear down structures that had been in existence since medieval times in order to build the Paris we know today. The center of the city was completely rebuilt—with wide boulevards, stately squares, and lovely parks—as a symbol of the Empire's prosperity and splendor. Although this urban renewal program aided the workers by providing employment and eradicating ugly slums, it also did away with the breeding grounds of revolution. The wide avenues made erecting barricades much more difficult, and permitted the use of cavalry and artillery in case there should be another popular uprising.[6]

Despite the perspicacity of many of Napoleon III's domestic reforms, however, "his foreign policy [showed] an unerring instinct for doing the wrong thing, causing domestic discontent."[7] The divisions which had emerged in 1848 between republicans committed to political reform and those favoring broader social change were exacerbated by the development of a virulent hostility towards all middle-class republicans, who were increasingly seen as "belonging to 'the obese bourgeois democracy . . . which had shot down the people' in 1848 . . . [so that] a substantial amount of support for violent revolution was building up."[8] Polemics between these groups became increasingly bitter, and tracts favoring socialism and communism became common (Marx's *Communist Manifesto* had been published in 1848). To counter the possibility of a domestic uprising, "the government, in time-honored fashion, would be only too ready to seek the distraction of a foreign adventure. In the summer of 1870, it came."[9]

The throne of Spain had been vacant for two years, and Bismarck, the Prussian Chancellor, suggested a German prince, Leopold. The possibility of German princes on the Pyrenees frontier, as well as on the Rhine, alarmed France so much that Leopold's candidacy was withdrawn. France, however, wanted more: a guarantee that his candidacy would not be revived. Bismarck also wanted more: the bonding together of the German federation into a unified nation, dominated by Prussia. He judged that a war with France would enable him to achieve this, and "had his ear well tuned to the prevailing tone in Paris."[10]

King Wilhelm refused to give the French Ambassador, Count Vincent Benedetti, a guarantee, and a telegram reporting on the interview—the famous Ems telegram—was sent to Bismarck. Before passing it on to the press, Bismarck sharpened its emphasis. This so enraged Paris that Napoleon III, urged on by the press and even his own wife, declared war on Prussia on July 15, 1870. The French mobilization was chaotic, and disaster followed disaster at the front. On September 1, "a sick and defeated Napoleon III surrendered to King Wilhelm at the head of his army in Sedan."[11] Thus ended a war begun "with little reflection, much patriotic fervor, and bold predictions of triumph."[12]

The republicans saw Louis-Napoleon's defeat as their great opportunity. The end of the Empire was proclaimed, and a new Republic was formed with General Trochu as president. It was assumed that the victorious Prussians would return home and leave France alone. But Bismarck had his own agenda, and the German press was shrieking for the destruction of Paris. Supplies of food, fuel, and ammunition were stored in case of a siege,[13] and those who had a residence or family in the suburbs left the city. Among these were Mathilde's aunt and uncle, Caroline and Hector de Cabanoux; in fact, the entire family left, except for Charles.[14]

On September 20, the siege began, and Paris was cut off from the rest of France.[15] For the first two months, things in Paris were not too bad: a provisional government was set up in Tours, new French armies prepared to attack the Prussians from without, and the Paris garrison prepared to break out of the city at the same time so as to seize the occupying army in a deadly vice.

Unfortunately, the only way to get messages out was by balloon; these were soon taking off at the rate of two or three a week, and included the mail. But the direction of their flight was unpredictable and uncontrollable. And as balloons offered only a one-way method for communicating, a sender could not be sure that a vital message had been received. Pigeons were tried, but of the 302 sent, only 59 reached Paris. Trochu sent a dispatch to Tours, setting November 29 as the day for the breakout, but the balloon carrying it landed in Norway, reaching Tours too late for the forces there to attack as planned. With the failure of the sortie intended to break the siege, morale in Paris plummeted, and hunger and bitter cold added to the general depression.[16]

On December 8, Charles, who had stayed at St. Thomas d'Aquin to serve his congregation and others in need of a priest, wrote to his parents that provisions were not lacking, although it was hard to cook. He inventoried available staples as follows: "no butter, no eggs, no dairy products, very little fresh meat, lots of cured (that is, salted) meat, rationed in small amounts, dried beans when one can find them, prepared in grease, and what grease! On the other hand, plenty of bread, coffee, wine, chocolate, sugar, pastries, pasta, liqueurs."[17] Charles added that he had made use of the jars of jam in his parents' empty apartment "without scruple." At the end of the month, wishing his parents—for the first time ever—a Happy New Year by mail, he recalled the New Year celebration of the previous year, when the entire family had been together, little dreaming of what would come: "What a dream, what a nightmare, what a frightful reality!"[18] He longed for peace, but accepted God's will.

On January 5, 1871, the Prussians began bombarding the forts and the civil population. The shells did not do a great deal of harm to the infrastructure, though some residents were killed. The bombardment ended because it outraged the rest of Europe.[19] Charles wrote that provisions were growing scarce, observing "we will keep a [Lenten] fast that will count!" They were eating "horse, donkey, mule (excellent), cat, dog, and brown bread." On the other hand, "religion is held in higher regard than ever before, thanks to the chaplains and the brothers who are everywhere, in the ambulances, on the battlefield, at the forts and the outposts."[20]

Although Mathilde, at 27, and her family in Gisors were spared the suffering of the Parisians, she was not oblivious to it. In a notebook into which she occasionally entered her reflections after Communion, she, too, marked the crisis:

> France is very low. . . . My heart bleeds within me when I hear the tale of her humiliations and miseries! I had not felt before how strong the sentiment of patriotism is. . . . I climbed to the top of our old grotto. . . . The sun was shining today as though it wished to console us. But below it, gloomy mists spread like a funereal veil; it seemed to me as though all the tears wrung from my poor country were mounting to Heaven to form these sad clouds; mine also fell at the remembrance of all who are suffering in France; I prayed for them, for us all, poor children of this dishonored land, and I came down again with my heart a little consoled but still very sad.[21]

Until the day of her death, Mathilde remained loyal to her country. However much she might deplore the anti-Catholicism of the Third Republic, she prayed frequently for the salvation of her nation and all its citizens. The proletariat, furious with what they saw as the ineptitude of the bourgeois administration, preferred to surrender rather than risk the destruction of Paris, and civil war threatened to erupt within the city.[22] In the face of this, Trochu sent an emissary to Bismarck to ask for an armistice. The peace negotiations were painful, and the Prussian terms harsh. Most infuriating to Parisians was Bismarck's insistence on a triumphal symbolic march along the Champs-Elysées. Paris endured it with drawn blinds and shuttered windows.[23] (Although the last Germans had left by March 2 and food could finally be rushed in, the danger was far from over.)[24]

At the end of March 1871, fearful that Thiers (who had succeeded Trochu as president of the Third Republic) and the new Republican assembly were making a deal with the monarchists to restore the old imperial regime, the Parisian left set up a new regime, the Commune de Paris. It was "a kind of diffuse rallying point for all manner of social, political and philosophical grievances against the establishment."[25]

The Commune was also fiercely anticlerical. Charles de Cabanoux was among the priests who remained to serve the people. His situation was especially dangerous because of his youth; he might be seized and mobilized by force. Yet the priests wore their cassocks and continued to carry out their ministry. In fact, Charles, on his way to attend someone near death, was seen by an insurgent and barely managed to avoid being captured.[26] On May 21, the forces of the Third Republic began pouring in. They entered the city from the southwest, the predominantly bourgeois Left Bank. The Communards, in desperation, began forcing passers-by to assist in the construction of barricades. But they were no match for the regular troops, who could shoot over the barricades from the top of the high buildings along the rue Royale. On the night of May 23, the Communards set these buildings on fire, and the fires burned all through the next day and into the night. Many historic buildings on the Right Bank, including the Tuileries and the Hôtel de Ville, were destroyed; Notre Dame barely escaped.[27]

On the night of May 25, as resistance was beginning to crumble, the Communards murdered Monseigneur Darboy, the Archbishop of Paris; the following two days saw savage killing on both sides. The remaining Communard defenders took refuge in Père Lachaise cemetery, and on May 28, Pentecost Sunday, Thier's army moved in for the kill. The last great siege of Paris was over. More than 20,000 Parisians died during that "bloody week," with 147 of the captured Communards shot in revenge for the death of the Archbishop.[28]

The year 1871 was a landmark, not only in France's history, but also in Europe's. A long period of peace among the major countries of Europe began as a new balance of power among them emerged. Both Austria and France were overshadowed by a Prussianized Germany; even Italy demanded recognition as a significant power in Europe. From this time on, "suspicion, rather than trust, characterized international dealings, and though there was to be no major war for forty-three years, the threat of war was almost always present."[29]

The conflict in France between monarchism and republicanism continued.[30] Republicans distrusted the left, on one hand, and the Church, on the other. In their minds, Catholicism was identified with reactionary politics.[31] Many Frenchmen were equally distrustful of republicanism: "On several occasions in the early years . . . the various royalist factions had come dangerously close to resurrecting the monarchy."[32] Only the split among the three monarchist factions, Bourbon, Orleanist, and Bonapartist, as well as the lack of an available candidate, prevented a monarchist revival. No practical solution existed other than to maintain a conservative republic.[33]

In grasping the condition of her nation, Mathilde was again a woman of her times. On September 4, 1872—the second anniversary of the founding of the republic—she prayed, "Do not permit our poor country to be always the prey of wicked men."[34] This was not, for Mathilde, a partisan stance. It was republican hostility to Catholic belief and worship (as well as republican abuse of power) that she found evil, and against which she prayed. She prayed just as earnestly for their conversion, as subsequent entries show. Mathilde would later describe her life thus far as "natural, suffering, militant, a life which happily, notwithstanding its mistakes and wanderings, was rooted in God."[35] She "knew [God], and yet knew [him] not, loved [him] and yet loved [him] not." She added that although she would never have deliberately offended him, her heart was still full of frailties and illusions.[36]

Although she had kept a journal for several years, it was not until 1882 that Mathilde began to keep it regularly, under obedience to her confessor. Thus, almost all of the earlier entries were written retrospectively. The only exceptions are the few composed between July 1870 and March 1873,[37] which were written as dated. On December 13, 1871, Mathilde and Thomas had a fourth child, Eugène. He was not born in Gisors, but in La

Roche Guyon, at the home of Mathilde's grandparents.[38] Was this, as we might expect, because she needed help in caring for her three older children as well as an infant? Was it because a fourth pregnancy in five years had been a physical strain on her, and she needed rest and care too? Was Thomas there also? We do not know.

Since she had given birth in 1866, 1868, at the beginning of 1870, and again in December 1871, it is not surprising that Mathilde had had little time to keep a journal! In October 1872, she says as much: "Why have I not written anything in such a long time, merely a few thoughts, the fruit of my Communions? . . . Many exigencies, some sad, others trivial but necessary, have absorbed all my time."[39] Some of the entries that do exist are the sort of thing any devout young woman might write: a prayer that God guide all her actions, a desire to be more faithful to her regular pious practices (her "rule," not further specified), a request that God empty her heart of whatever posed an obstacle to his grace.

Others refer to the psychological abuse she endured from Melanie and Thomas; she does not name these directly, but refers to both indirectly. Apparently, there were others who belittled her as well; we cannot guess who. The criticism seems primarily to have been based on others' lack of understanding of, and appreciation for, her focus on interior worship of God, rather than on the more exterior forms of devotion.

Mathilde's response to these personal attacks is not, as one might expect in a private diary, either blame or self-justification. Instead, she prays to forgive and love those who cause her pain, and for the grace to be indifferent to others' opinions of her and of those she loves. No masochism appears in these passages. Instead, Mathilde sees beyond the immediate to the greater good: "I should testify to the truth, but I should do so from pure love of truth and justice." "I must never excuse myself, even if I am in the right, if I cannot do so without irritation." Mathilde is also able to consider her effect on others: "I must never make an observation or reprimand without thinking of the pain it will give the person to whom I make it. . . . I must always reflect when I see the faults of others, . . . how much I fall short of my own good intentions. Others have, as I have, good thoughts, and have made resolutions which they find very difficult to put into practice."[40]

No conflict is seen in Mathilde's heart between her love for God and her love for Thomas. On Easter Sunday, 1872, she writes of the great joy she has had "going to Holy Communion with [my] beloved husband." She adds, "Never before had I felt so strongly the fusion of our two hearts as at that moment when our souls penetrated deeply into God." She prays to be more useful to her husband, more of a help to him and to her children, whose spiritual formation had been entrusted to her, observing that she would be unable to teach them how to be dedicated Christians unless she were one herself.[41]

In all of these early entries, Mathilde's emphasis is on what she herself must do "to strive efficaciously after perfection." Her understanding of what is required of her is very much in line with the teaching of Bérulle and the French School of Spirituality. Thus, she writes of her intention "to renounce enjoyment . . . never to seek enjoyment in anything." This can be difficult: "I see that this sacrifice is necessary, and I have not the courage to make it." She prays to accept generously "the crosses which God sends me," and adds that she is beginning to love suffering because it brings her nearer to God. Nevertheless, she confides, "How rebellious I often feel . . . and sometimes, like today, how weary."[42] One is reminded of St. Teresa of Avila's metaphor of watering the garden. She compares meditation to the human effort required to draw water from a well. Contemplative prayer, on the other hand, is like a continuous stream, watering the garden without human effort or skill.[43]

Mathilde concludes this section: "This is the last page written in my old life. I have not written anything concerning my soul since then because I did not know whether it was the will of God. What I am about to write now is engraved only in the memory of my heart, which desires to be eternally grateful!"[44]

Mathilde was now twenty-nine years old; readers familiar with the work of C. G. Jung may recall his conviction, based on his work as a therapist, that a significant shift in psychological development, which manifests itself especially in the person's spiritual maturation, normally occurs around the age of thirty, a conviction that seems to be supported by the lives of many of the outstanding religious figures in the history of mysticism.[45] In this respect, Mathilde was no exception; the shift which she experienced was so great that all that had gone before appeared, in retrospect, to "belong to another life."[46]

CHAPTER THREE:
A NEW LIFE, 1873–1879

Mathilde had been accustomed, since her sixteenth year, to making her morning meditation on *The Imitation of Christ*, a book very popular among devout persons right up to our own time.[1] Doing so, as usual, on Friday, April 25, 1873, she had an experience that was not at all usual; it was so powerful that she thereafter referred to this day as the Feast of the Vocation. Writing about it nine years later, she says, "Suddenly these words flashed before my inward eyes: *God alone*. It may seem strange to say that one sees words, and yet it is certain that I both saw and heard them inwardly, but not in the ordinary way in which we see and hear; indeed I am conscious how imperfectly I am expressing what I felt, although the memory of it is very clear."[2]

It is significant that this occurred quite suddenly and unexpectedly. Mathilde was untutored in ascetical or mystical theology, and neither hoped for, nor even knew about such experiences. Nevertheless, she describes her experience precisely, in a prose that, in the original French, is fluid and lyrical:

> It was at one and the same time a light, an attraction, and a force. A light which showed me how I could, though living in the world, belong entirely to God alone, and how until then I had not grasped this fact. An attraction which ravished and subjugated my heart. A force which inspired me with a generous resolution, and placed in my hands, as it were, the means of carrying it out; for with these divine words, utterance and operation are one. These were the first words which God deigned to speak to my soul, and which, through his mercy, became the starting point of a new life.[3]

Mathilde found words inadequate for recounting her experiences, and prayed that, in her writing, she be preserved from error in her efforts "to express what is so far above our natural understanding."[4] Nor did she write, as did many earlier women mystics, to communicate a message to other women or to the Christian community,[5] but in obedience to her confessor. Mathilde called this day, whose anniversary she would thereafter celebrate with humble thanksgiving, the Feast of the Vocation "because it was then that God called me, and that I gave him my heart irrevocably."[6]

There is no indication, either in this entry or later, that Mathilde, after her entry into the mystical life, saw any conflict between her love for God and her love for her husband. God and the Church were recognized by the culture as "women's domain," just as business and politics were men's. In both town and country, women's religious life formed a distinctive subculture. The church provided women with their major focus of sociability in the male-oriented communities of the day; it was the primary place outside the home normally allowed them. Upper-class women had an additional outlet through charitable and humanitarian work, and there were also various lay associations to which women could belong. And many men, even anticlericals, believed that religious practice was an important source of support for the "feeble" sex.[7]

The next entry in Mathilde's notebook, also written retrospectively, is dated July 16, 1874, fourteen months after the description set out above. She records that she had been ill nearly all that past year, and was very often deprived of Mass and Communion. During one six-month period, she had been unable to go out at all. For this reason, she had felt sad and complained to God that he had abandoned her. On the Feast of Our Lady of Mount Carmel, as she was sitting alone with some needlework, she was suddenly flooded by the divine presence, which made itself felt to her as a reality: "God was there, close to me; I could not see him, but felt the certitude of his Presence as a blind man is certain of the presence of someone whom he can hear and touch. My heart was overflowing with peace, devotion, and a divine joy! This was the first time I felt the presence of God in this manner, but it was not the last. It endured for about an hour.[8] Mathilde was so consoled and fortified by this divine favor that she could not consider it to be an illusion, although, at that time she was very ignorant concerning spiritual things. In her journal, she called this experience "The Feast of the Holy Presence."[9]

After the stay at La Roche-Guyon, the Boutle family moved to Mantes, but this, too, turned out to be only a temporary residence. In the fall of 1874, Thomas arranged to purchase a printing press and weekly journal in Vernon, a town about 65 kilometers northwest of Paris on the Seine.

Adolphe Alcan, who in 1868 had married Henriette, Thomas's youngest sister, may have suggested this; he was a printer and publisher himself.

Whatever the reason, on January 1, 1875, Thomas acquired both the printing press and the paper, *La Gazette de Vernon*, becoming its "Editor in Chief."[10] This publication contained, among other things, local news, a serialized love story, and a listing of theatrical performances. It tended to be religiously conservative, even "clerical" in tone. It usually employed between seven and ten typesetters and lithographers; about 1,200 copies were printed each week. It would not have been practical for the editor to be living in Mantes, so in December 1874, Thomas moved his family to an apartment in Vernon at 27 rue d'Albuféra. There was another reason to get settled in Vernon before Thomas officially took over as editor; Mathilde was pregnant for the fifth time. Their last child and second daughter, Elisabeth, named after Mathilde's younger sister, was born on February 3, 1875.[11] This birth came nearly two years after Mathilde's first mystical experience. Mathilde's pregnancy serves as an unmistakable testimony that virginity is not a necessary condition for, nor marital relations an obstacle to, mystical experience—despite traditional clerical beliefs.

Toward the end of 1874 and the beginning of 1875, Mathilde began to feel her soul overpowered by divine love whenever she received the Eucharist; it was so strong that she at first feared it might cause her death. She abandoned herself to God, and was immediately reassured by an experience of profound peace.[12] Having been surrounded with selfless love in her natal family, she had developed a warm and affectionate temperament herself. Thus, we should not be surprised to find that her experience of God's presence was equally ardent. (God respects and works through the unique personality of each of us.) She names April 29, 1875, the "Feast of the Mysterious Embrace," and struggles to find adequate words to describe the experience: "With what words shall I tell how my poor soul feels enfolded within the embraces of your divinity?"[13]

Mathilde attempted to express what she felt only because she was under obedience to do so. She compared her latest manifestation of God's love with that of her First Communion, saying that the latter "was like the dawn of a coming day, the first rays of the rising sun which foretell the heat and ardor of its noonday splendor compared with what . . . my soul felt in that Communion of April 29, 1875."[14]

But Mathilde was also aware of the danger of letting her feelings run away with her. In a brief entry, dated May 1, 1875, she stated, "In this year, I wrote down the following thought which dominated my soul: My

God, I will try not to feel either joy or pain immoderately any more; I will try to feel only you."[15] This was not easy for her; in the next entry, she recorded "feeling very anxious about certain persons and certain events." Her habitual practice in such circumstances was to carry her troubles "to the feet of Our Lord."[16]

She recalls, but does not date, one occasion when she was feeling "more oppressed than usual." At that time, she interiorly heard Jesus say to her, "My daughter, there is no one in the world but you and me." "And the others, Lord?" she asked. Jesus replied, "For each soul in this world there is only me and herself. All other souls, all other things are nothing for her except for me and through me." These words so filled her with strength and consolation that she "acquired a certain degree of self-control over [her] feelings, which until then [she] had not possessed, and which helped [her] to make great progress in the virtue of patience."[17]

Although Poulain does not comment on this entry, it is significant for several reasons. Foremost, it is the first time Mathilde mentions an actual interior conversation with Jesus. Secondly, Jesus' words sum up admirably the way in which all believers are united in love with one another in loving God. If understood as "I love you only for God's sake," this would not be genuine love. Instead Mathilde sees loving others in loving Jesus— and for his sake—as implying not less, but an even greater loving service to family and friends, as her next entry indicates. Remembering how, on November 8, 1875, she had first experienced Jesus as her consoler, she adds that it was not yet the forgetting of all things in him, even though he was transforming, upholding, and comforting her in a way no human being could have done. She has been unable to write down all the acts of thanksgiving she has made for this grace, because "I believe that it is your will that I should take into account the duties of my state of life and these leave me only rare moments for writing."[18]

The care of her family was not left to Mathilde alone; all upper-middle-class families had servants at that time. The Boutles had the help of a young woman who lived with them and freed Mathilde from the usual domestic tasks of cooking and cleaning. This servant would not have had to do the laundry; poor women would have picked it up, and returned it washed and pressed. But Mathilde never left the care of the children to a servant; she considered motherhood her responsibility and duty. In an entry dated 1875–1876, she writes of this:

Although I have always looked upon marriage from the standpoint of faith, I now see it under a new aspect . . . : we cannot
doubt, we married Christians, that God calls us to exercise the
pontificate which he desired to entrust to man when he made
him lord of creation, and this, therefore, obliges us to offer him
that which is the most perfect thing in the world, namely, a
human being. The child belongs to us, and we belong to the child
by virtue of the holy bond of marriage, but we Christians may
not surrender ourselves to one another for any other end than
that of rendering glory to the sovereignty of God. The exercise
of our free will is the faithful expression of his Sovereign Will,
and we can only accept the supreme tribute of trust and love,
paid to us by another creature, in the light of a homage laid upon
the altar of our soul as an oblation to God.[19]

Mathilde also put her duties as wife and mother ahead of her devotional practices. She scattered brief moments of prayer throughout the
day, instead of setting aside longer periods, as she might have preferred.
These duties included, at least on occasion, the socializing customary for
women of her class, among which appears to have been going for walks
together. Here is her rather humorous reflection on this practice: "We went
for a walk, fourteen of us. I noticed that to associate with many Marthas,
men or women, does not affect me. One leaves them to talk, putting in a
word here and there, but in reality one remains quite free to continue in
prayer. But to be with one Martha only, what a terrible thing! Being only
two, one is obliged to talk nearly all the time. Assuredly this does not hinder
one from being united with God, but to speak of him is not the same as to
speak to him."[20]

Nor did Mathilde speak of God "as much and in the manner [she]
would like." Had she dared to speak, others might have been moved to love
God more, which "would [have been her] greatest happiness." However,
she kept silent, fearing that, were she to tell anyone the depth of her love
for God, "people might be too scandalized afterwards when they see all
my imperfections." This silence seemed to her a sort of martyrdom.[21]

Usually, Mathilde was able to get to Mass daily, as all weekday
Masses during this period were celebrated in the early morning, owing to
the fast (then, required from midnight) for those wishing to receive communion. Mathilde would thus not have been prevented from having break-
fast with her family upon her return, nor would attending Mass have
conflicted with other family plans afterwards. Whenever possible, she

would make a visit to the Blessed Sacrament in the afternoon, but this she would shorten, or even omit, in order to attend a local concert with the children or just spend time with them before dinner.

The next entry in Mathilde's notebook is dated specifically: Low Sunday, April 23, 1876. Referring to the gospel for the day, John 20:24–29, Mathilde calls it "the Feast of Peace," since it commemorates the day on which "the gentle Savior gave his peace to his Apostles." It stood out in her memory because "he himself brought that divine peace into my soul." She adds that she remained in this peace for two weeks, without knowing either how to thank Jesus for this gift or how to give this peace to others.[22] Surely she would not have recalled the experience so precisely had there not been a lack of peace earlier, but she says nothing of this. Poulain, in a footnote, comments that she does not write at length about her sufferings, because her director knew of them already; he was interested in understanding how she bore them.[23] We, however, are left to wonder, in view of her later difficulties, if she were enduring the disapproval of Melanie and Thomas.

The next entry, written two months later, on June 24, 1876, Mathilde calls "the Feast of the Sweet Union"—an experience of Jesus' love and kindness which, while it filled her with wonder, never left any room for doubt in her heart. Because she spoke of these experiences to no one until November 1879,[24] she would not have been troubled by anyone else's doubts. Her own doubts, when she later had them, came from her humility.

Mathilde's next recollection is of Pentecost a year later. Experiencing "being profoundly recollected in the Holy Spirit and united to that adorable Person, I felt drawn to a life of prayer." Her response was a resolution to kneel down and recollect herself from time to time during her ordinary daily life. She adds that this proved a most efficacious help.[25] There is nothing abstract or neo-Platonic about her spirituality; she prays with her whole being, both body and spirit!

In the autumn of 1877, she had her first experience of passive prayer. Making her thanksgiving after Communion, she found herself unable to express her love in any words. "Feeling her will fixed in God and powerless to formulate the simplest act, she no longer sought to make any, but remained in that state of deep repose in God in which the soul no longer seeks because she has found." Poulain called it "the ligature of the powers." Mathilde herself had no name for it, although she recognized it as a state of recollection that is a great grace, "most efficacious for furthering the spiritual life." She added that, since that day, this experience of passivity was repeated each time she received the Eucharist, but not always with the same intensity, observing that "this state has many degrees."[26]

There are no further recollections for 1877. In May of 1878, Mathilde had a new experience, which she recounts very simply. She had been obliged to go to a party, and noticed there how her imagination had been more attracted by certain traits of created beauty than she thought proper. Therefore, she spent a few extra moments in prayer, asking for the grace not to be distracted by created beauty. The next morning at Communion, this grace was granted. She had a sensible impression of the beauty of God: "The whole world became as nothing, and terrestrial impressions vanished once and for all before that divine charm."[27] This experience stayed with her for an entire week.

In the seventeenth century, Jansenism had taught Catholics to distrust earthly beauty. By contrast, Mathilde gradually came to see earthly beauty as a participation in Uncreated Beauty, writing, "I sought you . . . in all things beautiful, and in all things I found you. I sought you at the hands of all creatures, and they all replied: Behold, he is here." In a long passage reminiscent of St. Augustine, Mathilde lists all the forces of nature: sea, mountains, forest, wind, thunder, dawn and twilight, springs in the valleys, the songs of the birds, sun, flowers, and stars, "and they all say, in their own language: Behold, He is here. . . . Glory be to God!" While none of these things appeared less beautiful to her than they did when she was younger, once she had been given a glimpse of the beauty of God they seemed pale in comparison. She writes, "I gazed on sea and land and saw only God."[28]

Poulain comments in a footnote that the divine attributes were beginning to manifest themselves in Mathilde's prayer life. Such self-referential observations were entirely foreign to her, however, even had she been familiar with classical mystical categories—which, at least at that time, she was not.[29] She merely states what she has experienced, as she has been asked by Father Grieu to do. While a detailed account of each new vision may be of interest to specialists in mysticism, our interest here is in observing the way in which Mathilde's growth in union with God enabled her to retain emotional stability, and even a sense of humor, in spite of unremitting psychological distress, occasioned by factors that would range from political upheaval to chronic verbal abuse within her home. Therefore, we will limit our attention to those visions which manifest her growing human and spiritual maturity in surmounting tribulation while being faithful to her responsibilities.

Without any spiritual companionship, let alone spiritual direction, Mathilde responded to each new divine initiative with simplicity and trust. Being, so far as we can tell, unfamiliar with monastic practices, she had, at first, to figure out for herself how to embody each new grace in her daily life. No doubt she had learned from her reading about the ways in which earlier Christians had prayed, but had to adapt them to her own circumstances. Because she was unable to set aside a room in her home for an oratory, she prayed in her room, kneeling and facing the parish church, where the Eucharist was reserved.

At the end of 1878, she had begun to practice what she later learned was called mental prayer: "Yielding to the impulse of grace, I recollected myself for a few moments, after my evening as well as my morning prayers."[30] She had become accustomed to reciting, daily, a number of vocal prayers she had memorized as a child; beyond these, she prayed in her own words. This new prayer was wordless. She described it as "a simple glance," adding that, from time to time during this prayer, [God] "would plunge my soul into the same passive state as at Holy Communion."[31]

Writing about this for her confessor, more than a year afterwards, she added an explanation: "At that time I could not have expressed in words that which I am writing today, at least not in the proper terms. I did not know the nature of these graces God was giving me, and [I] was like the daughter of a king who finds herself covered with . . . precious stones of which she does not know the value. Nevertheless, as these graces helped me sensibly to advance in virtue I could have no doubt as to their origin, and my soul, walking in all simplicity, felt that she was meeting her God."[32]

In her next recollection, Mathilde explains further what she meant by "passive prayer." She recounted being for "a few weeks" unable to feel any joy in receiving the Eucharist, yet remaining "in one act of speechless, motionless adoration." These Communions gave her much strength and peace, as well as "a sense of great security, because I could not attribute the deep recollection in which I found myself to any sensible fervor—which I did not then feel—and therefore I was forced to consider it as the direct action of God."[33]

Melanie, Mathilde's oldest child, was confirmed on June 24, 1879; she was thirteen years old. Praying for her daughter and for all the other confirmands, Mathilde writes that she "received the grace of union with the Holy Spirit, a union which imparts a powerful love to the soul and raises her above all perishable affections. Since then, this grace has been repeatedly renewed."[34]

The summer of 1879 was a busy time for Mathilde. Her children were out of school, and although she does not mention Thomas's foster mother, it is likely that she would have visited often. Melanie, at thirteen, was the eldest; Albert was eleven, Adolphe, nine, Eugene, nearly seven, and Elizabeth four years and four months old. Keeping them, their friends, and, probably, assorted visiting cousins happily occupied would have been a challenge for any woman. Mathilde wrote plays—none of which, regrettably, are extant—for them to perform. She was also the producer, director, stage manager, impresario, costumer, fitter, and publicity agent for these productions.[35]

Fitting in her times of prayer as she could, Mathilde includes only a single recollection for the summer of 1879: "In one of my Communions I had a sudden interior illumination, and in that light, . . . caught a glimpse of the power of God, and at the same time of [his] infinite gentleness. . . . If that divine gentleness had not then been revealed to me, I would not have been able to endure the sight of God's supreme power."[36] In the nineteenth century, perhaps still influenced by Jansenism, most Catholics, even those in the religious state, were more motivated by fear of God's justice than dared to trust in his mercy and love. Perhaps this is partly the reason Mathilde found the sight of God's power so unsettling. Nevertheless, as we will see, this reaction fades as she becomes more aware of God's kindness. Most of all, it is love that inspires her. She comments that "no book, nor any kind of instruction, could ever make God known to the soul as he is made known through those flashes of interior light; this knowledge sets the soul on fire with an unspeakable love and fills her with a burning desire to serve God at all costs."[37]

Life in a little town, then as now, meant a smaller, more tightly knit community, where ingrained opinions could exert great power and cause much unhappiness for those in any way different from the rest, as Mathilde certainly was. She found support in her prayer experiences, and describes one such occasion, which occurred on October 18, 1879. That morning, at Communion, she had been penetrated with a deep sense of the strength of God. Mathilde was filled with admiration, even though she did not understand this strength.[38] What she did grasp was this: "God's strength does not need to actively overcome human obstacles as we would. It is, and by the mere fact that it is, its existence overcomes everything opposed to it at the very moment when he wills it."[39] She felt uplifted by this sentiment, which lasted even after she returned home.

Mathilde writes that for the rest of that day, "[I] had to suffer certain trials which are generally very painful to me, but on that day they appeared very light. In the evening, the person who had been persecuting me remarked how sweet-tempered I had been." She did not name the person, but added that there was no merit in her sweetness, because she had felt carried by God, and was only too happy to have something to offer him.[40]

Reflecting further on this, Mathilde observes that, although kindness had not been shown to her as one of God's attributes, it is actually the common ground and character of all the manifestations of the Eucharistic presence. "Our poor souls need kindness above all things, and Jesus knows this well! It is by . . . his kindness that he attracts and captivates us. As for me, that divine kindness seemed to be the atmosphere upon which my soul fed."[41] This important insight, articulated here for the first time in her notebooks, is one which she would continue to ponder and deepen as her union with God grew.

Returning to her account of that day, Mathilde comments that, when God gives her the gift of supernatural prayer,

> he takes it away at his own good pleasure, but does not permit it to be suspended by any extraneous cause. Thus, when I left the church after my thanksgiving at the time appointed for my returning home to my other duties, my soul . . . carried her treasure through the streets to her home, where . . . the best part of herself remained in the company of the divine guest as long as it pleased him to make his presence felt, whilst all the faculties necessary for the accomplishment of all exterior actions recovered their liberty in the exact degree required in order to do them according to the will of God.[42]

Thus God, who desires—above all—loving union with his children, accommodates himself to human needs, schedules, and duties.

CHAPTER FOUR:
A WISE GUIDE, 1879

Once classes began again in the fall, the Boutle boys would have been back in school—sent to one of the minor seminaries, or to one of the collèges in Paris. The minor seminaries accepted not only boys aspiring to the priesthood, but any whose families wished them to have a Catholic, instead of a secular, high school education. These schools, many of which were run by the Jesuits, prepared boys for the naval and military academies.[1] Mathilde had more time for reading now, with only Melanie, a teenager, and little Elisabeth at home. In October 1879, she was reading Abbé Bougaud's hagiography *The Life of St. Chantal*, in which he describes the saint's manner of praying: "It was a very intimate union into which she was plunged as soon as she began to pray and which no longer left either to her mind or to her will the power of making any act."[2] Mathilde was startled and deeply moved, for she recognized at once "the mysterious state into which my soul had been plunged during the last two years!" She writes,

> A few lines in particular described perfectly the characteristic feature of this state of my soul: "My spirit in its extreme summit is in a very simple unity. It does not unite because when, on certain occasions, it desires to make an act of union, it feels a strain, and perceives clearly that it cannot unite itself, but can only remain united. The soul has no desire to move from this state. She neither thinks nor acts in any way, except for a certain imperceptible deepening of her desire that God should do with her and with all creatures, in all things, all that he wills.[3]

Bougaud adds the advice of St. Francis de Sales and other reflections of St. Chantal, on the subject of passive prayer.[4]

Mathilde's first reaction to these words was one of joy, "that joy which the spirit experiences when it clearly recognizes truth, and this was followed by a transport of love and an act of thanksgiving." Her second reaction, however, was one of confusion: "Who was I to pretend to the same favors? I felt like an intruder . . . who had strayed inadvertently into the palace of a king!"[5] Since Bougaud's book exaggerates the holiness of St. Chantal at the expense of her humanness, it is small wonder that Mathilde was troubled!

What comforted her was the Gospel passage in which Jesus states that the halt, the maimed, and the blind are called to the feast given by the king, "and it seemed to me as if he desired to make good my . . . great poverty with his . . . great mercy; . . . then my heart could doubt no longer."[6] She prayed fervently for guidance, and a month later, decided to ask her parish priest for counsel. This good man accepted her account of her soul, and proved capable of understanding and encouraging her for nearly thirty years, until his death on March 15, 1908, a month before her own death. His name was Eugène Grieu.

Before proceeding further, it might be helpful to briefly review the dominant trends in French spirituality during the nineteenth century. Pre-revolutionary France had seen outstanding spiritual leaders. St. Francis de Sales (1567–1622) taught that "God wills to save all humankind, not only an elect few . . . but . . . it was up to each person to cooperate with the grace so fully offered."[7] He came to represent *devout humanism*, "the belief that human beings possess 'relative sufficiency' to act on behalf of their own salvation. Though wounded in the Fall, human nature retains a natural orientation to God as its end. Humans may exercise their essential goodness and cooperate with grace towards that end."[8] Francis understood his work as a bishop to be that of "raising up many devout people in all walks of life as leaven in the loaf of Christendom. Devotion . . . was simply living a life surrendered to love; prompted by the love of God, the devout person sought to love his or her neighbor."[9] His first and most famous work, *Introduction to the Devout Life*, was addressed to a laywoman.[10]

Pierre Cardinal de Bérulle (1575–1629), John-Jacques Olier (1608–1657), and John Eudes (1601–1680) were leading figures of the French School of Spirituality, which had been, in part, a reaction against the dogmatic aridity of late-medieval scholastic theology. This school fostered an interest in mystical and spiritual thought and practice, returning to an emphasis on interior, rather than exterior, observance.[11] Pierre Cochois lists the characteristic themes of Bérulle's teaching as "the spirit of religion and theocentrism; mystical Christocentrism, . . . keen awareness of the sovereignty of the Mother of God, [and] the exaltation of the priesthood."[12]

Both the Salesian tradition and that of the French School became honored and permanent parts of French Catholic spirituality. A third, which also developed during the seventeenth century, was not so lucky. Jansenism originated from a Latin study entitled *Augustinus*, written by Cornelius Jansen, a former theology professor at Louvain who died as a bishop in Flanders. The work was published posthumously in 1640. Jansen had devoted his life to the study of St. Augustine, especially the latter's teaching on the mystery of redemption through divine grace. He had concluded that, having lost its original justice through the fall, humanity had been restored by redemptive grace. In Jansen's view, however, this universal grace was no longer sufficient for salvation. Instead, an additional, efficacious grace was necessary to enable believers to overcome their otherwise irresistible inclination towards evil. God does not offer this grace to all, but only to those whom he had predestined in the death of his Son, provided that they cooperated actively with it through good works. The book reopened the disputes over the relationship between grace and free will that had rocked the theological world until Pope Paul V imposed a ban on them in 1607, and so it was condemned.[13]

That might have been the end of it, had the work not influenced both the nuns in the monastery known as Port Royal and Blaise Pascal (1623–1662), whose *Pensées* was the movement's finest achievement. This book conveys "an impression of unqualified pessimism about human nature. . . . The theme of human 'vileness' keeps returning. Suffering and humiliating misery constitute the human condition. . . . The union of our human nature with Christ's divinity holds no general assurance of redemption."[14] "Only from God himself, (in faith) can one learn about a total, intrinsic redemption that sanctifies one's attitude and grants merit to one's work."[15] Having "come into contact with the high idealism and stern righteousness of Port Royal," Pascal had been seeking "a genuinely loving relationship with a wrathful God."[16] His "second conversion" on the night of November 23, 1634—the "night of fire," a powerful experience of the presence of the God of Abraham, Isaac, and Jacob, not of "the philosophers and intellectuals"—convinced him that only by total submission to Jesus Christ and to his spiritual director (the spiritual director of the monastery of Port Royal) could he hope for salvation. He saw this as an eternity of bliss, "in exchange for a day of hard training in this world."[17]

Louis Dupré, the T. Lawrason Riggs Professor in the department of Religious Studies at Yale University, asserts that Port Royal was not, during its early period, a heretical community. Rather, it was "a group of deeply committed Christians . . . whose main innovation consisted in a more radical attempt to return to the pure sources of [Catholic] tradition."[18] It was cruelly suppressed, and finally destroyed by Louis XIV's guard, but this could not destroy its spirit, a piety that continued to speak to generous Catholics well beyond the destruction of the monastery and the movement's official condemnation.[19]

The Carmelites and the Jesuits had brought their own traditions to France as well.

Gerald N. Alford, O.C.D.S., formerly an appointed member of the First Provincial Council of the Oklahoma Province and Director of Formation, describes Carmelite spirituality as a Christocentric spirituality whose orientation is Trinitarian:

> It is the Christ who steadfastly sought silence and solitude in which to experience prayerful union with his Father that the Carmelite above all seeks to imitate, and from that union seeks, again in imitation of Christ, interaction with the world in community and service and apostolic witness. Thus, Carmelite spirituality has a basically two-dimensional charism: contemplative and prophetic–apostolic. Formally, this spirituality began to originate when, in the late thirteenth century, a group of laymen, mostly ex-crusaders, established an essentially eremitical settlement on Mt. Carmel to live a life based on the prophet Elijah's ideal of dwelling continually in the Presence of God in silence and solitude and experiencing from that awareness of God's Presence a spirit of great zeal for the Lord God of Hosts. The eremitical dimension of the budding Order tended at that time to be its primary focus.[20]

Alford further explains that when the Order was forced to migrate to Europe to escape religious persecution, it had to mitigate some of this ideal in order to survive. These mitigations tempered some of its ascetical and eremitical practices. Becoming known along with the Franciscans and Dominicans as a mendicant or "begging" Order, it engaged more in active ministry to sustain its existence. Consequently, there has developed a dynamic tension in the Carmelite's effort to balance his/her contemplative attraction and orientation (with its need for silence and solitude) with communal living and interaction with the world. St. Teresa of Jesus (known to many as St. Teresa of Avila) wished initially to return the Order to its original eremitic ideal. However, as she became more and more sensitive to the apostolic needs of the Church, she incorporated in her reform an awareness of, and opportunity for practicing the prophetic–apostolic dimension that has always been inherent in the charism.

A comment from Alford summarizes the result:

> Carmelite spirituality is rooted in the God-given capacity of the individual to seek and dispose him/her-self first and foremost for a mystical, that is, a direct experience of God as the center of one's existence and from that encounter to be zealously fruitful for the needs of God's Kingdom. For the Carmelite, the ascetical "nada" described by John of the Cross has always been for the mystical "toda" he describes—the *All* of God's Presence. The Carmelite seeks through the discipline of its asceticism the elimination of any and all attachments that are obstacles to the sanctifying work of God's Holy Spirit that prepares for this union. Its teaching concerning detachment has never focused on detachment as an end but as a means for attachment to God first of all, and in the resulting union with God Who is Love, finding and loving all creation anew with His Love and for the praise of His Glory.[21]

According to Philip Sheldrake, William Leech Professorial Fellow in Applied Theology at the University of Durham, Ignatian spirituality is characterized by the conviction that God is encountered primarily in the practices of daily life. The fundamental pattern for Christian life is the life and death of Jesus Christ, who revealed to us that God is not a stern and demanding task master, but one who offers us "healing, liberation and hope." Sheldrake states,

> Spirituality is not so much a matter of asceticism as a matter of a deepening desire for God . . . and experience of God's acceptance in return. The theme of "finding God in all things" suggests a growing integration of contemplation and action. . . . Following the pattern of Jesus Christ focuses on an active sharing in God's mission to the world—not least in serving people in need. Finally, at the heart of everything is the gift of spiritual discernment—an increasing ability to judge wisely and to choose well in ways that are congruent with a person's deepest truth.[22]

The Church of the nineteenth century was conflicted in its own self-understanding. Due to the Revolution—and its aftermath, the First Republic—a process of de-Christianization had begun. A whole generation had been deprived of religious education, and an antagonism between "republican egalitarian ideals and the ideals of a besieged Church" had been created. Despite this, nineteenth-century spirituality was "still strongly hierarchical and clerically dominated, viewed the world in general and the body in particular as sources of evil, and concentrated on salvation in another world." [23]

But there had been changes. The emphasis on the fear of a wrathful God and attempts by the clergy to impose a rigidly ascetic ideal had weakened a great deal. Pastoral emphasis was increasingly put on the love and forgiveness of God, and divine–human love was seen as reciprocal, expressed particularly in the Eucharist.[24] A wide variety of devotional practices developed in response to the Catholic perception that modern society was threatening the destruction of "the sacred canopy of traditional religious symbols."[25] In response to the perceived guilt of modernity, the devout were drawn to the idea of redemptive suffering and the importance of "victim souls." "The ideals of poverty, simplicity, and humility functioned as a critique of modernity's unbridled pursuit of wealth, rationalism, and social protest."[26]

Wright states that Francis's *Treatise on the Love of God* "even became the backbone of priestly formation in some seminaries," and the moral theology of Alphonsus Ligouri, who had been greatly influenced by Salesian spirituality as a seminarian himself, was being taught in many Catholic seminaries. It exposed seminarians to such very Salesian themes as the love of God, conformity to his will and confidence in his mercy. St. Francis had also maintained that all are called to sanctity, regardless of their state in life, and manifested by word and example that the most successful way for pastors to win the hearts of their people was through gentleness.[27]

Thanks to Sister Catherine Marie, the Archivist of the Evreux diocese, we do have some information concerning the spiritual traditions which would have been influential at its major seminary when Eugène Grieu, who had been born and received his earlier education in a nearby village, studied there.

The seminary had been founded directly by St. John Eudes, and was under the Eudists until the French Revolution. After the Concordat in 1801, it was entrusted to the Lazarists—also called Vincentians.[28] John Eudes was the youngest member of the original French School of Spirituality, and the one most influenced by the writings of St. Francis de Sales and Jane de Chantal, to whom his own spiritual vision is more indebted than that of the other founders of the French School. "He believed, like de Sales, that his listeners could be drawn to the love of God 'heart to heart'" and followed Francis by using the term *devotion* rather than *religion* (as did the other members of the French School) in referring to the practice of the spiritual life.[29] The Lazarists, or Vincentians, were founded by St. Vincent de Paul, a slightly younger contemporary of Francis de Sales. The two had first met in 1618, and they remained in contact throughout Francis's life. Francis had a profound influence on Vincent, who was impressed with Francis's "irenic and charitable pastoral approach," developing a gentler style himself.[30]

According to Sr. Catherine Marie, other spiritual influences at the seminary during Grieu's education there would have been that of the Sulpicians and the Oratorians (Salesians), founded by John Jacques Olier and John Bosco respectively.[31] As a child, Olier had known Francis, developing a profound veneration for the latter which he passed on to his spiritual sons well into the nineteenth century.[32] John Bosco (1815–1888) had also been influenced by the writings of Francis de Sales. In fact, composing his resolutions on the eve of his ordination to the priesthood, he wrote, "May the charity and sweetness of St. Francis de Sales guide me in everything."[33]

It would seem, therefore, that at the major seminary of the Evreux diocese, as elsewhere in France, "the rigorist moral theology of the eighteenth century was softened. . . . Increasingly, pastoral emphasis was put upon the love and forgiveness of God."[34] Eugène Grieu was ten years older than Mathilde; he was ordained in 1859. He came to Vernon on November 22, 1874, and remained there for the rest of his life. His obituary in the *Semaine Religieuse du diocese d'Evreux*,[35] April 4, 1908, describes him as a model priest: firm and at the same time conciliatory, never taking risks but never drawing back, zealous and devout.

Father Grieu began each day with Matins (the Office of Readings), "drawing from this the lights and the graces which should give him clarity and fortify him for all the day's duties." He did not delay it for any reason, although there must have been times when it would have been more convenient for him to have prayed the Divine Office later in the day. He explained his reason for this to a friend of thirty-five years: "The manna disappeared when the sun rose; it is above all on our prayers at the beginning of the day that God sheds his blessings."[36]

Love for God was the foundation of Grieu's life. He had a special devotion to the Sacred Heart, which he regarded as a powerful means of salvation for souls. His love for the Blessed Virgin inspired him to lead parish pilgrimages to her shrine at Lourdes. He fostered vocations to the priesthood, maintained a warm and obedient relationship with his bishop, and was totally dedicated to the good of his parishioners, especially the children and the poor. Nor did he neglect practical matters. He saw to the restoration of the parish church, which, like the town, had existed since the Middle Ages. (The diocese itself was even older, having been established in the third century.) Grieu restored the church to its original simplicity, improving the heating system and the lighting. He acquired a building in which to establish a free school and maintained it out of his own pocket as long as he could. During the conflict over the religious schools, he fought for their survival, at least in Vernon, and even tried to set up a free school for girls. He welcomed a nursing order, and located a building in which they established their mother house.[37]

Even when Grieu began to fail physically, he never lessened his activities. On Saturday, March 7, 1908, he remained in the confessional until 9:00 in the evening. The following morning, he was unable to stand up, and the doctor gave him little hope of recovery. Diagnosed with pneumonia on Wednesday, he received the Last Rites of the Church, thanked his assistants, and made his last recommendations. He continued to pray the Office, and on Saturday evening, dictated Sunday's announcements. At 5:00 PM Sunday, he died peacefully.[38]

Such was the person to whom Mathilde turned—a person of genuine holiness. That this apparently ordinary parish priest would have the requisite degree of wisdom and discernment is, as anyone who has looked for such help in vain can testify, quite unusual, and provides evidence of a special grace of God to each of them. Mathilde did not date her talk with him precisely; she noted only that it was after a month of prayer that she approached him. This would put it in mid-November 1879, five years after he had come to Vernon, during which time he would have had ample opportunity to notice her attentiveness during religious services.

We do not know how often they met; perhaps it was only in her fortnightly confession. Not until the beginning of 1882, when she was 38, did he ask her to keep an account of her prayer experiences. Thus, all the entries dated earlier were written retrospectively. As might be expected, they are less numerous than was the case later. Only the significant spiritual events are included.

Mathilde began her journal, as she did everything, with prayer. Addressing Jesus, she stated that she had been requested "to set down in writing the graces which, of your pure mercy, you have lavished on my soul, in order that the remembrance of them, recorded on paper, might nurture this poor mendicant, should she ever be deprived of them."[39] Due to her family responsibilities and the duties expected of her social position, however, she seldom had the leisure to describe a new grace for her director as soon as it was given. Hence, many entries were written after, sometimes long after, the experience related. Unless otherwise specified, the date given here is that of the writing, rather than of an experience's occurrence. Grieu read what Mathilde wrote and added comments before returning the journal to her.

There are no more entries for 1879; the next is dated March 4, 1880. At least part of the reason for the long silence is that Mathilde had been ill, confined to bed. She reports being "very sad at being deprived of Holy Communion." She continues, "I constantly directed my heart toward the Blessed Sacrament, and prayed to the best of my ability." She had told Our Lord often in the past that she would willingly remain hidden, deprived of glory for all eternity so long as she was hidden close to him. Now she saw that this showed a great ignorance on her part: "While at prayer this kind God [filled] my soul with his light and said to me interiorly 'I myself am the glory.'" Immediately she was dazzled by the splendor of heaven, and she understood that the blessed are bathed in the light of God; he himself is their robe of glory.[40]

It is easy to forget that Mathilde was educated at home. Her intelligence, her ability to describe her experiences precisely and clearly and to make distinctions, is so obvious. Yet where could she have gone? There were only a few secondary schools for girls; these *pensionnats*, as they were called, were boarding schools conducted by nuns. "There they dispensed an education compounded of piety, sexual repression, and the social graces, which even anticlerical bourgeois men found appropriate as a way of ensuring that their daughters would be virgins at the altar, and subservient wives and mothers thereafter."[41] It does not appear that Mathilde spent any time in such a school. She states in her letter to the Superior of Adoration Réparatrice that she is educating her daughter at home, as her mother did her.[42] Nor would it have given her any exposure to philosophy or theology. Some of her insights are worthy of a Thomist philosopher, but not until Leo XIII's encyclical *Aeterni patris* (1879) did even seminary education include a study of Thomas Aquinas. Nor would she have been allowed into a seminary. And, lacking any knowledge of Latin, she would not even have been able to study theology on her own. Like Teresa of Avila before her, she received her "theological education" in her dialogues with God.

Mathilde herself comments on the way in which Jesus guided her. Sometimes his words were full of tenderness, sometimes they would dissipate distractions (which she believed to be caused by the devil) at Communion or instruct her regarding daily conduct. But at other times, his words enlightened her, either "about people and things of daily occurrence, or in a more general way." She tells us explicitly:

> This advice given to me interiorly never caused me to deviate in the least degree from the directions laid down for us by the Church. On the contrary, on hearing certain counsels of perfection either from my director or in sermons, or else through my own reading, I often remembered having received them before in the words of the good Master, spoken to me interiorly, and I was profoundly touched by the divine goodness which desired to teach me itself. And what a grace these divine instructions bring with them![43]

Nine years later, she refers again to this grace. After she had made her confession, Father Grieu had spoken to her about the importance of detachment and humility lest the graces she was being given might constitute a danger to her soul. She adds, "It is very touching to see how God anticipates such external advice with his interior advice."[44] How Mathilde knew that her instruction came directly from God, she also explains:

> The divine words carry with them an inexpressible sweetness by which the soul recognizes in some manner the voice of God. Moreover, they impress themselves forcibly on the soul and bring about what they utter. I had observed this before I read about it. These interior accents cannot bear any comparison to those words which are sometimes formed by the imagination. Moreover, very great benefit always accrues to the soul from these divine interior words, whether they enlighten her, instruct her, fortify her, or console her.[45]

These graces did not remove Mathilde from ordinary human experiences. Not only was she subjected to verbal abuse by Melanie Bellanger and Thomas, but she encountered the same difficulties with which all devout persons struggle from time to time, especially when praying. She does not describe these struggles further than "temptations and obsessions" which, owing to her lack of experience, often terrified her. One evening in May 1880, during the customary devotions in honor of Mary, upon finding herself thus distracted, she begged Jesus and his mother to deliver her.

Immediately her prayer was answered: "Our Lord's glance pierced my soul like a flash of lightning, and dispersed my enemies as light disperses shadows. . . . For a whole fortnight those banished phantoms left me in peace; at the end of this period, as they assailed me anew, I was given the same peace, and I was freed for . . . two [more] months." She added that she did not see Jesus distinctly, but did see interiorly the great power of his glance, which greatly increased her love.[46]

Nevertheless, Mathilde felt that she was doing great violence to herself in daring to speak and write about these divine favors: "Nothing less than duty can constrain one to do it. . . . [O]ne does it with fear and trembling as if handling something sacred. . . . What is more, one feels that one does it badly, like some ignorant and clumsy sculptor who mutilates and disfigures the masterpiece he wishes to produce. At least, so it is with me."[47]

Albert, the oldest son and second child of Thomas and Mathilde, was confirmed on May 16, 1880. Mathilde was again granted the grace of union with the Holy Ghost, "with much greater force than in the preceding year." Sometimes, while adoring the Holy Trinity, she felt herself deeply united to the three divine persons. At such times, her soul was able to perceive "by a light which she cannot comprehend, the relations which unite those three adorable persons." Mathilde was so moved by the beauty of their union that she forgot herself and everything else: "Were it not that we can never be sure of our salvation, I would believe it absolutely impossible for anyone who has had such a vision to eradicate the love and reverence due to God from his heart."[48]

In June 1880, again after Communion, Mathilde was given an impression of the purity of God. This insight gave her "an immense and efficacious desire to be pure, so that she might be pleasing in the sight of her beloved."[49] If these words sound strange to us, more appropriate to a nun than to a married woman, it is because we have forgotten the social conventions of the time. The socially sanctioned distance between the genders did not encourage emotional intimacy, which is a large component of romantic love. Mutual respect and fulfillment of the spouses' duties to each other, the family, and society were sufficient to ground a marriage. Sexual passion was no requirement in marriage, the education given neither gender included sexuality.[50] "Good" women were not expected to find marital relations pleasurable, and "married women were not supposed to enjoy sex. . . . The idea of a wife and mother having an orgasm was deeply scandalous."[51] Any conflict we might imagine between Mathilde's love for God and her love for her husband and family would therefore be grounded in the contemporary view that an ideal marital love establishes a hierarchy in which the conjugal couple serves as each other's primary beloved. In this view, each marital partner serves as the other's exclusive love.

The love expressed in Mathilde's writings establishes an entirely different concept of love. Mathilde loves God in an exclusive way, with her whole heart and soul. In return, Jesus loves her in her uniqueness and is present to her. This does not prevent Mathilde from loving her family any more than a love between husband and wife prevents them from loving their parents and their children. Nevertheless, the love of complete abandon does not occur between Mathilde and Thomas, as the romantic model would posit, but between Mathilde and God. Despite this, or rather, concurrent with her gift of self to God, Mathilde can love her husband, experience full conjugal relations, and exercise the duties of a wife of her time and place. Mathilde's profound experience of a loving union with God that permits a full engagement with human marriage, not as idealized in romantic conceptions, but in lived experience, is an extremely important facet of her mysticism.

The distinctions in love that her writings illuminate are extremely important, lest we reduce Mathilde to a "married monastic." These distinctions resist easy clarification, particularly because "love," understood as romantic, is typically contrasted, not with a disinterested love, but with feelings based primarily on a self-centered desire to sexually possess the beloved—lust. Such an understanding is limiting.

Commenting on a passage in *Raïssa's Journal*, her husband Jacques explains that for his wife, real love is always disinterested, unlike *amour concupiscentiae* or the love of covetousness. There are two types of disinterested love. Raïssa calls one "the love of friendship," and the other, simply "love."[52] She writes,

> — The essence of love is in the communication of oneself, with fullness of joy and delight in the possession of the beloved. The essence of friendship is in the desire for the good of one's friend,

strong enough to sacrifice oneself for him. . . . God loves us with friendship by providing for all our necessities and by dying for us on the cross. God loves us with love by making us participate in his nature by grace—by making the sanctified soul his indwelling.

— And what does he demand of us ourselves?
— Our heart.

— How can I prove my friendship to God?
— By keeping his commandments.

— How can I prove my love to him?
— By giving myself to him from the bottom of my heart in such a way that no other love ever dwells in it. In this sense, God is jealous. He is not jealous of our friendships. On the contrary, he encourages them. But he is jealous of that particular gift of the heart, which is love, and which is total and exclusive in its nature.[53]

Jacques, in the *Notebooks*, adds an explanatory note: friendship is "the love of mutual goodwill"; mad, boundless love (*amour fou*) is "the love of total self-giving."[54] For Raïssa, "The friend of God keeps his commandments, but the lover of God goes further, giving himself from the bottom of his heart in such a way that no other love ever dwells in it."[55] Jacques develops this distinction: mad, boundless love is by its very nature exclusive. "It is the very person of the lover which is the gift, simple and unique and without any possible reserve, made to the beloved."[56] This love "does not exclude loving others in addition, but it does exclude loving them *in this way*."[57]

Mathilde certainly respected Thomas, and came to love him. However, she did not love her husband with the *amour fou* that would relativize all other loves, but with, to borrow Jacques' terms, "a unique and perfect friendship, rooted in charity."[58] Nothing in Mathilde's education or upbringing would have led her to seek passionate love. Given her pious upbringing, her early desire for the religious state, and her concern since childhood for a personal relationship with God, it appears that she had grown to love God in an exclusive way prior to her marriage, without perceiving this as any obstacle to the relationship expected of her in marriage.

Neither did Thomas love Mathilde in an exclusive way; it may be that the person who mattered most to Thomas was neither God nor his wife, but his foster mother. It was she who had rescued him after the death of his own parents, and she would thereafter exert the greatest influence on him. Thomas's affection for and gratitude to Melanie is understandable, since he owed her so much. The problem for the Boutle marriage was that Mme. Bellanger appears to have been quite unaware of how possessive her love for her foster son was. As her behavior throughout her lifetime showed, she expected Thomas to agree with her in everything, and to be available to her at any time. Further, it appears that Melanie was unable, either to love Mathilde herself, or to allow Thomas the emotional freedom to "cleave to his wife," as recommended by Ephesians 5:31. Keepsakes found long after Thomas's death nevertheless argue that he valued his marriage and honored his vows to Mathilde as he understood them.

Later in 1880, Mathilde began to feel, at various times, united with Mary. She perceived the Blessed Virgin as "a bond of love, a divine instrument between herself and God." It was her conviction that it was to Mary's intercession that Mathilde owed all the graces which God had given her. Taught by her mother, Mathilde had been devoted to Mary since childhood. When she was ten years old, she had prayed that Mary's Immaculate Conception would be proclaimed, and rejoiced when it was: "Thus my heavenly Mother lost no time in attaching to herself the heart of her child forever."[59]

This way of seeing Mary was commonplace. Catholics who still retained the eighteenth-century view of God as a stern judge found Mary a sympathetic and loving figure, the personification of God's love for humankind.[60] Devotion to her was very popular in the nineteenth century. Since she did not share this view of a harsh God, Mathilde had much less need of a protector to shield her from him than her coreligionists, but her closeness to her earthly mother made it easy for her to relate to Jesus' mother as well.

At the end of July, someone—she does not say who, but we may suppose it was her director—asked her to visit a dying person who wished to have a civil, rather than a Catholic, burial. Out of humility, she felt unequal to the mission, but because she "had abandoned herself entirely to God's will, and often offered herself to do his good pleasure," she went, "begging his love to make me suffer whatever might be pleasing to him for the salvation of that soul." She also asked to be given what she should say to the person. To her great joy, the "gentle Savior touched the heart of the dying man, who returned to him." Taking no credit herself for his conversion, she "admired the ways of God, who always loves to make use of the humblest and weakest instruments. . . . It is also very probable that some devout souls had been praying for that dying man."[61]

The property that Thomas had purchased in May 1876 at 52 rue Albuféra, for 32,000 francs was not small. It included a residence for a caretaker and a lodge. It had 2,500 square meters, and also access on rue Ricquier. In 1879, he added to it a piece of property on the latter street contiguous with it, and in1883, Melanie Bellanger bought a small piece of property adjoining it. On June 30, 1880, Thomas acquired another house at Le Tréport, a coastal town on the English Channel, for 50,000 francs, and in the same year, he bought 86 square meters of land at Bray-et-Lu, a little town situated on the Epte, on which to construct a country house.[62]

Meanwhile, Mathilde's prayer life, all unnoticed by her family, continued to deepen. In August 1880, even the pain which others' insensitivity caused her was turned to good account by her offering it to Jesus who "made known to [her] the balm which lies hidden in the cross." The union effected between Jesus and her soul through sorrow, she said, was ineffable, and both changed and fortified her at the same time. "The soul feels ready to suffer anything for love, and this without any effort on her part." Jesus responded to her offering with these consoling words: "Souls who consent to suffer everything for my love are not destined on that account to suffer more than others, but love makes their suffering more meritorious, lighter to bear, more glorious to God and more fruitful for their own salvation and for that of [others].[63]

Mathilde also experienced a deep sense of Jesus' presence in the Blessed Sacrament. She writes, "By faith we believe in the real presence as though we had actual testimony of it, but with the grace of which I speak, this . . . presence makes itself felt with the same certitude we would have if someone stood beside us and spoke to us while our eyes were closed." When she asked Our Lord why he gave her such happiness, she was told that it was to detach her from all creatures. Indeed, she had become indifferent to many things which, although interesting in themselves, appeared to her more and more futile.[64]

Sometimes Mathilde felt "at the very gates of ecstasy." She seemed to herself like one standing by the open door into a hall filled with things of great beauty. Although she perceives how she might enter it, she is not invited in. Ecstasy would have caused her to lose all consciousness of self in God. "But," she adds, "God did not grant me that grace and I would not have dared to ask him for it, knowing how unworthy I was of those [graces] which I had already received."

Nevertheless, she did ask him if he would never grant her this grace. Jesus asked her in turn whether she could bear the crosses attached to such graces. What these crosses would be he did not specify. Although she felt herself too weak to bear great crosses, she longed above all for a deeper union with Jesus. Her reply reflects her lack of pride: "If you would only strengthen my weakness I would willingly suffer all it might please you to send me in order to be united more closely to you." Jesus told her to have perfect faith in his love, "which I did with all my heart, and all was well with me in consequence."[65]

In September 1880, experiencing a return of the distractions which had earlier troubled her at Communion time, Mathilde turned to Our Lord. This time Jesus came to her help in a different way than he had earlier. While she was deeply united to him in Holy Communion, he showed himself to her as "the sovereign good, and at the same time I understood that evil is only the *negation* of good, *pure nothingness*." Thomas Aquinas could not have said it better. This sight reduced all the suggestions of the evil spirit to nothing, so that she no longer feared them at all. This "intellectual vision," a technical term she must have just learned for an imageless insight, helped her understand as well how dismayed those who have loved what is evil will be at death, to perceive that what they loved, praised, adored, and lived for instead of God was actually nothing; a pure nonentity.[66]

Yet further, Mathilde saw clearly how mistaken they are who see purity of soul as a negative quality, a mere nullity. "On the contrary, this purity is a lovely flower blossoming for eternity, a treasure of incomparable beauty, and a soul who has lost it has only emptiness." In this vision of God as the sovereign good, Mathilde found great love, strength, and happiness. A year later, while reading the Conferences of Father Monsabré, she "was greatly interested to find a definition of evil analogous to that which I had seen with my inward sight."[67]

The next entry, dated "end of 1880 and beginning of 1881," shows how her mystical experiences helped her to deal with her difficult family situation:

> Several times during prayer, Our Lord spoke words which sank
> deep into my heart, bringing with them peace and consolation
> to my soul, as well as certain lights from which sprang very
> practical resolutions. Their principal effect was always to make
> me know our adorable master better and to attach me more

firmly to him alone. "I am the interior life. I am the better part. I am Charity." On that last occasion I saw and admired interiorly the charity of Jesus Christ irradiating and influencing souls, and this sight set my heart on fire. That day I had something to forgive, and returning home, feeling the charity of Jesus within my heart, I had the joy of effecting a reconciliation. How wonderful it is to see interiorly that tender and powerful charity of Jesus, which embraces, as in a net of love, the just and sinners alike. None can escape him except, alas, those *who absolutely will it.*[68]

In addition to the psychological distress to which Mathilde was subjected, there were physical problems. In February 1881, she fell ill and was unable to visit the Blessed Sacrament. She describes it in her journal as a slight illness, during the first six days of which she "remained in the prayer of permanent union, except for short intervals; [her] soul was in Jesus, and never left Him." She believed that if one could remain in such union, "whether ill or well, earth would already be Heaven."[69] The illnesses she mentions periodically may indeed have been partly due to her stressful home life, but this would not explain the trouble she had begun to have with her eyes. She was only thirty-six years old; because visual difficulties would make it more difficult for her to fulfill her duties as well as limit her ability to read, this must have caused her anxiety.

In March 1881, Mathilde underwent an eye operation that apparently did not improve matters, nor is it clear exactly what was wrong. She refers to it as "a veil," but in the beginning it came and went. Poulain refers to it as "an eye infection," but he is no authority on diseases of the eye. Whatever it was, Mathilde described the preparation for the surgery as fatiguing, making any sort of concentration very difficult. Trying without much success to pray during the Exposition of the Blessed Sacrament, she deplored her inability. At once she was "as it were, taken possession of by God and drawn into the depths of the Blessed Sacrament." Hearing the words "All is there," she saw "marvels, treasures, beauties" which, while distinct from one another, are yet all Jesus himself. "It was my very God unveiling himself and allowing himself to be felt and dimly perceived." She continues, "My soul remained thus ravished (I am probably using the wrong term, but I cannot find a better one to express my thoughts) for what . . . seemed to me to be about ten minutes, but which had in fact lasted more than half an hour. During that time I had not lost consciousness, only I was too absorbed to hear a big bell which it is ordinarily impossible not to hear, and which must have rung during that half hour."[70] Is it not poetic that, as her outward sight began to fail, she "saw" such beauty interiorly?

Mathilde adds that this experience would have given her a special attraction to the Eucharist if she had not had it already. She felt very unworthy of all these graces, and wondered whether Jesus could not find better servants on whom to bestow them. Reflecting further, she admits that "it would grieve me deeply to think that others do not serve you better than I do myself." Still, it was intolerable to her that others might love God better than she did, "May my poor heart at least love you as much as it is possible for a human heart to love!" Even this is not enough; she prays to bring others to love God also, and that none might love her "except for love of you." She asks that Jesus give his love to all those for whom she prays, adding: "Since it is your will that I should live in the world among those who replenish and renew your Christian people, grant, O Jesus, that to the end of time there may be other hearts born out of mine to bless, serve, and love you."[71] It seems to this author that, within her family and beyond it, by example and through writing, her prayer has been granted.

Mathilde concludes this last long entry by commenting that she had resolved to write down "only the few necessary notes, and now I have allowed myself to be carried away." But the mere remembrance of God's goodness to her "enflames my heart and makes me aspire to a love of which I will never be worthy." Yet, she adds—a frequent acknowledgement in her journal—that God has gratuitously given her so much already.[72]

CHAPTER FIVE:
ADORATION RÉPARATRICE, FOUNDED IN 1854

Mathilde had, besides her spiritual director, one additional spiritual support. Her maternal cousin Marguerite de Cabanoux had entered Adoration Réparatrice in 1868, taking the religious name Sister Marie-Thérèse de St. Pierre. Train service between Vernon and Paris was (and still is) excellent; Mathilde could easily travel to Paris and back on the same day. Although there is no mention of it in her journal, at some point during the spring of 1881 Mathilde had, at Marguerite's suggestion, decided to ask the order's Mother General to accept her as an *agrégée*. This is a congregation unlike any other of the women's orders founded during the early nineteenth century; it became a significant part of Mathilde's life. Therefore, it is important to describe it in some detail.

The woman who became the foundress of Adoration Réparatrice, Théodelinde Dubouché, born in 1809, was a woman well ahead of her time. The spiritual family she was called by God to establish anticipated Vatican II's Constitution on the Laity (1968) and could not be fully realized during her own life.[1] At her birth, women were still seen as subordinate creatures in both the household and the Church, and were barred from significant participation in public life.[2] Upper-middle-class women either married a man chosen for them by their parents or entered one of the cloistered women's monasteries. Dr. Janet Ruffing has suggested that the reason for this may have been primarily financial. The family provided the young woman with a substantial dowry, but once the nun had made solemn vows, she no longer had any claim on the family's wealth. Since women in teaching and nursing orders did not take solemn vows, their status with respect to their family's fortune would not have been as clear. Also, these sisters, especially those in nursing orders, would have been doing work usually done by servants in upper-middle-class households—work not seen as suitable for the daughters of such families.[3] For the rest of her life, the nun would be under obedience to a religious superior, who was herself under

53

obedience to a male cleric. Independence and creativity in assessing and responding to what a woman saw as the religious needs of the day were neither expected nor appreciated.[4]

Théo's family was only nominally Catholic. How this gifted artist, who could easily have had a professional career as a painter, ended up founding a religious order reveals much about her understanding of the needs of the Church in nineteenth-century France, and helps to explain her vision for the order. Her mother considered church attendance a social duty and wanted her daughter to participate in it for this reason. The Corpus Christi procession first introduced Théo to the Eucharist, which became more and more important for her as she matured. She made her first Communion at the age of twelve, as was customary; it was her own idea to prepare for this by a three-day private retreat. Three years later, in spite of all the objections heard around her, she made her Confirmation.[5]

From sixteen years of age, Théo had devoted herself seriously to the study of art, first in Orléans, where she was allowed to work in an unused tower of the art museum. In 1833, when she was twenty-four, her family moved to Paris to enable her to continue her studies. She chose to work under the guidance of Monsieur de Juinne, and the following year she was joined by Louise-Coraly Leconte, a younger woman who became a lifelong friend. They worked together for ten years, being drawn together not only through their work but also through their mutual desire for God. Coraly later became an Ursuline nun and wrote a book about her memories of Théodelinde, whom she described as the most intimate friend of her youth.[6]

Challenged by two of her Protestant friends regarding the contradiction between the belief Catholics proclaimed to have in the real presence of Jesus in the Eucharist and their practical neglect of the Blessed Sacrament apart from Mass and other communal services, she committed herself to a daily visit.[7]

The general spirit of religious indifference around her made Théo distrust her growing attraction to prayer, and she feared any form of spiritual direction. Nevertheless, those "she chose as friends were people who by their birth and culture belonged to the Catholic France of a former age. . . . Through them, she began to see things in a new light, and the long hours she spent alone in her studio gave her much time for thought. She came to see that art is not divorced from spirituality, and almost without realizing it, was constantly thinking of God. The move to Paris opened new doors. She saw her future as full of promise and flung herself into her new life with enthusiasm, excitement, and expectation. There is an early self-portrait of her that shows a very attractive young woman, with dark curly hair and a slight smile, looking directly at the viewer.

Théodelinde Dubouché, as Mother Marie-Thérèse, would later say of this period, "I wanted to see everything, know everything," adding that this inquisitiveness "resulted in a thousand imprudences which could have caused my ruin had not God himself preserved me."[8] But it also showed an independence of mind and heart which enabled her, later, to resist the pressure of clerics and even friends who did not understand the nature of the new religious community she felt called to form, and who kept trying to use her "to sew a piece of new cloth to old and worn ideas."[9]

Respected even by her agnostic art teacher for her integrity and innocence, and perceiving how much good—or harm—other aspiring young artists were capable of, Théo formed an association of artists dedicated to St. Luke. The members went to Mass and celebrated together on his feast day. At the same time, she was working very hard, spending eight to ten hours each day in her studio. Even though devotion to art and love of God already held first place in her heart, she had not yet renounced her worldly ambitions. Through her friendship with a distinguished physician and writer who praised her talent as a painter, she was introduced to many prominent persons, whose portraits she was commissioned to paint. Even though this was the realization of her dearest hopes, it led to disillusionment. She found her clientele so full of stupid vanity that her illusions about human glory were shattered. Torn between a growing attraction to a more intense spiritual life and her love of art and music, she threw herself into her work . She had determination and energy, and longed to accomplish great things.[10]

Théodelinde was a true artist; painting was not just her hobby or career, but a strong part of her life and vocation. Even many years later, she still spoke of the joy she felt in taking up her palette. She said that for her, painting was a way of giving, "of making use of something that overflows in my heart and my spirit. . . . I think that, but for prayer, I could not, humanly speaking, do without it."[11] What her life might have been had she not responded to grace we do not know, but we do know that a full half-century later, another Parisian artist of immense talent, also a young woman, was destroyed at least in part by limitations imposed on young women in the arts by her society.

Camille Claudel (1864–1943), sister of the poet Paul, was a talented sculptor. Despite this, in the waning decades of the nineteenth century, she was not allowed to enroll in the École des Beaux Arts because of her gender. She studied with Rodin, eventually becoming his lover, but he was not willing to divorce his wife to marry her. Apparently, after the end of a pregnancy, claimed by some to be an abortion, by others an accident, she went into a deep depression, became isolated, developed a strong sense of being persecuted, gave up sculpting and destroyed much of her artwork.[12] Confined to a mental institution by her mother and brother, she wrote of her own travails in art: "It is the exploitation of women, the crushing of the artists whom they want to make sweat blood and tears."[13] Odile Ayral-Clause, in a 2002 biography, comments, "Her refusal to sculpt was also an opportunity to reassert her personal freedom. Everything had been taken away from her, everything but her willpower."[14]

For Théo, the recognition she had attained as a painter by the middle decades of the nineteenth century, the vanity of art patrons rendered visible by that recognition, her own genuine love of painting, and her thirst for a closer union with God continued to fuel a tension that deeply troubled her. "By chance" she bought a book entitled *The Christian's Manual,* containing the Psalms, the Epistles, and the Gospels, none of which she had read in their entirety. The book moved her profoundly and, not without a struggle, she decided to speak to a priest whom she knew to be both wise and holy. She expected to be sternly scolded; instead he astonished her by asking if she had ever thought of joining a religious order in response to the graces with which God was showering her. He told her that she should receive communion very often: "God loves you and wants you for himself."[15]

Théo was stunned. Surely one of them must have lost his mind! She resisted the suggestion with every possible argument, but the words "God loves you" burned in her heart. Because nineteenth-century French Catholicism was influenced by Tridentine spirituality as well as Jansenism, and tended to regard God as stern and demanding, the idea that God could love her was a powerful and life-changing revelation. She felt unworthy, but realizing that it is Jesus who is the Savior, she turned totally to him. For one of her temperament, as for St. Augustine before her, only an unconditional dedication was possible. The Eucharist became, and remained, the center of her life.[16]

She also developed a growing recognition of Jesus' presence in others, however, especially the sick. She began to visit them, inspiring some, moved by her kindness, to be reconciled to God before they died. This included her own mother, whom Théo cared for day and night from the time of her diagnosis with cancer until her death four years later. Their mother's return to the Church and her patient endurance of her suffering so impressed Théo's sister that she, too, returned to the practice of her faith, and a year after his wife's death, her agnostic father was converted as well.[17]

Théo was now thirty-three. On the night her mother died, she had cut off her hair and promised to consecrate herself wholly to God. But her father still needed her. He asked her not to leave him as long as he lived, and she promised that she would not, even though this meant an indefinite postponement of her intention to enter the religious state. Yet her longing grew stronger every year.

Perhaps to protect him from the religious indifference of the time, Théo's sister sent her son to be educated by the Jesuits in Belgium. During a visit to him, Théo had the opportunity to speak to one of the priests. This discussion turned her from Jansenist influences, which were still prevalent at the time, and obtained for her the privilege of daily communion, rarely granted to the laity or even the vowed religious at that time.[18] The priest told her, "Jesus is not in the least angered by your desire to receive him. . . . He desires you much more than you desire him."

This wise counselor kept in touch with Théo by mail thereafter, and remained a devoted spiritual friend.[19] From him, she received prudent counsel. He tempered her tendency to superlatives and recommended simplicity in everything. He also told her to forget a lot of her notions about God, whom she, along with most of her contemporaries, still tended to see as a terrible taskmaster, satisfied only with the greatest sacrifices, rather than a father who is delighted by his children's efforts to be good.[20]

In 1845, she was able to make a retreat with him. According to Coraly, he told her, "The saints have manifested the sanctity of God; allow him to manifest in *you* his kindness, gentleness and mercy." He advised her to be more prudent about the soul's food than about bodily food. "All truths are not suitable for you. In sermons or spiritual books, don't apply everything to yourself. . . . *Choose* what helps you. Read the writings of St. Francis de Sales and of Saint Chantal. His letters are pure gold; his doctrine is sound and ordinary."[21] That Théo took his advice to heart is evidenced by a letter she sent to one of her young art students along with a copy of *Introduction to the Devout Life*: "Read this every day, my dear child. Your heart will love the gentle and solid piety of the lovable St. Francis de Sales."[22]

During Holy Week, 1846, one of the great treasures of Notre Dame Cathedral, a relic believed to be Jesus' Crown of Thorns, was exposed for veneration. Théo attended Mass there daily, and one morning, while making her thanksgiving after receiving Communion, she was filled with the thought that the Eucharist is greater than all relics, even those of the Passion. Looking again at the reliquary, she saw beside it a Host, unsupported by any ostensorium. She buried her face in her hands, but no effort on her part caused the vision to disappear. She felt "love, fear, and an interior conviction that all things are possible to Our Lord" as well as confusion over her own unworthiness. The experience was unforgettable. She said of it, "My heart, already so strongly drawn to the Holy Eucharist, was thenceforth as if linked to the Tabernacle. My prayers became a single act of burning, silent love."[23]

The tension between her promise to become a nun and her promise to her father caused migraines. During Mardi Gras the next year, they were so intense that she was unable to pray, so she simply offered her pain in reparation for the licentiousness associated with Carnival Week. During the night, she dreamed of seeing a statue of Jesus, wearing the Crown of Thorns, come to life. He was suffering, but divinely beautiful. In spite of her distrust of extraordinary experiences, she was deeply moved by it. At Mass the next morning she saw Jesus' face again, as if within her soul, and later, while making the Stations of the Cross, she saw the vision a third time. She prayed that Jesus would imprint his image on her heart as he had on Veronica's veil.

Indeed, his image remained within her, but this troubled her as she felt unworthy of such a grace. But when she told her confessor what had happened, he reassured her, and a week later, she was reassured by Jesus himself. Again she saw him, but now the sense of his presence was too strong for fear or doubt. Interiorly she heard him say, "You are my wellbeloved; I have chosen you" as he gave her two drops of his blood "for sinners."[24] Théo regarded this grace as an indication of her vocation, and later, of the religious family she founded—a vocation of total self-sacrifice in union with Jesus.

At the beginning of 1848, Théo and her father moved near the Carmelite monastery so that she could lead a more secluded life before seeking admission there. She placed herself under obedience to the Prioress in preparation for the day when she would be free to enter the community. There was unrest in Paris. The republicans reproached King Louis-Philippe with having hindered the reestablishment of a republic, and opposition became so strong that on February 24, rioting broke out in Paris.[25] This soon developed into serious fighting. King Louis-Philippe fled for his life, and the mob sacked the Tuileries before order was restored. Convinced that the conflict was the result not only of social and political discontent but also of the loss of faith by so many Christians, Théo initiated a "Forty Days of Reparation" in the monastery chapel. The response to her appeal for others to join her was so great that many felt a permanent Association should be formed. By the beginning of June, over two thousand had been enrolled.[26]

The last and worst phase of the rioting began on June 23. Barricades were set up in the streets, and the violence was dreadful. Although it was during the octave of Corpus Christ, no Parisian church dared to have Exposition. In spite of this, the Associates got permission to have the Blessed Sacrament exposed each day until eleven in the evening, and twice all night long, in the Carmelite chapel. They themselves were the only guard, and they took great risks coming through the battle-torn streets to pray. Only the death of the saintly Archbishop while attempting to negotiate a truce so affected both sides that the conflict was brought to an end. By June 29, the last day of the Octave, the government had regained control of the city. The Associates spent the day in prayer and thanksgiving, and were given permission to continue Exposition for one more night.[27]

Théo's watch was from one to three in the morning; it was June 30, the Feast of the Sacred Heart. Again she had a vision of Jesus. She saw him upon the altar as if on a throne, a golden light flowing from his heart to hers, immersing her in the experience of his love. Then he made a request for a new community—one centered on reparation by Eucharistic adoration. Those who dedicated themselves to this purpose would be filled with his life as well, and empowered to communicate this life to all persons of goodwill with whom they would come in contact. Théo gave the Prioress an account of her experience, and with her encouragement suggested the establishment of a "Third Order" of Carmel devoted to Eucharistic adoration and reparation. "At this particular point, she did not envisage the foundation of [a new] religious congregation: [a] Carmelite Third Order . . . with a regular and a secular branch, seemed to offer a framework wherein Our Lord's request could be realized, especially if the new establishment could have Perpetual Exposition of the Blessed Sacrament." Because it seemed an answer to the urgent needs of the times, both the Mother Prioress and the ecclesiastical authorities were quick to welcome the suggestion.[28]

Thus, on August 6, Théodelinde and her eight companions gathered in the monastery parlor. From behind the grille, the Prioress spoke to them about the sublimity of their vocation to a life of love and sacrifice of which the Blessed Sacrament was to be both the source and center. Théodelinde was to be their Mother Superior. It was, however, an unusual arrangement; she was still keeping house for her father, and the eight postulants lived upstairs. They had neither habits nor religious names, and she who was their superior was making her novitiate along with the rest. Clearly, such a situation could not continue indefinitely, but Théo believed that, in time, the Congregation would no longer need her presence, and that she would be free to enter Carmel at last. A year later, on Pentecost, 1849, with her father's consent, she and her companions received the brown serge habit of the community, similar to that of the Carmelites in its cloth and color, but sufficiently different in its pattern to distinguish it from the parent order. Two days later, she professed her vows, and became Mother Marie-Thérèse of the Heart of Jesus, the name by which she was known for the rest of her life.[29]

It was necessary at once to give this beginning community a characteristic form, to define the spirit which was to animate it. What Mother Marie Thérèse envisioned was unlike any of the existing orders—not simply a religious order, but a spiritual family. It was to be a society of people living according to the Gospel, different from other communities by the absence of anything out of the ordinary in its way of life, and distinguished from other Christians simply by the dedication and devotion they brought to whatever state in life to which they were called. She recognized that it would be precisely this "simplicity of means" that would be the obstacle: "The sublime is rarely attained because it is always simple, and fallen man has no taste for anything which would make him whole without using complicated means."[30]

The order was to consist of three different branches. The regular sisters remained within the convent. Vowed to a life of worship and Eucharistic adoration in a spirit of reparation, they prayed the Divine Office in common. Even though their choir in the church was separated from the public area, the sisters were not hidden, and there were no grills. Nevertheless, the foundress insisted that an interior attitude of recollection was to be their enclosure, together with an uninterrupted life of contemplation and adoration. This insistence was not well understood in her own time. The convents were to be the foundation stone for the other branches: "the convents were founded . . . to be a support for the secular members of the society, whom Our Lord has called to witness to the Gospel in the world."[31]

The secular branch consisted of two groups. First, there were those living in the retreat house (house of solitude) attached to the convent. They were consecrated to Eucharistic adoration, but were not required to participate in the Divine Office, and were free to go out to shop, carry on the convent's external activities, and provide for the sisters' needs. These sisters were to be equal to the regular sisters in every way; manual work was to be shared by all. The distinction was intended to be one of "function," not one of subordination.

The second group consisted of women who wished to have a close relationship with the sisters while remaining in the world. They were to devote themselves to the interior life, to Eucharistic adoration in a spirit of reparation, to attending Mass daily, praying the rosary, and spending some time each day in spiritual reading and one day each month in Eucharistic adoration, preferably in the convent chapel. Each had a formal commitment ceremony, and each year, on the Feast of Corpus Christi, they had a celebration in which they renewed their consecration. They lived in their own homes and kept the Evangelical Counsels according to their state; married women were not excluded.

Both groups existed from 1854 on, although not mentioned by Mother Marie Thérèse in her letter to Rome in 1862. Perhaps she did not wish to generate confusion on their account. The third branch was the Priests of Nazareth; this was never established as a group, although there have been individual priest-affiliates.[32]

The new community soon faced bitter opposition. A religious pioneer, Mother Marie-Thérèse was seen by many as a dangerous innovator, and even those sympathetic to her goals found the community's uniqueness troubling. Although the community grew, and was asked by the Cardinal of Lyon to found another house in his diocese, she was constantly pressured to "regularize" her community, to make it like existing religious orders. She understood the puzzlement of such people and wrote to a sympathetic priest, "It is not my fault if my path is blocked by the world's preconceived ideas and especially by attachment to outward forms. It is nobody's fault— we are all conditioned by the times in which we live."[33]

Her refusal to conform was adamant, yet even she was unable to establish the full religious family as she saw it. Writing to a supportive priest in 1860, she explained her "stubbornness": "Up to now, everyone has tried to make use of me to sew a piece of new cloth to old and worn ideas, which although good and useful in other ages, have become detrimental in our day. The aspect of our poor Work which has given rise to fear and opposition, and which has been choked, is precisely that which would make it useful and lead to its expansion, if our ecclesiastical patrons and especially our own regular and secular sisters were willing to enter into it unreservedly."[34]

What was the big problem? It had to do with the two secular branches, referred to by Mother Marie-Thérèse as "The Priests of Nazareth" and the "Secular Sisters." Both branches were to develop the Gospel spirit of freedom, drawing their inspiration, in each individual instance, from the simple life of the Holy Family in Nazareth. She is quoted on this concept as follows:

> I have often been advised, by people who wanted to make the secular branch more perfect, to add detailed regulations to their constitutions. These experiments have only impeded their work. Their constitutions are sufficient and provide for each one's particular needs by the following important point which has not been grasped: the complement of the Rule of Life, particular to each one, is decided in collaboration with the Superior according to circumstances, character, health, abilities, and degree of grace.[35]

> If this Rule of varying the personal pattern of life and action according to the individual is not followed, and instead elaborate constitutions are developed for the secular branch, the Work of God will be destroyed. I repeat that emphatically. Those whom God, for his own special purpose, had chosen precisely for unforeseen and providential action, would find their work hampered by narrow restrictions.[36]

This view of the potential of the laity within religious life was more than nineteenth-century Catholicism was ready for. All that was then possible was an association of laywomen. Even that was modeled on a more traditional pattern, since members received a religious name, a cross, and sometimes also a ring as signs of their commitment. Mother Marie-Thérèse put her trust in God, for whom all things are possible. In 1854, she wrote to a friend, "If my poor family is destined to produce a new Nazareth, my one action will be to have believed. I have done absolutely nothing except prevent others from paralyzing the action of God who is the only Founder. . . . I have met with much opposition to the secular branch which is so important. I persisted passively, waiting for the hour to come. . . . If it has come, God will make it clear."[37]

The order's Constitution was first approved by the bishop of Paris in 1851, at which time the foundress and her sisters were living in the annex of the Carmel. This arrangement was already becoming problematic, however, and a separation of the two was being discussed. Mother Marie Thérèse grieved over this, calling it a heavy cross. In a circular letter to her sisters, she asked, "Who will ever succeed in separating what is united in the love of God?" She counseled them, "Have courage. This is very much in accordance with our vocation. . . . Only what Jesus wants will be good for us."

Although the members of the third order lived by the doctrine and spirit of Carmel, its openness to laypeople and the exposition of the Blessed Sacrament became a cause of anxiety for some of the French Carmels. To Sister Anne, the first superior of the new foundation in Lyon, she wrote, "I must have faith that, if Our Lord wants to make a foundation through us, he will guide me."[38] The final decision was that the Third Order of Carmel should have the status of an independent congregation, although this caused some tension at the time. This tension no longer exists, and the two Orders now remain bound by ties of charity and prayer.[39]

The new convent was first located in what was formerly an Ursuline convent. Its first chapel was destroyed in 1855 by a fire in which Mother Marie-Thérèse was severely burned as she tried to rescue the Blessed Sacrament. She survived, but remained scarred on her head, face, hands, and shoulders. She was never able to close her eyelids completely thereafter. The chapel was rebuilt, but this "baptism of fire" that destroyed so much—including her first painting of Jesus' face as she had seen it in her vision—she saw as a grace, reminding them that material glory, which can be so quickly consumed, is not the true glory given by God. "It is a holiness that is everlasting that is needed," she told her daughters.[40]

The rue des Ursulines was expropriated in 1861, during the reconstruction of Paris during the Second Empire, and a new street was laid out. Consequently it was necessary for the community to relocate and a new convent was built nearby, on the rue d'Ulm. The last two years of Mother Marie-Thérèse's life were devoted to supervising the building of the new mother house. Although so ill from the cancer which finally took her life that she could hardly stand (at this time there were no painkillers such as we have today; even aspirin was not patented until later in the century), Mother Marie-Thérèse had lost none of her artistic sensibility. She oversaw every aspect, even the colors of the paints. On August 28, 1863, she arranged to be moved into a small room in the half-finished convent. Besides intense physical suffering, she experienced profound desolation of spirit. She who had so longed for total union with Jesus was sharing in the darkness of his last hours. But on the morning of August 30, she lay calm at last. Her look of agony had been replaced by serenity and peace. Raising her eyes, she said, faintly but clearly, "I see . . . . I see . . . ." and breathed her last.[41] This room has been kept as a memorial, and a number of items belonging to her are still displayed in it.

The order received the approval of the Holy See in 1865, two years after her death, although the status of the secular branch was left unclear. Both secular groups were officially suppressed by Rome in 1883. Those living in the "house of solitude" were forced to become extern sisters, an arrangement which Mother Marie Thérèse never wanted at all. Those living at home became *agrégées*. The new spirit in the Church after Vatican II inspired the hope of reestablishing the secular branch as originally conceived, and in 1965 the general chapters of the order set to work drafting a "Charter of the Secular Fraternity." This was presented to Rome in 1982, and has received tacit approval. In 2002, there were twenty of them; they promise chastity while single, and sexual fidelity to their husbands if married, as well as obedience to the superior general.[42]

At the present time, the regular sisters maintain the retreat house in Paris and are available for those wishing to make a private retreat. One sister is assigned as guest mistress to care for guests' physical needs. The Blessed Sacrament is exposed in their chapel from early morning until late in the evening, and lay persons are free to spend time there in Eucharistic adoration; usually there are several adults. Children participate as well; a good group of them has developed. There is also nocturnal adoration. But the nuns have no external ministry, which has seriously limited their numbers, and they are now an aging community. Young women attracted to the religious state are far more likely to consider religious orders with younger members and a means of support other than donations from friends and retreatants. Nonetheless, there seems to be a growing hunger among many lay persons for the opportunity for Eucharistic adoration and contemplative prayer—exactly as Mother Marie Thérèse envisioned for the regular sisters.

The original chapel was situated perpendicular to the street; its main entrance was on rue d'Ulm. A passageway alongside of the church led into the courtyard onto which both the convent and the "house of solitude" opened. These were connected above ground by another completely enclosed passageway. In 1977, the property on rue d'Ulm, including the chapel, was sold. It was too large and difficult to heat, and was not easily adaptable to regulations after Vatican II. Moreover, both the convent and the retreat house were in need of major renovations. These have been done, with an entrance on rue Gay Lussac. The original courtyard and the lovely walled garden of the sisters have not been changed. Both the retreat house and convent entrances are from the courtyard, as is that of the new chapel. This chapel is exquisitely simple, with no distinction between the choir and public sections. Mother Marie Thérèse's tomb is in a little alcove on one side, and an entrance to the convent leads directly from the chapel. There, Eucharistic adoration continues as before. All who wish are welcome to join the sisters for the Divine Office, Mass, or private prayer.

In a leaflet printed by the order for distribution at the Adoration Réparatrice mother house, there is a description of the nature and spirit of the "secular fraternity":

— The fraternity . . . forms part of the Congregation founded in 1848 by Mother Marie-Thérèse of the Heart of Jesus.

— Adoration is much more than a simple devotion. By taking part in the Mass and by adoration of the Blessed Sacrament, fraternity members strive to be *united with Jesus* in his perpetual self-offering to the Father for the salvation of the world. Their hearts are open to receive from the crucified and risen Saviour that life which he wishes to communicate, through them, to the world. By their consecration to Jesus in the Blessed Sacrament, they share in the Congregation's mission in the Church: to cooperate with the Saviour in his work of Redemption.

— Before accomplishing his sacrifice on the Cross, Jesus spent thirty years at Nazareth, living a very ordinary life. There, he began by *living* that Gospel which he would one day *proclaim*. Fraternity members seek union with Jesus in his saving work by striving to carry out the Father's will in the detail[s] of their own everyday lives.

— By adoration of *The Eucharist* and by shaping their lives according to the *Word of God* in Scripture, fraternity members can radiate God's love to others. They communicate that love which they themselves have received from its source—the Heart of Jesus in the Holy Eucharist.

— In their family lives or in their professions, they are called *to witness to Gospel values* by their way of life.[43]

This description provides a very exact summary of Mathilde's prayer and practice. Indeed, one author, who published a selection of excerpts from Poulain's book with her own commentary, entitled it *Lucie-Christine: L'Ostensoir sous le voile*.[44]

CHAPTER SIX:
DIVINE EDUCATION, 1881–1882

I n January 1882, in an entry expanding upon her experiences of mysticism for her confessor, Mathilde Boutle, with characteristic modesty, introduces the context of these experiences: "One day, when I had come, sad and full of cares, to pray before the Blessed Sacrament, and my soul began to expand under the sweet and invincible rays of that divine glance, the good Master told me to fear nothing, for His divine glance was *a veil, a rampart, and a shield* to my soul."[1]

As an upper-middle-class woman, living within a comfortable home in a small town apart from but accessible to Paris, Mathilde's need for protection might seem small to us. Familial accounts from differing sources agree, however, that it was in fact within this home—and specifically in the relationships with her mother-in-law and husband—that she was most in need of protection. Melanie and Thomas were respectable people, no hints of physical abuse or deprivation are raised, and Mathilde was clearly able to exercise her responsibilities as a wife and mother freely within their community. But a chronic, escalating pattern of verbal abuse aimed at Mathilde emerges repeatedly in family stories, punctuating the ordinary course of days and signaling the imperative under which this daughter-in-law, wife, and mother labored to preserve steadiness of mind and dignity in her deportment.[2]

Mathilde's spiritual life strengthened her to cultivate personal patience, model the fruits of faith for her family, and grow into a greater interiority in her religious practice. These efforts opened her to a surprising mysticism within the most ordinary duties of daily life. Devotion to God allowed Mathilde to endure the ceaseless derision and criticism of Melanie and Thomas, as well as to carry out the family responsibilities and social obligations that frequently prevented her from going to church to pray before the Blessed Sacrament, as she would have preferred. She was compensated, in the summer of 1881, by beginning to feel Jesus' presence in the Eucharist "across great distances." This could last for several hours.[3]

Repeatedly, Mathilde, whose descriptions are marvelously precise, complains of the impossibility of finding words adequate to convey mystical experience: "When we speak of something human, one word helps to explain another until finally the idea is expressed. . . . Here, it is just the contrary; words only serve to weaken what I wish to express." For example, she relates the experience of praying in church during the novena in preparation for the Assumption and feeling Jesus' loving glance, but regrets that she cannot describe what she has felt to her confessor. This vision lasted "for about half an hour," and the sense of union remained with her as she walked home.

Reflecting on such visions, she added, "It is the nature of these divine touches to penetrate the spirit with the awareness of its own misery," even though the action of Jesus is all gentleness and tenderness. Mathilde notes that all her pride was crushed, but that she simultaneously was filled with love "for so great a God who comes to seek so small a creature."[4]

Even though Mathilde did not go into much detail regarding her position and treatment at home, neither dwelling on it at length nor attempting to justify herself against the criticism to which she was continually subjected, she did—at her spiritual director's behest—try to explain how she coped with it. In a journal entry, written during October 1881, she recorded being "troubled with many annoyances," and relates that, when she received Jesus in the Eucharist, he asked her, "What do people matter to you?" This gave her such a strong sense of God's greatness that "everything else vanished before it." Its effect on her was that it became "easy . . . and almost natural, to disregard everything human except those things which God desires me to take into account." A few days later, again after Communion, Jesus repeated the same words, with "great tenderness," and she "felt that [my soul's] Beloved was indeed all things to her." It is not hard to imagine how such reassurance from Jesus could place into context the lack of respect and affection that she encountered from her husband and his foster mother.[5]

Such reminders of her significance to God allowed Mathilde increasingly to tolerate her mother-in-law's lack of affection and respect for her. Further, rather than diminishing Melanie's value as a human being, these experiences enabled Mathilde to see that her mother-in-law and husband were also the objects of God's love. Her endurance was thus not based on obsequiousness or stoicism, but on active love.

Echoing—probably quite unconsciously—St. Paul, Mathilde writes of her soul that "she is as if she were not . . . as if she had no longer her own life but were living in God and through God." This grace brings forth abundant fruit:

> The will remains so united and at one with the will of God [that] she [the soul] no longer has any personal views or interests . . . concerning this life or the next, except the desire for her salvation. . . . She will accomplish the divine will in this life as much, as long, and as perfectly as she can, and in the manner most pleasing to God; but she is unable to think either of merit or of reward. . . . Knowing how unworthy she is of the graces she receives, she can depend only on the mercy of that good God who already in this life gives her such strong incentives to trust in him, and such powerful and touching proofs of his love.[6]

Mathilde then realized that an exchange had occurred. Inasmuch as she had surrendered all her personal interests to God, the interests of God had become her own. "From that moment, the soul becomes far more sensitive to everything that touches God, whether to glorify or offend him, than to that which touches herself." These affronts, including the ills of the Church, the tepidity of the faithful, and the deficiencies of some of the clergy, "are like so many cruel burdens which constantly weigh [my soul] down, making it pray and weep, and offer itself to God in reparation for so many evils, although it well knows the small value of this offering. But if it had more it would give more; it offers all that it is and all that it possesses."[7]

Mathilde writes of this realization at some length; she reports suffering "in the souls of sinners, where she feels her God . . . imprisoned and ill-used." For example, whenever obliged to associate with persons that she had grave reason to believe were not in the state of grace, it seemed to her as if she were seeing so many dead persons walking about. Feeling deep pity and love for them, she implores God to restore them to life. Similarly, she mourns for "impious men of learning . . . buried in their false science as in some tomb dug by their own hands," talented writers and artists who have used their gift "to produce degrading masterpieces of evil,"[8] and actresses too, sometimes marvelously gifted, interested only in wealth and applause.

The latter were filling the papers with the report of their talents and scandals—Jane Avril, the toast of Paris, was becoming an icon through the work of Toulouse-Lautrec, while Ellen André had been portrayed in Degas' *Absinthe* in an alcoholic stupor. Mathilde laments that genius which cares "only about the ovation given their latest triumph, and remain[s] deaf to the call of God, . . . miscreants who play with the soul of France, who wish to snatch out of . . . children their budding faith" and who dare to place seemingly insurmountable obstacles "between God and the dying."[9] It mattered to Mathilde that artistic representations of human degradation, glorified in the press and repeated by many, be recognized as a confusing of creative power with popular appetites for a vicarious, and thus supposedly safe, participation in the abject.

Mathilde's prayers are for the speedy return to God of "all these unfortunates running to their eternal damnation." She asks God "not to give them any truce," even if they have to be brought to him through misfortunes, "which are really blows of God's mercy." For Mathilde, the only real misfortune is to live and die without knowing the love of God. Therefore she regards it as a kindness for God to move to prevent such a catastrophe, even if the means he must employ in the face of human freedom includes trouble and suffering. We might today call this approach "severe mercy."[10]

Mathilde, at this time, was growing to see her own suffering as a participation in Jesus' redemptive mission, dramatically portrayed in Matthew's gospel through the parable of the lost sheep (Matthew 18:10–14). In this parable, Matthew elides the distinction between an earlier mention of the ignorance of children (Matthew 18:1–6) and that of souls continuing heedlessly on the path to perdition. Jesus' expression of the unique value of each individual to God closes this parable: "Your father in heaven is not willing that any of these little ones should be lost" (Matthew 18:14).

Mathilde, "urged by the interest of God who desires his glory and the salvation of souls, . . . unites her feeble offering to the divine action." Her reflection closes, "Thus through God's very goodness, the soul which is united to him is identified with his cause and, so far as she is able, she devotes herself wholeheartedly to it."[11]

Mathilde's reflections about modeling Christian quiet (a refraining from chatter and gossip) before her family, as well as her prayers for divine intervention on behalf of public figures, serve as witness to her concept of God's use of trials to further the salvation of souls. She herself had had no theological education. Most of what she learned she attributes to Jesus' personal instruction. But she also learned from her spiritual director, as well as from the community of which she became an *agrégée* in December 1882.

Over a year before the prayers that she had so urgently offered for the conversion of the luminaries of French secular society, Mathilde had written to the Superior General of the Adoration Réparatrice community, asking to become a candidate for membership. Her letter of May 9, 1881 is preserved in the archives of the Congregation at the mother house in Paris:

Dear Reverend Mother,

Sister Marie Thérèse de Saint Pierre recommended that I write to you. I would be very happy if I could become an *agrégée* in your order. Since my childhood, I have had a lively and deep attraction towards the Blessed Sacrament, and I'm hoping that you will help me to respond to it.

I think that I should tell you the milieu in which I live. I have the happiness of having a Christian husband. Of our five children, three are with us. The eldest is a girl of fourteen, whom I am bringing up myself, as my good mother brought me up. Even though my life is fairly busy, I still have the freedom I need for my devotions, and my husband does not object to this [lit.: does not put any obstacles in my way about this]. However, in his family there is more *strict* faith than *piety* [what she seems to mean is that faith is seen more as a matter of external observance than as an inner spirit of devotion]; this has a disagreeable influence on my husband and causes me some difficulties. It results in certain delicate situations—in action and especially in conversation. I try to do all I can to bring my husband to devotion—he is not naturally opposed to it—and I would like to bring the others to it as well.

I should also submit to you my Rule of Life. Once a week, out of prudence towards my husband, as well as for other reasons concerning the children and the servants, I deprive myself of Holy Mass. I confess every fortnight. Since last year, I have had the joy of receiving Holy Communion five or six times a week, as far as my duties allow. Oh, you must find that a lot for a poor soul like me, and doubtless it is one of God's great mercies towards me. I spend a quarter hour of mental prayer in the morning, and a quarter hour or more in the evening. I use l'Abbe Hamon's book, *Meditations*. I do my spiritual reading in several stages, so as to counteract the distractions caused by my temporal activities: I read either *The Imitation*, or a few lines of Rev. Eymard on the Blessed Sacrament at noon, at 3:00 PM, at 5:30, and in the evening.

After lunch and after dinner, I seek a moment of privacy in which to kneel down and adore the Blessed Sacrament from afar, and I go to make half an hour of adoration in church during the day when that is possible for me. I make an examination of conscience at noon and again in the evening, as well as in each of my actions as I come to them. I try also, both in the morning and throughout the day, to foresee the evil to be avoided, and the good to be done. On one day each week, I receive Communion with the intention of adoration and reparation.

There, my good Mother. All this is the pattern of my daily life. It is the result of a very pious upbringing and all God's graces. But what is all this, if I lack the *spirit* of adoration and reparation? Can I say that I have it? Assuredly not. I would be far too afraid to be mistaken, and to mislead you. But I will say that I seek it; that I want to seek it with all the strength of my soul. I feel that God is drawing me to continual adoration and to a life of recollection and union with Him in all things.

As to making *reparation*, if I have something that I can offer for others, it is done; it seems to me irrevocably so. Assuming that grace gives me some merit, I want nothing of it for myself. I pray to God to do with it whatever He wishes for others. Grace makes it easy and pleasant for me to commit myself wholly to His will, and to hope for nothing in this life or in the next, except for His love and His mercy. Besides, it is more prudent than counting on my merits. But it is not out of prudence that I do it—no, truly I don't think so. It is rather because if I were to bargain, however little, with Divine Goodness, and to stop abandoning myself to it entirely without any reserve, this would no longer be called loving it; I would feel myself even more unworthy of it.

For the last three and a half years, always at Holy Communion and often during mental prayer, I have found myself in a particular state of soul. I will discuss it with you, Mother, if you think fitting, and if you consider that these matters can be dealt with in letters. In all things I think that your counsels will be precious to me, and I am ready to reply very simply to the questions that you find appropriate to ask me, recognizing in you our adored

Lord and Master. I sense that it is he who has put my soul in touch with yours, in order to give me, through you, the graces and insights that I need. And I thank his mercy for it.

Receive, then, Reverend Mother, all my filial respect in Our Lord,

M. Boutle (Elisabeth's sister)
5 rue Riquier, à Vernon.

Mathilde's introduction of herself through her younger sister is part of the original letter; why the superior should have known Elizabeth, however, is unclear. That Mathilde did meet with the Superior General then in charge of Adoration Réparatrice is evidenced by a briefer letter, written some six months later on November 12, 1881, and also preserved in the archives of the mother house:

Dear Reverend Mother,

I had great pleasure in seeing you and in talking with you, so I am really grateful to you for making it possible, through [the intermediary of] my dear cousin, Sister Marie Thérèse, for me to make the next retreat in your holy house. How happy I will be to spend a few days at the feet of Our Lord; I hope, with the help of your counsel, to come back [home] a little bit better. I had written to you in the spring, but it appears that [it was at a time when] you were not able to reply. I ought to have written again since then, but my family obligations sometimes make it necessary for me to postpone writing for a long time. Nevertheless, I offer you my apology. I still have too little time to myself to write in greater detail. And especially if I can have the joy of speaking with you next week, it is not necessary to write [now].

As I look forward to these desired days, permit me, my dear Mother, to renew the filial expression of my respect.

M. Boutle

There is no mention of this retreat in Mathilde's journal, perhaps a result of the retrospective character of these early writings for her confessor. Key events, rather than each step toward them, were recalled and interpreted.

Not only did Jesus support and strengthen Mathilde in the midst of her difficulties, he also prepared her beforehand. On November 6, 1881, while praying before the Blessed Sacrament, she had an interior vision of the face of Jesus. "I could not distinguish the divine features, but the whole impression was so beautiful . . . that nothing human could ever give an idea of it. My soul seemed to be outside herself." She added that this vision was restored to her each time she could kneel before the Tabernacle for three days thereafter, and was even repeated in the midst of various occupations; she experienced "a very marked feeling of love and recollection."[12]

During those three days, it also became necessary for her to travel to Paris. Approaching the city, she venerated, as was her custom, Jesus present in all the churches, and "saw his beloved head rising above the great city which seemed covered with the fumes of sin." Because of his face "the arrows of divine justice were turned aside." Further, she saw Jesus' face "rising from all points of the globe" and understood that it was what protected the world. These days were "days of heavenly joy; I was almost too happy for this earth and felt that the cross was bound to come. It came. . . . Leaning on the infinitely kind heart of Jesus, my heart acquiesced in all that God willed or permitted."[13]

What this cross was, she does not discuss, just as she does not explain why travel to Paris was necessary. The occasion would not have been for the retreat at Adoration Réparatrice, since her letter of November 12, 1881 speaks of this as a week away.

In the next entry, dated January 1882, Mathilde notes that, from time to time while at prayer during November, December, and January, she has perceived Jesus looking at her. Even when his glance is only dimly recognized, it brings light, devotion, and peace to her soul: "It fortifies, consoles, calms, and uplifts; should she have felt forsaken, it restores her to joy in one single moment." Mathilde writes that a person need not be aware of his look for it to bring about a change, but only "must not give him cause to withdraw it." That would be a great misfortune, causing the person to fall into darkness.[14]

Attempting to explain this, she likens it to the action of the sun on the visible world. But the analogy is weak, because there are "poor, little far-away corners" which the sun's rays never reach, whereas "Jesus looks with love and predilection on the small, the worthless, and the unknown ones of this world! O, what wonderful mercy!"[15]

Mathilde's theological education was furthered through these mystical experiences. On February 12, 1882, she made the following entry:

> I received the following interior instruction: When a soul is in a
> certain degree of union . . . which is not the perfect union, the
> imagination and memory are very active and cause much trouble
> to the soul. This state continues as long as God permits it, the
> will not being able to quit its divine object in order to try to bring
> back the other powers; often a momentary grace brings them
> back and then they likewise share in the joy of union. But what
> I heard interiorly was that the will is fortified by this very oppo-
> sition which the other powers of the soul offer it, and is more-
> over purified since the will has remained attached to God
> without enjoyment, or at least troubled and disturbed in its en-
> joyment.[16]

Poulain calls this "the prayer of quiet" and comments that it can
approach more or less to full union. As he explains it elsewhere, the prayer
of quiet is the stage of mystical union in which "the divine action is not yet
strong enough to hinder distractions."[17]

The next day, Mathilde reflected on what she had learned: "I observed that the division alluded to above often produces a very salutary effect in the superior part of the soul, for it enables her under normal
conditions to rule more easily over the movements of the inferior part."[18]

This must have been a relatively tranquil time for Mathilde, as
there are five more entries for February 1882. On February 16, after receiving the Eucharist, she experienced being caught up into what she describes as "the Purity of God," adding that all day she remained penetrated
by it. "At the same time, Our Lord enabled me to understand that each favor
he grants enriches the soul with a degree of grace and glory which will be
hers for all eternity, unless she loses it through her own fault." The entry
ends, as we might expect, with an earnest prayer that Jesus preserve her
from such a misfortune and ingratitude.[19]

Later in that week, Mathilde wrote that "Jesus asked me to be
'prodigiously charitable.' He has since repeated this." She added that Lent
was approaching; her heart was full of sorrow "because of the wounds inflicted by men on the infinitely kind Heart of Jesus." It would have been
Mardi Gras time, originally a period in which all food forbidden by the
Lenten fast that would not keep for six weeks would have been eaten, a
sort of "fortification" for the lean meals to come. Mardi Gras had thus quite
naturally assumed a festive air. As religious observance declined, however,
it lost its original significance and became more and more characterized
by licentiousness. Small wonder that Mathilde was concerned about the

behavior of so many! She expressed her sorrow to Jesus, who, she wrote, "accepted the feeble compensation which I offered Him, and lavished his tenderness on me."[20]

Later in the month, Mathilde received a most consoling instruction "for [those] who have not yet entered the way of union. 'When he [Jesus] gives a soul an immense desire to possess him, and the soul corresponds with it, he finds himself forced to accede to [this] desire and to grant this intimate union.'"[21] One of her sorrows, as often seen in her journal, is that so few are even aware that such a grace and joy is possible.

Her mystical life continues to develop, but now Mathilde describes experiencing "a certain division in my soul . . . during prayer, as though the superior part of my soul separated itself from the rest and remained transfixed in God." This is what she felt, even though she knew that the soul is indivisible. She adds, "Prayer under these conditions is very profitable. I need not say that this is due to the action of God and not to that of the soul."[22] Poulain understands her to mean that the soul is so immersed in God that she no longer receives any sensible impressions, adding that "this would be an ecstatic state which through humility she dared not call by that name."[23] Throughout Mathilde's journal, she manifests a healthy reluctance to classify her experiences, name them using traditional terms, or measure her own growth in mystical prayer. It is only when traditional terms or classifications help her to explain these experiences that she uses them. Her focus is always on God and his grace, not on herself.

In her effort to fulfill her spiritual director's request, Mathilde attempts to describe an experience which stumped even Poulain: "Once, at Holy Communion, my soul was filled with a great interior light and was penetrated with a deep sense of the Identity of God. I beseech Our Lord of his good pleasure to give me the grace to explain this if it be agreeable to Him." Poulain substitutes "the 'intimate Being' of God" for 'Identity', suggesting that this is what she wished to convey.[24] But let us allow her to speak for herself:

> Generally speaking, our knowledge of God is negative rather than affirmative, for it is easier to understand what he is not than to understand what he is. For instance, believing him to be *eternal,* we say that he is without beginning and without end; believing him to be *infinite,* we say that he knows no limits; but when we put these terms aside and try to explain what God the *eternal* and *infinite* is, our mind at once feels its limitation and

stops short. This is not the case with created things. I know light not only because I distinguish it from its contrary . . . but also and especially because I know and apprehend directly what light is. Ask a child for a flower; he will know quite well how to distinguish it from a piece of wood. . . . Now it was this very simple and impressive vision of himself which God gave my soul on [that] day. . . . No word was spoken to me, neither was any divine attribute in particular shown to me, but God withdrawing my poor little soul into himself caused her to see and to feel *what he is.*[25]

Poulain warns us not to reject these visions as illusions. They are common to all ecstatics, as may be seen, for instance, in Angela of Foligno and Ruysbroeck. He believes them to be an essential part of all ecstasy.[26] Mathilde does not trouble herself with such concerns; hers is rather the admission that she is unable to describe the experience more clearly: "It would be useless even to try. No doubt everything I have said so far is full of imperfections, but I could not pass over in silence this great and incomprehensible grace, this intimate vision of God which leaves the heart inflamed with love and filled with the desire to devote itself to his service."[27] We do not need Poulain's warning. The effects of this grace attest to the genuineness of Mathilde's experience. As he notes further on, these graces are always followed by an impulsion to virtue: "This is an essential characteristic of all orthodox mystical states. Hence, directors can always judge the tree by its fruits."[28]

But on February 24, Mathilde wrote of having been placed "in a painful circumstance," and of succeeding, by the grace of God "in preserving the sense of his presence lovingly, notwithstanding what [she] had to listen to." We may conclude that her husband and/or Melanie were criticizing her in their usual fashion. She "pondered over his divine tenderness with gratitude" and was immediately attracted towards the Blessed Sacrament, adoring from afar. So absorbed was she that she seemed more with Jesus than with them, which lasted about ten minutes. The family members present thought it was "a quite natural half-swooning fit."[29] Mathilde writes of "a certain languor" which lingered, but did not hinder her from performing necessary actions while she continued to be "turned toward Jesus in . . . tenderness and intimate union." Thus God both enabled her to endure harsh words and prevented her critics from discovering her deep prayer life, which Melanie, at least, would likely have mocked.

On this occasion, Jesus also gave Mathilde "a profound insensibility towards all earthly things, with a great facility to be patient when occasion arose, and a firm resolution not to care about success in anything except . . . fulfilling the divine will in all things." By drawing her to his own heart "so powerfully and tenderly," was not Jesus shielding her from the worst effects of living with constant criticism?[30]

In her writing at the beginning of March about her experience of union with God after Communion, Mathilde states that it was so complete and profound that all her powers were suspended in God. Reflecting on the way in which people are drawn to glimpses of love and beauty here on earth, she asked how many ever think of their Source, and wished to live only to make God more loved, as well as to bring others to love him. "Those who speak according to the spirit of the world appeared to me to be blind and mad. I should have liked to be able to say to them all, 'If you only knew what God is!' My secret burned my lips and yet I knew I must keep silent." Nevertheless, after these reflections, she felt "quite renewed."[31]

When considering Mathilde's commitment to silence, we must consider both her humility and the reception likely to have been given to any discussion of her experiences, since she had had no formal schooling. She was a wife, mother, and daughter-in-law, making her way through the social circles in which her family moved. Mathilde's comportment within them, and particularly within the sphere of a critical family, provides an eloquent testimony that sanctity is simple. It is not a matter of blind imitation, but of integrity, discovery, and developing the unique gifts of one's own personhood. We make it complicated, but it is really "Thy will be done," no matter what occurs. Be a saint where you are!—this is the call to which Mathilde endeavored to respond.

Only a few days later, while praying before the Blessed Sacrament, Mathilde saw Jesus "as if through a veil, a sort of luminous atmosphere." He said to her, "I love you; what else matters?" This increased her indifference to what others thought or said, so that she was "ready to be humiliated and to suffer" and sought in everything to become whatever would make her pleasing to God. That this grace was indeed given is evidenced by its results: "Later I found myself in circumstances hard for nature to bear, and heard things calculated to wound profoundly, but I was unable to pay any attention to them, my soul being still so filled with sweetness by reason of what I had seen and heard, and I could feel only charity toward my brethren. I think they profited by it; as for me, I had not the slightest merit."[32]

During this time, she "made several resolutions relative to certain details concerning the duties of [her] state of life." Leaving the church felt like returning to everyday life from another world; she added that this re-action had occurred several times since, and that the whole experience had been so powerful that she felt she would have been able to take even the most crushing sorrow in stride. At the moment of seeing Jesus, her awe was dominated by her love, but later, thinking of those who willfully offend God, she felt fear: "The Devil tried to make use of this fear as a temptation against confidence in God, but prayer drove him away, and the next day's Communion confirmed my soul in perfect peace and confidence."[33]

Mathilde learned about the many ways through which God can lead a person to the sweetness of union. One approach is through *generosity*. This comes about when a person renews a total abandonment to God by an act of love, forgetting self entirely and embracing all that God wills, even while suffering, by *willing* that suffering because God *wills it.* Then God, the soul, and the person's prayer become one, "and this prayer is trans-formed into the ineffable prayer of union."[34] A second way is the union of *simple purity*. At the moment of absolution [in the Sacrament of Reconcil-iation] "Our Lord takes possession of the soul [after which the penitent] seems to have acquired a transparency, through which the rays of his Di-vinity shine." Mathilde calls this a union of complacency: God is mirrored and delights in that soul, "seeming to cherish it all the more because he is the author of its innocence." She adds that the person feels "an exceedingly sweet and intense joy, which sometimes lasts for a day or two, and is a powerful protection against the least voluntary negligence."[35]

A similar union is often granted after the evening examination of conscience. When, "at the close of a day which has been difficult, arduous, fertile in small trials, when exterior circumstances have been pulling at the soul in all directions," one recollects oneself before God, reviewing every hour of the day in his sight. First one thanks God for his graces, and for everything which has occurred during the day, "since all has been either willed or permitted by him." Then one looks for any faults, and finds "none which could have separated [the person] from God," the person's faithful Guest through all the difficult hours of the day. Then one humbles oneself for all one's hidden omissions, and for all the faults of one's life. One feels that the mercy of God desires to overlook them, however. God is well pleased, and unites the person to himself with a look of love; this is a pure gift of love and mercy, relieving all weariness, and bringing consolation and rest.[36]

The fourth approach is through the mediation of the Blessed Virgin Mary. "Mary presents the soul to Her Son, and he receives [it] tenderly out of love for [his] Mother." "Sometimes the soul can continue her prayer to Mary with an intimate sense of the presence of Our Lord. More often, vocal prayer becomes transformed into that more complete union which suspends the powers of the soul. . . . As for me, I cannot pray to that beloved Mother without her being the means of bringing back to me the intimate presence of Our Lord if I am deprived of it, or if I already possess it, of rendering it even closer and more profound."[37]

On the Feast of the Annunciation, Mathilde found herself "sad and cast down at the sight of her wretchedness before God." Our Lord told her that when this sadness amounts to an obstacle to prayer, it is a temptation. It is better to lean on him than to brood too much over ourselves. Since we are all sinners, all "our" virtue comes to us from God. Jesus drew her into himself: she appeared like a little, tarnished grey stone which, being plunged in the light of God, changed into a diamond.[38]

Because her first mystical experience occurred on April 25, 1873, Mathilde always celebrated its anniversary. But in April 1882, she was ill and deprived of the Eucharist for sixteen days. She writes that "during this painful deprivation, my good Master sustained me by his intimate presence in . . . my soul. . . . There I adored him, as fever prevented me from visiting the church even in thought. This union was frequent during the first week. . . . But the characteristic grace of this time of sickness . . . was the union of my soul with the Holy Ghost." She adds that this is a very precious grace, which carries the soul straight to God, and that since this time she has had a special attraction to the Holy Spirit, "so little known and so little invoked, although he is more intimate to our souls than we ourselves."[39]

Following Communion on May 9, the Lord gave her an experience of his peace which not only supported her but, she writes, *established her in him.* She describes being dazzled by the divine beauty of Jesus' Humanity on another morning and reflects that, beside the sweetness of these encounters, all other sweetness, even spiritual ones if mediated by human agency, appeared no more than borrowed. Jesus complained to her that his longing to give himself to his children "with lavish generosity" has been often frustrated by the shallowness of many. Thus he is obliged to keep back the treasures of his love and his graces, which he so longs to give.[40]

Yet prayer was not always a consoling experience; there were times of aridity. Some of these times Mathilde describes as being like a cloud between herself and God. He is silent and hides himself. Such times are a kind of purgatory. At other times, one may be occupied and detained by exterior cares; then one feels as if deprived of one's vital element. Even so, she persevered. She asked Jesus how to become holy, and received this reassuring reply: "Don't vex yourself. It is I who have begun your sanctification, it is I who will accomplish it."[41]

At the end of May, Mathilde was ill, this time for five days. Nevertheless, she remained, as she describes, at the Feet of Jesus. On May 24, he took possession of her so strongly that she had to close her eyes. "But," she adds, "I was surrounded only by my children, who did not notice it. If other people had been there, I think that the good Master would have seen to it." Jesus reminded her that while it is good to regret not being able to receive the Eucharist, he is always present in his divine nature. She still felt free to chide him. She replied that he instituted the Eucharist for us, so that we could possess him wholly here on earth, and begged him not to allow her to be unable to receive him in the future.[42]

Before Communion, three days later, Jesus told her, "No created force can give an idea of the desire by which I attract souls to myself in the Sacrament of my Love." Later, he manifested himself in what she had learned (from reading) to call an intellectual vision. Poulain defines these as "visions perceived by the mind alone, without any interior image."[43] Mathilde's own definition is this: "that intimate and penetrating knowledge which imposes itself on the soul with an authority above all certitude, and which she feels can only be imposed on her by God himself."[44] The vision caused her briefly to lose consciousness; returning from church felt, as she had observed before, as if she were returning from some other region. This grace left her fully satisfied; it seemed to her that she had enjoyed a perfect good.[45]

The first mention of Mathilde visiting the convent of Adoration Réparatrice is on June 8, 1882; she notes that it was the feast day of Corpus Christi. She was able to attend Mass and spend the entire day there, a grace for which she had often prayed, but for which she had not had the freedom earlier. After Mass, a profession ceremony took place in the chapter room behind the sisters' choir. She joined in the prayers of the nuns, asking with them to die to all things and to suffer for the love of him whatever came to her. In her description, she adds that this is not in the least conformable to her natural weakness, but "what [else] can the soul do when the love of

Jesus sets her on fire?" Praying to bear her crosses as he wishes, she understood that at these times Jesus wills that she rest on his heart, and he gave her "his heart, in such a manner that [it] surrounded and interpenetrated [hers] and made it his."[46]

At that time, Corpus Christi would have had an octave; that is, the celebration would have been prolonged for a week. On the fifteenth, attending a musical party, Mathilde was thinking of the solitude of Jesus in the Tabernacle since all the ceremonies were over. She asked him to repose still in her heart. Adoring him there, she prayed for all present at the performance, "especially those . . . most exposed to danger and those whose falls, alas, are only too well known." And she was filled with a sense of his presence "which dominated all exterior impressions." He appeared both great and tender, "above and beyond all our trivial daily occupations."[47]

While praying before the Blessed Sacrament at the beginning of July, Mathilde saw that God's nature is absolute unity—Truth itself—and that the divine will is one single act which is eternal. Our actions should be a prolongation of that one, eternal act, but sin breaks the mysterious chain. This observation filled her with a vivid horror of sin. Later, during some particularly trying days, Mathilde made an act of love for those who were persecuting her, and Jesus consoled her by his presence. At the same time, he encouraged her to preserve her peace when others were causing her pain, and explained that she should regard her persecutors as instruments which provide the thorns and crosses which are a necessary part of the contemplative life. He also advised her to take care, whenever she spoke to them, that her words were full of charity. She promised that through grace she would, for his sake, "remain silent when [her] blood was boiling, act according to duty without any probability of meeting approval, and offer [her] soul for those who torment her."[48]

One might expect that such constant verbal abuse would cool Mathilde's affection for Melanie and Thomas, but this was not the case. Only a day later, she recorded an incident that substantiates her affection. She and her husband were in great anguish concerning the health of an unidentified young relative, and they went to the church to pray for him. There the sweetness of her prayer lifted the weight of her sorrow, and thinking of "the beloved soul who was praying by [her] side, and still suffering that anguish," she asked Jesus to take the consolation he had given her and give it to "this dear soul so sorely afflicted." Jesus replied: "I will grant your request in another manner for the good and strengthening of that soul, but I will not take back the grace I have given you because I find my glory in this."[49]

The extent to which Thomas was able to consider Mathilde a "beloved soul" is questionable. He certainly did not always seem to treat her as one. Her next entry, written only three days later, recounts a dialogue with Jesus regarding "these days of excessive torment." In her distress, Mathilde had said fewer short prayers during the day, for which she reproached herself. Jesus reassured her: "Fear no longer; your very suffering, accepted for the love of me, is in itself a prayer, and through your will, which remains fixed in me, you continue united to me almost without feeling it." She adds, "O blessed words!" and regrets that she is unable to repeat them to all who suffer. Their effect was so consoling that it seemed as though "I could never lose my peace, even in the midst of trouble and anguish."[50]

Her union with God did not deliver Mathilde from all temptation; mystical literature confirms that the contrary is the case. Whether the source is understood as satanic or a mystic's human nature, mystics are subject to various attempts to dissuade them from persevering. Worse still, ordinary temptations and temptations afflicting people more advanced in the spiritual life differ in that the former temptations are attractive, while the latter are not attractive at all. They are very distressing. Mathilde records one such attempt to hinder her determination to be faithful on August 4. While she was praying after Communion, she reports, "the Tempter tried to display before me some of his vain imaginings." God foiled this attempt; she was given an insight into the Trinity. Mathilde "was fully satisfied" and also understood that "in the Father who proceeds from none a great mystery is contained, so great that [even] in eternity we will understand it [only] up to a certain point through the Son and the Holy Ghost."[51] Regarding a similar attempt in early September, she writes that such abominable images do not really tempt, but only harass the soul. Jesus always delivered her from this sort of annoyance when she turned to him.[52]

Problems with vision continued, and on August 13 Mathilde speaks of her eyes as being "covered with a veil." She has had to write her notes in pencil, then copy them later. While traveling on the previous day, she had hoped to be read to, since she could not see to read herself. But this proved unimportant. Jesus, knowing her need, gave her a strong sense of his presence without preventing her from paying necessary attention to exterior circumstances. Her spirit had not been nourished by reading for an entire week, so Jesus nourished her himself.[53]

Mathilde's devotions in no way diminished the joy she found in the love of family. On the contrary, her anticipation of a family reunion on the Feast of the Assumption (a major holiday for Catholics in France) was so great that, during Mass, she "had some difficulty at first to entirely forget that joy . . . and think only of my Savior." After Communion, Jesus made her understand "how his kind Heart loves to see the union and the joys arising from the affection of a Christian family." He also told her that since she would probably not have any humiliations during the following days (suggesting that the gathering was to last several days), it would be good to make acts of humility instead. During the rest of the Mass, she remained absorbed in Jesus' presence; she adds that this grace was granted to her very often when she could not read.[54]

Mathilde was repeatedly filled with confusion when she thought of Jesus' great kindness, the holiness of the saints, and her own unworthiness. Jesus asked her, "Why are you disquieting yourself? I love and cherish you quite as much as my dearest friends." Moved with love for God's goodness, she felt a great increase in her desire to serve him every minute and to please him in all things.[55] When she asked Jesus how to change so as never to displease him, he replied that she should aim to do little things well, since these are the foundation for the big things, the opportunity for which is much less frequent. By attention and fidelity in small matters, Mathilde would find peace, in spite of all difficulties.[56]

New theological insights were given to Mathilde, and she was more and more moved by them, especially after Communion: "We shall die without having fully known the Kindness of Our Lord."[57] Without realizing it, she was herself acquiring a great kindness toward everyone, especially Thomas and Melanie.

Conflict between monarchists and republicans characterized much of the nineteenth century in France. Since the Catholic Church had been permitted greater freedom of action under monarchy, republicans, though not necessarily atheist, saw the Church as hostile to democracy and feared it might overthrow the Republic. Hence the government was anxious to break the Church's control of education. Catholic schools, as seen from this point of view, were the surest guarantee of the Church's continued influence, and a reduction in that influence was seen as essential to the Republic's future. This outlook was fundamental to the debate over laicization in the 1880s.[58]

The influence of the Church in education was in fact, not inconsiderable. For example, in 1870, close to 40 percent of French children were being educated in church schools. Catholic boys were educated either in one of the eighty or more minor seminaries, or in one of the three hundred *collèges*. Approximately three-fifths of the girls were taught by nuns.[59] This is the situation the republicans aimed to change.

The goal of reducing the influence of the Church in education was pursued gradually, however. In fact, "legislation passed in July 1875 [had] allowed Catholics to set up their own universities" and five were set up in different parts of the country, including Paris. Initially they were permitted to confer independent degrees, but in 1881 the schools were deprived of the right to call themselves universities. Nevertheless, "the Catholic institutions of higher learning carried on successfully as 'Instituts Catholiques,' their students proceeding to degrees by taking the national examinations."[60]

In March 1882, the French parliament voted to secularize schools. Primary education was to be free, obligatory, and lay. Their curriculum was to include the teaching of "duties toward God," as manifested in different forms in different religions, whose rules, it stated, are known "in conscience and reason."[61] Not surprisingly, this caused considerable concern among Catholics. Mathilde's spiritual director requested her to ask Jesus about the future of the Catholic schools. She did so, confiding all the little children of their school into his hands. He surrounded these little ones with kindness, but did not answer her question. Instead, he gave her a message for her spiritual director: "Tell my priest that I am with him." She writes that the words "my priest" were spoken with special affection, and adds that many times thereafter, when she was praying for her pastor, Jesus gave her the same reply.[62]

It would not be until "after the First World War had destroyed the bitter old anticlericalism" that the situation for Catholic elementary education improved. In fact, "after World War Two the State was to go so far as to give subsidies to Catholic schools," a concession which would have been unimaginable in 1882.[63]

Most of Mathilde's education took place after Communion. On September 18, 1882, she was enlightened regarding the way in which all things are in God as their principle. She saw a very pure spring flowing down onto the earth and dividing itself into very many little streamlets, whose purity was dependent on the surfaces over which they flowed. Crowds were trying to drink from these muddy little trickles, but very few went to draw water from the pure spring itself. Those who did were able to find all things in their perfect mode in God. When she expressed regret at being unable to visit the poor because her present duties prevented her,

Jesus replied that because so few think of him, he himself was one of the poor of this world.[64]

St. Thomas Aquinas wrote that humans learn most easily through the use of concrete examples which embody a universal principle; it was in this way that Jesus, the model of teachers, educated Mathilde. She saw him placing what looked like a nugget of gold in her soul. When she asked what it might be, he told her that it was "peace in the midst of crosses, peace in the midst of all things." These images, she explains, appear very suddenly in the soul when the mind is not busy. This is how they differ from images stored in the memory or formed by the imagination.[65] Sometimes she came to Mass weary in body and mind, but when Jesus manifested his presence, she felt renewed and full of courage. At such times, she wished she could tell the whole world, so that it might adore God along with her. She asked Jesus to give this same peace to other souls weary with the burden of life "and much more worthy than I am." She included a prayer for those who are, as yet, blind to the kindliness of God: "Let the scales fall from [their] eyes, that they may see you through faith, and worship you."[66]

A vision on October 8, 1882, during Benediction was similar to the one Mother Marie Thérèse had had in 1848, on the Feast of the Sacred Heart. Mathilde saw a great stream of fire pouring out of Jesus' heart and flowing towards all who were present. From several of them, a stream of love flowed back into his heart, but in many others, the stream was too weak to reach him. She also saw Jesus enlarging her own heart, so that the stream of love flowing out of it might serve as an intermediary to unite these others to him.[67] Thus she was gradually learning how she might lead others to a greater love of God.

Again, in November, she referred to verbal abuse in her home, and the divine presence comforted and strengthened her. Alluding to the person who was afflicting her, Jesus told her, "Forget yourself entirely, my beloved one, and think only of doing good to that soul." At the same time, he showed her the love with which he had died on the Cross for those who caused that death.[68] On some level, she began to find it appropriate that in God there are three Persons: she experienced each separately, yet as a unity, and felt *at home*. She was told that when her exile weighs too heavily, she should seek her rest there.[69]

It appears that Thomas was often away at Le Tréport. Their daughter Melanie kept a number of letters which he had written to her from this coastal town. In a letter dated October 2, 1882 (Melanie was then sixteen), he tells her that he had received her letter upon his return from a fishing trip with Eugene, her youngest brother, then about ten years old. They had just dropped off her uncle Adolphe (Thomas's brother-in-law, husband of his youngest sister, Henriette) at the railroad station. Adolphe regretted having to leave such a beautiful village. He closed with "I embrace with all my heart my dear little world of Vernon, my good Toutoute [nickname for Melanie] and the little mother."[70]

A year later, in another letter to Melanie from Thomas, also from Le Tréport, Thomas reports receiving a letter from Eugène, in which he has found several mistakes. These he corrected, returning the letter, apparently to Mathilde, whom he criticizes for "having pretended that it was free of mistakes." He adds in the letter to his daughter, "If I have returned it [Eugène's letter], it is evident that it was not without any reason." Also evident is Thomas's irritation with his wife, and willingness to express that to her eldest child, over what appears to be a very insignificant matter! Appended to Thomas's letter to Melanie is a postscript, written in another hand: "[Your] godmother embraces her dear goddaughter with all her heart."[71]

From these letters, we learn that Thomas's foster mother accompanied him to Le Tréport, while his wife remained in Vernon. According to Marguerite de Cabanoux, Mathilde's cousin, the elder Melanie was a woman of action, dynamic and authoritarian. She had been very generous to the orphaned Boutle children, for which they revered her all their lives. Mathilde, on the other hand, clearly was at home in the inner world of prayer, apparently as warm-hearted and sensitive to others' feelings as Melanie was unyielding.

Marguerite, Mathilde's maternal cousin, stated that "the habit of criticism and of stinging jokes which Melanie had developed in regard to her daughter-in-law, and which manifested itself unpleasantly in the behavior of Mathilde's husband, only [further] inflamed the situation." Alain Le Touzé concludes, "It seems evident that, in the course of similar stays at Le Tréport, Thomas again came under the dominating influence of his mother, who must have incited him against his wife," leading to the acid remark mentioned above. Marguerite, given her own choice of the life of an enclosed religious, would quite naturally have sympathized more with her cousin than with Thomas or his foster mother. Therefore, she may have been harder on Mathilde's mother-in-law than was justified.[72] We need not suppose that Melanie was intentionally cruel to Mathilde. As likely, she may have been merely "object-oriented" rather than "person-oriented"—

believing that there were only two ways to do things (her way and the wrong way) and quite insensitive to anyone else's opinions or feelings.

Mathilde, however, felt such behavior—today we would call it "psychological abuse"— very keenly, as a journal entry for April 5, 1883, makes clear:

> The hurts which come from without have for some time taken on a certain amount of bitterness and frequency. The person whom I believe [to be] the original source and first cause of these difficulties said to someone else that I have the patience of an angel. That's one of those very elastic ways of speaking, conventional expressions which it would be very naïve to take literally. However, I am delighted to think that at least on one point she is not scandalized concerning me. Alas, if I had [even] a little bit of virtue, and I was capable of edifying her I could perhaps do some good to [this] soul to whom my own soul owes so much beneficial suffering. My God! You know how many times I have asked you, and first of all for that other soul who is so dear to me, to convert into graces for those who attack me every distressing thing which they can do to me.[73]

CHAPTER SEVEN:
A VEILED OSTENSORIUM, 1882–1884

Mathilde made a retreat, November 16–21, 1882, no doubt at the convent in Paris, although she does not say so in her journal. She called it a "retreat of union" with God and prayed for the grace to concentrate her whole attention on God alone. On November 18, she heard these words from Jesus:

"I am mindful of you alone."

"And the others, Lord?" she asked.

"In me there is no division. I give myself wholly and entirely to you and to each soul in particular. Therefore, you should give yourself entirely to me."

Mathilde's retreat resolutions included keeping her attention fixed on God with unshakable confidence, despite any interior difficulties and troubles that might afflict her, as well as trying to answer everyone so gently that they would be forced to recognize God as the one able to make such humility possible, and worship him.[1]

Traveling several days later, passing through a town that served as a railway hub, Mathilde compared it to one who receives special graces. The railway lines cross the town so as to go beyond it; similarly the one to whom God has given special graces should not think them given for herself alone. Her outlook must be wider and more just: they are given for the sake of many others. In fact, "God chooses a *little* soul for his great designs [so] that all may know it is really *he* who is active in bringing about [every] good." He can accomplish whatever he wills with a small and imperfect instrument.[2]

Towards the end of November and the beginning of December, however, the sensible presence of God was withdrawn from Mathilde. She felt only isolation and emptiness, although her faith remained steady. She was attacked by hideous and discouraging thoughts; her confidence in God appeared as presumption, her will to serve him, illusion. "If she calls upon Jesus, she thinks he turns away from her." She offered all this darkness to

God, resigning herself to it for as long as he willed. Finally, peace was restored: Jesus asked her, with great tenderness, "What troubles you, my beloved daughter, my friend? Abide in me."[3]

Why this sudden turmoil? Perhaps it was because she was preparing to become an *agrégée* on December 8, 1882, the Feast of the Immaculate Conception. This would be a public ceremony, a deeper commitment of her entire self to God. It is common, before a major step—a different job, a move to a new city—to hesitate, even to become reluctant to make the change. When it is a major spiritual step, there can be active resistance, if not from the individual, certainly from the powers of darkness. Mystical literature repeatedly warns that the closer one is to God, the stronger these attacks. Jesus told Mathilde that her consecration would be the spiritual marriage of [her] soul with her God. Poulain adds, in a footnote, that this is not to be understood as designating the transforming union which he defines as the fourth and last stage of mystical union.[4] Mathilde didn't classify it at all; she simply resolved to make each day until then a day of retreat and preparation, honoring God in each of her family members.

Walking from the train station to the convent on December 7, she was praying. Once she arrived, she was told that on the next day she would receive not only a cross, but "also the *ring* of the spouses of Christ." This was a great favor, and she was deeply moved by it. On the morning of the feast she was absorbed in the prayer of union; it was nearly noon before she was able to say her morning prayers. Jesus said that he wished to give her this pledge of her union with him in order to assure her of her close alliance with him, and to unite her to him even more closely, but only through death would this union be consummated. Mathilde added that, had she done something for God, she would long for death, but so far, she had done nothing. Later that day she expressed her joy in being told, as she was given the ring, "It is *he* who gives it to you." She was given a religious name as well: Sister Marie-Aimée of Jesus.[5]

Mathilde was convinced that it was God who had placed her in the world, rather than in a convent, yet she longed to belong entirely to God as much as any nun. It should thus not be surprising that she still yearned for some visible sign of her inner devotion. She had asked Jesus to ratify his reign over her by some special consecration, and had regretted being unable to transform her desire to be wholly his into any concrete act. Thus, the ring, a symbol of his love and empire, was very precious to her as Jesus' affirmation of her commitment.[6] Thereafter, she noticed a change in her relations with Jesus: "Since my Beloved has called himself my Spouse he is obedient to my call. Before this, I did not dare call him so freely; now he condescends to my desires, and if he is not present within me he comes as soon as my heart calls him. Doubtless, there will still be periods of absence and trial, . . . but where could I better find the strength to bear them than in those relations of sweet familiarity with my Lord and my God!"[7]

Mathilde was convinced that it was because of her insignificance that God had loaded her with so many graces—too many to enumerate. She writes, "That a genius should be tempted to pride is, humanly speaking, conceivable. . . . But if a thought of pride presented itself to a poor little woman like me, . . . not only would such a thought be *wrong* but also *ridiculous*, and . . . a sense of the absurdity of such a pride is the best guarantee against it."[8]

There was, however, no change in her outward relationships. On January 4, she noted that during the previous few days she had been molested, humiliated, and miserable. Humorously, she thanked Jesus for not having forgotten "the New Year gifts" for his spouse. The end of one year and the beginning of the next was celebrated with various gatherings, which she could not avoid. What made her really suffer was being obliged to listen, even for half an hour, to trivial worldly conversation. She felt estranged by all the insignificant things she heard, to which she had to make some reply. Although she tried her best, she supposed that others must have believed her to be absent-minded, and found her as strange as she found them. But for the grace of God, she would have been no different than they. She then prayed that they might be brought to know God better.[9]

Jesus assured Mathilde that she loved him with a unique love— that is, a love which prefers him to all other persons and things, a love for him alone. He told her that he loved her, and not only her, but each unique human being in a way as unique as each is. God's love, as Mathilde expressed it in her journal, is not a universal, homogenous love, divided among many, but a particular love. (A Thomist might say that God's love is individuated according to the openness of each recipient.) Only God can love in this way; God's love embraces the entire world, giving it being. Thus, even the person whom we love best, whom we have most obviously been given by God, "will never be *necessary* to our heart with anything more than a *secondary* necessity, resulting from the place which God has marked out for the person in our destiny."[10]

This does not mean that there need be any conflict between one's love for God and one's love for other humans. But Jacques Maritain describes the way in which one's love for another person can become so consuming that there is no room for God. Such a lover will resist any claim, even by God, on the beloved's devotion.[11] That is, by idolizing another human being, one can create a conflict, but if one loves God as God, and other humans as human, there is no problem.

Being obliged, as she wrote, to go to the theatre, Mathilde nevertheless remained in God's presence: "What does the spectacle of human passions, even when most *idealized,* count when compared to the memory of Jesus solitary, in the loneliness of the church, at night?" Recalling the vision of Jesus' white robe, given to her the day before, she could visualize it more clearly than the performance before her bodily eyes.[12] Mathilde's references to being tried by her "fellow creatures," and sometimes also by having no sense of God's loving presence, appear frequently, although his presence is usually restored to her during her morning and evening vocal prayers, which consoles her.

Attempting to describe her inner state in times of turmoil, Mathilde compares it to the interior of a ship rolling violently in a storm: "Everything it contains is in disorder, except those things which, being suspended, remain . . . vertical . . . perpendicular both to the surface of the sea and to the vault of heaven. Thus it is with my poor soul, everything is confused, upside down, save the straight line of the will which remains fixed on God."[13]

Mathilde then considers that this painful state, against which reason is powerless, is the result of a resolution she had made after Confession the previous evening to *seek occasions* in which to sacrifice nature to God. "It would give the Tempter a great advantage if he were able to trouble us, or just distract us a little from [carrying out] our resolutions by such activities." He would like to *humanize* her thinking, causing her to look at herself rather than attend to God. To do so, she believed, would be a sacrilege. But if God were to leave her to herself, she would be unable to resist the temptation, in spite of her resolution. She was certain, however, that her Spouse would never abandon her.[14] After several days, "Jesus healed her by impressing on her the glance of His love." She stipulated that this was no imaginative vision. She likened it to the light and heat of the sun shining on a blind person, dying of cold and fatigue. Though he cannot see it, he can feel it; it gives him a new vigor. This, she writes, is not an adequate comparison, but no earthly comparison could be adequate.[15]

These temptations could go so far as to challenge her faith and confidence in God: "At times an absurd and unreasoning discouragement takes hold of me. . . . Jesus hides himself almost continually." Such trials, frequent among mystics, caused Mathilde to fear that she had consented to them.[16] But she writes that Jesus delivered her from her torment by asking, "Don't I cherish you as my very dear one?" This expression of approval sustained her amidst these disturbances.[17]

Here is her explanation of how she distinguished imaginative visions from the ordinary working of the imagination. In ordinary imagination, an *idea* exists in our mind *before the image*. But in the visions given by God in prayer, the reverse is true: "The soul sees interiorly *first an image* and the light to comprehend what she sees is given *subsequently*."[18] Unlike many mystics, Mathilde did not have visions of Jesus' passion, but on Good Friday night she awakened, terrified, from a nightmare of hearing a voice that ordered her to the stocks and condemned her. She thought that perhaps Satan was amusing himself, but decided it was probably just the work of her imagination, since she had been meditating on Jesus' Passion earlier.[19]

Mathilde, given an insight into the perfections of God, is also shown that God's perfections are not distinct from him. She writes, "*God is what he has. Jesus himself is his Amiability.*" Jesus sheds some of the rays of this Amiability upon the earth to make the ugliness of life more bearable.[20] Still a Frenchwoman, Mathilde continued to pray for France. Jesus showed her the love with which he desired to save her country and told her, "It is [the French] who do not, as yet, wish to be saved." He also showed her his love for sinners. She writes that, if we were to see the love with which he forgives us, we would never be able to offend him.[21]

Mathilde greeted February 12, her thirty-ninth birthday: "One year less between me and Your Eternity, O my Jesus!" Not a very common reaction, even among devout Christians; fear of meeting God was far more common. What accounted for this difference, she writes, is that Jesus had so often manifested his kindness to her, so she could not fear him.[22] She writes about the ability to be absorbed in prayer even while busy about her duties—walking through town, speaking with others, shopping—without anyone being aware of it. As finding even a quarter of an hour to make a visit was often a challenge for her, this was no small blessing.[23]

Later, after an exceedingly trying day, Jesus told her, "If you choose, I will give you empire over all those around you." Instead Mathilde chose his own empire: the cross and humiliations. She was reluctant to dwell too much on the graces which she had received, "because nature would run the risk of seeking itself in them; neither can she dwell always in the thought of her crosses, because this would prove too burdensome to nature." Rather, she should dwell on God himself above all graces and crosses.[24]

At the beginning of March, Mathilde had a vision of the Trinity. She specifies that this was not an imaginative vision, but what she had learned to call an intellectual one: "that intimate and penetrating knowledge which imposes itself on the soul with an authority above all certitude and which she feels can only be imposed on her by God himself."[25] Poulain defines intellectual visions as "visions perceived by the mind alone, without any interior image."[26] All Mathilde's visions of the Trinity are of this sort. She writes, "It is only in that prayer of union with the Three Divine Persons that the idea of Trinity and Unity becomes so simple and luminous to the soul."[27] Poulain comments that this intellectual vision of the Trinity recurs often in her journal.[28] Mathilde later noted that a single intellectual vision compensated her a hundredfold for all the harsh and bitter struggles she endured—in fact, for all the sorrows of life.[29]

According to an earlier Church calendar, March 14 was the Feast of St. Matilda, her patron saint. On that day in 1883, Mathilde noted this.[30] She said no more about the saint, so we do not know what she knew about the latter. But there are striking parallels. The saint was well-brought-up, married the King of Saxony, and bore him five children. She was kind and gracious to everyone, generous to the poor, and loved her husband and children. Her husband died after only twenty-three years of marriage, as would Thomas. One big difference between them, however, was that St. Matilda "was the joy of her husband who trusted her in all things."[31]

During a visit to the Blessed Sacrament, Mathilde found herself, against her will, prey to a thousand distractions and preoccupations. After about fifteen minutes of struggle, Jesus rested his hand on her head, which ended all the tumult. He drew her into a union which "left me just enough consciousness of my existence to allow me to feel that, [had he] chosen to take my soul for all eternity, she would have gone to him *without . . . bestowing a thought on the world.*" Making a special Communion of reparation or of petition for the salvation of souls often plunged her into an interior state of "indescribable anguish" even though the summit of her soul remained intimately united with Jesus. It felt like "the chill and silence of death." She accepted this as his will.[32] The more she advanced in prayer, the more frequently was she subject to attacks from the evil spirit, especially after Communion. When she offered the torment for other communicants, it ceased.[33]

During Passion Week (the week preceding Holy Week), Mathilde was suddenly assailed by temptations against the faith which were so violent that she felt as if all her limbs were being broken; Jesus delivered her by uniting her with himself. But whether or not she experienced God's sensible presence, her one desire was to serve him as wholeheartedly when he seemed absent as in times of consolation. On Holy Saturday, she experienced more temptations against faith and confidence in God: "At times an absurd and unreasoning discouragement takes hold of me" when Jesus hides himself. "Yet at moments he shows himself and uplifts me."[34]

Again, at the beginning of Holy Week, fearing an increase of public offenses and violence against God and the Church, she prayed for France, offering to God the innocence of the singing birds, uniting herself with them and with the priests, monks, and nuns who were awake and praying, and expressing her willingness to take the offenders' deserved punishment on herself. "Reign over the souls of France, . . . but do not avenge yourself with rigor. . . . Do not crush our poor nation utterly. . . . Treat her with . . . mercy and love."[35]

It would be a mistake to think that Mathilde was beyond anger when unjustly criticized. When, after a very busy day, she had to listen to some harsh words, she wrote that while her will was saying *fiat*, "nature was rampant within me." But when she began her evening prayers, Jesus, "with great sweetness," said, "Tell Me your sorrows; you can say anything to me. To complain to me is still a prayer." This so comforted her that she "had no desire to complain anymore."[36] When she was too hard on herself, he reprimanded her: "Be patient with yourself since I am patient with you!" And he taught her not to be astonished that his goodness left certain imperfections in order to preserve humility. Jesus' reprimand was so gentle and loving that it calmed and encouraged her. She asked for the grace to reprimand others, when it was her duty, in the same gentle way.[37]

Mathilde took great joy in the piety of her children. Melanie, her eldest, at sixteen, had not become distracted by "a taste for pleasure." Elisabeth, who was eight, asked always for "stories about the good God" and confided all her little secrets to her mother. Eugène, her youngest son, seemed at twelve to have displayed too much "natural vivacity" for his mother's comfort. As the day of his First Communion was approaching, she prayed especially for him.[38] But she also took human delight in them: "Today [May 6, 1883] was the first real spring day. My daughters were wearing dainty light dresses and I took some pleasure in watching the one with the graces of her sixteen summers, and the other with her childish charm." She feared that she had taken too much pleasure in watching them, and reproached herself for it. Jesus responded by showing her the divine beauty, which is the source of all created beauty.[39]

Eugène made his First Confession on May 19. While praying for him, Mathilde felt guilty for a moment of indignation several days earlier, during which she had spoken sharply to someone for repeating "for perhaps the fiftieth time," an unjust comment about someone not present to refute it. She scolded herself, "I must never forget that those who speak like this suffer themselves from their mood." She would have liked to confess this fault, but her pastor was busy with the children. Her regret troubled her, but Jesus forgave her while forgiving her son.[40]

Under the republican government, religious practice steadily declined in France. Fewer Frenchmen and women were fulfilling even their obligation of an annual communion at Easter time, although the percentages varied in different regions. No figures are available for the diocese of Evreux, to which Vernon belongs, but according to the figures for Paris and environs, the total number of Easter Communions was less than 15 percent of the population.[41] This indifference was a grief to Mathilde. She wrote that on May 26 she was "praying with great anguish . . . for the souls of France." Jesus assured her that "he could not permit one of those souls to be lost for lack of help, since he does not allow even . . . infidels, if they seek the truth sincerely, to lose God for lack of the means to know him." She protested, "Think of the perils and evil influences of our troubled times." The response she recorded for her confessor was, "I will ask less of those who have lived in these days. But do you know to what degree I can draw good out of evil?"[42]

In the summer of 1883, most of the family took a trip. Thomas wrote to his daughter, Melanie, from Le Tréport that during the trip she would be sharing a room with his sister, her aunt Henriette. Albert was at School in Paris, and Elisabeth remained in Vernon, perhaps considered too young to accompany the rest of the family. The two younger boys, Adolphe and Eugène, were included, as was Mathilde. Thomas's foster mother may well have been included also, but this is not clear. The family left on June 16 and reached Tours in the evening. Mathilde managed only a short visit to the little church while they were taking a walk in the evening.

During this trip, Mathilde had very little time to herself, and very little opportunity to engage in the spiritual practices she maintained at home. There, in addition to daily Mass, a typical day included attending vespers and benediction in the afternoon, as well as the rosary, spiritual reading, and fortnightly confession. While traveling, Mathilde had little opportunity to pray regularly, and almost none to keep her journal. She was expected to share in whatever the others were doing, which seemed mainly to be sightseeing. Sometimes she was able to get to Mass, but not always. Yet she did not lose the sense of Jesus' loving presence. He told her, "Wherever you go, there My Heart is ready to receive you." Nor was she spared the usual "tirades and raillery on the subject of devotion," as she later described in her journal. Jesus reassured her, "You were not created *for them*, but *for me*."[43]

On June 17, the family went to Poitiers, and the next day, to Rochefort, which they reached in the evening, but left too early the next morning for Mathilde to attend Mass. This saddened her. She offered her deprivation for those who either do not receive Communion or who do so without devotion. In her hotel room, she prayed that Jesus would give all those who might sleep in that room a grace corresponding to their dispositions in Holy Communion. On the train the following day, she adored Jesus in all the churches where Mass was being celebrated. He united her to himself, and she would have liked to attend to him alone, but was not allowed to: "I am interrupted. . . . I must discuss politics a little . . . then share in some slight joke . . . then open my eyes to see a ruin, a river, a view, all things interesting in themselves, but just at this moment I should like to see nothing!"[44]

On the afternoon of June 22, the travelers reached and apparently spent several days at Romaneau. Thomas described it as "an excellent estate abounding in flowers and shade. There are hundreds of nightingales and everyone smiles at us." He added that not only were the inhabitants pleasant, they were respectful and religious.[45] They were staying at a chateau which had a chapel in which the Blessed Sacrament was reserved. Mathilde took refuge in it as often as she could. She prayed that Jesus' charity would overflow from her onto others, that it might be the particular characteristic of all she said and did. Even when she had no opportunity to attend Mass, Jesus covered her with his mantle, and when she rejoined her companions, she was still as recollected as if she had been in the convent chapel in Paris. She remarked that it meant a lot to her to be sleeping under the same roof that sheltered Jesus.[46]

On July 3, however, she was unable to receive Communion since the priest in the neighboring church was ill. The family was to leave early the next morning, but she was promised that if the priest was able, he would give her Communion before they left. Mathilde mentioned her intention and completed all her preparations for the journey before going to the church. Despite her efforts to avoid inconvenience for her family, she writes, "There was some unpleasantness on my return. This worried me; I feared lest I had offended God and scandalized my companions. . . . I think I would not mind appearing *mad* myself if only it did not reflect on holy devotion."[47] Mathilde feared that by insisting on her own desires to attend Mass, she may have been perceived to have failed her duties to her family. Her concern was not for her own reputation, but that her conduct would discourage "holy devotion."

On the way to La Rochelle, they visited the coast. There was an old chapel, still in use, on an island offshore, where Mathilde was able to pray. She was glad of this, since they returned to the mainland too late for her to visit the church. From La Rochelle they proceeded to Nantes. it was a Sunday, but she was unable to be present at the High Mass because it was dinnertime. At the time for vespers, the family went for a walk in the Botanical Gardens and she admired the trees, offering the coolness of their shade to their Creator and uniting herself with the Divine Office during the conversation. Despite their intention of participating in the service, they reached the cathedral just as it was ending. She said that she did not want to blame anyone for this. She must have been tired, for she wrote that it was with difficulty that she remained standing, and prayed not to wobble visibly. Fortunately, they were only there for a quarter of an hour.[48]

Their next stop was Le Mans. Mathilde noticed that some fellow travelers who had earlier been sending her little sneers were now occasionally going to morning Mass. On July 13, at Caen, Mathilde learned that Albert, her eldest son, who was at boarding school in Paris, was seriously ill, and she was unable to go to him at once. Although she willed whatever God wanted, she was very anxious. The next day was Bastille Day, a legal holiday (Mathilde called it an impious celebration), so she could get no news concerning her son. During Mass on the following day, she prayed earnestly for him, asking only what was best for him. Turning to Jesus, she asked him to be with the child in her place, since she was unable to embrace him tenderly herself. She felt as if she was in the Garden of Olives with Jesus. Still, no news.[49]

On July 16, the Feast of Our Lady of Mount Carmel (a special day for her, as it was the anniversary of her first experience of the presence of God nine years earlier), she arrived in Paris. To her great joy, Albert was beginning to recover. He had told his professor "I don't see why the Blessed Virgin hasn't cured me! She certainly can, and she wants to cure me!" The priest who had been caring for him said that, in his opinion, if it wasn't a miracle of the first order, it was at least a miraculous event. Mathilde poured out her gratitude to Jesus and to Mary. The latter's protection gave her confidence that he would mature well, in spite of his flightiness. Her eldest son was now Mary's child more than her own.[50] A few days later, Thomas took the recovering Albert to Le Tréport. From there he wrote to his older daughter that her brother was still not strong, but was improving every day. The doctor had recommended lots of cod-liver oil, drunk with beer. They must have been fishing, as he was sending her some fish, and hoped they would reach her in good shape.[51]

Back home in Vernon, Mathilde's life went on pretty much as before. Jesus counseled her to serve others with "divine kindness." This might seem excessive by human standards, but Mathilde would actually be giving herself to God through her service.[52] At the end of July, she wrote that she had come to church full of worry and with a violent headache. The Holy Spirit advised her to regard her sufferings as her cross, and accept them as Jesus had accepted his cross—that is, with love. God's words always empowered her to do what she was asked; she felt able to love beyond what she would have believed possible.[53]

Near the beginning of August, a natural disaster had occurred on the Italian island of Ischia, killing thousands almost instantly. Mathilde was moved by this, and while she prayed for them, asked Jesus why he had permitted so many to die so suddenly and so terribly. His reply, which seemed to satisfy her, was that in those moments of agony they had shortened or eliminated their time in purgatory.[54]

During a prayer of intense union, the Holy Spirit instructed her to love especially those who afflicted her since they caused her distantly to resemble Jesus. She saw Jesus in the Eucharist as a hidden victim; this made it possible for her to view her own situation in a way that gave it meaning. "This is how I ought to be, whether the cross comes directly from God or through the instrumentality of men . . . a hidden victim, unknown to the world, seeing my intentions misunderstood."[55] She added that a single intellectual vision compensated her a hundredfold for all the harsh and bitter struggles she had endured, in fact, all the sorrows of life.[56] Jesus taught her how to distinguish her own mental activity from God's action. During the time of passive prayer, Mathilde explains, normal mental activity tends to make the person quit the passive state whereas any word, light, or intellectual or imaginative vision which comes from God increases [the person's] peace and delight and makes [the person] penetrate more deeply into God. It also renews the person's strength.[57]

That God was never included in the conversations Mathilde had with those she loved best saddened her.[58] She also observed that, whenever she had prayed earnestly for someone, she immediately had to suffer either at the person's hands or on the person's account. This made Mathilde happy. She reasoned that if God had not wanted to hear her petition, he would not have added a little sacrifice to her poor prayers. Moreover, she realized that she should not turn her attention from God on account of her suffering, which is inseparable from love in this life. She understood that her task was to suffer for love, but the thought of love is to predominate always.[59] She struggled to chase away all thoughts, however innocent, which did not have God as their object.[60] At the end of a week of interior trials, Jesus said to her, "Fear not. It is I." And he covered her with his white mantle. This delivered her from all those temptations, and she thought no more of them.[61]

Later that same month, Mathilde was to visit a house where she had spent part of her childhood. She was anticipating seeing it again with great pleasure. Jesus warned her "with great kindness" not to be so attached to it. She remembered his telling her that dwelling on such things was a hindrance to union.[62] Again, at the beginning of September, she was terribly tempted by doubts against faith, and by despair; an impression of the Divine Simplicity dissipated them. Jesus told her, "Take everything that leads you to me and leave all the rest." [63] Even when Jesus said nothing, his mere presence brought her peace.[64] He also taught her that just as we are pleasant to the relatives of those we love so as not to grieve the hearts of our friends, he also looks with loving care on those his friends love, and gives them gifts which his friends desire for them—but cannot give them themselves.[65] A vision of Jesus adored by the angels helped her to understand how we will enjoy our friends in heaven without it affecting the union of our souls with God.[66] Seeing all those angels, she implored them to pray for France.[67]

Mathilde specifically mentions the scriptural reference to Mary and Martha. In spite of the fact that the Marthas of the world (including, perhaps, Melanie Bellanger) did not appreciate her more interior form of worship, Mathilde held them in high regard. She prayed to be given a little of their virtue, but did not regret that she could do so little for God. "I am content to do all I can to fulfill my daily duties well; I am content with my inferiority."

The family and friends of Mathilde were puzzled that she prayed without using a book.[68] Aside from the vocal prayers she had memorized in childhood, she prayed spontaneously, reflecting on his counsel: "Do with love the little things which call forth daily unselfishness, do them with a love which can be seen and felt. Always look pleased with others." She blamed herself for her occasional impatience with her children. "How tiresome you are! This is soon said, but is it divine amiability?"[69] No matter how much a mother may love her children, normal children are trying at times. Nevertheless, Mathilde noted in September that the noise her children made was not getting on her nerves as it had the last year.[70] Such patience and tolerance can have a powerful effect on children!

Mathilde described her life at this time as one of vicissitudes; her exterior life was overly driven and often troubled, and her interior life alternated between deep peace and temptations, desolations, and even the fear of being reprobate. She dealt with this fear by begging God to at least let her serve him in this life. It was God the Father who calmed her on this occasion. He said, "My child, my beloved daughter." She states, "If only others knew what a good and loving Father they have!" But she further comments that it was not often that the Father spoke to her; usually it was Jesus or the Holy Spirit.[71]

A woman had asked Mathilde to come and play a little on the piano for her. She felt obliged to go, "lest they think that piety is not kind." But it was a sad experience, because the family for which she played seemed to have lost the Faith. Mathilde felt as if she were playing before a corpse, and so prayed for them the whole time she entertained them.[72]

Adoration Réparatrice sponsored an annual retreat for the *agrégées* at the convent. In 1883, it was scheduled for November 17–21, which was the Feast of the Presentation of Mary. It was also the day on which the nuns renewed their consecration. Mathilde's prayer at the beginning of the retreat was for a deeper knowledge of God's will, so that she might always do it. Jesus replied that his will was to keep her united with him, no less in suffering than in joy. After communion on the second day of the retreat, the kindness of Jesus was shown to her. She described it as a "unique, an unspeakable kindness." She contemplated his kindness for the rest of the day.

The instruction next day included these words: "If God has given you the spirit of religion while leaving you in the world, it is so that you can sanctify it." These words rekindled Mathilde's habitual desire to do good to those outside her own immediate circle. She would like to visit the sick and speak to them about God, help the dying to make a good death, teach the little children, trying to make them aware of God. She recognized that in her present situation such service was not practicable, but if God willed it, he would open a way.[73]

Still, despite Mathilde's understanding that God had willed her to be in the world, she felt a persistent sadness in her heart that she was not as wholly God's as were the religious sisters. In this regard, she resembled the mother of St. Thérèse of Lisieux. Rejected without explanation by the Mother Superior of the religious order to which she had sought entrance, Thérèse's mother "had to face the fact that, denied bridehood with Christ, she might have to reconcile herself to the second-class status of Catholic women, motherhood."[74] Mme. Martin (mother of Thérèse) was born in 1831, thirteen years before the birth of Mathilde. The higher value accorded to religious consecration for women—by people, *not* by God—lasted well beyond these two mothers' lifetimes, at least until Vatican II. Their sense of regret was occasioned by the belief that, as married women, they were not fully consecrated to God.

Jesus consoled Mathilde with these words: "In your marriage, your heart remained virgin." At the close of the retreat, she noted its fruits: a much deeper peace and abandonment to God's will in all crosses, whether interior or exterior, both those in the present and those to come.[75]

Being charitable did not mean being blind to human foolishness. Mathilde reflected on the banality of so much interpersonal dialogue, the ease with which people "chatter about all they know and much that they don't know, amusing the company with clever sayings which agreeably dissect the character of absent friends, until it is their turn to be absent. . . . All this is scarcely admitted to be a fault at all. It is common currency, and always tolerated even when it is not approved." On the other hand, to converse with the "Lord of heaven and earth, that is intolerable, or at least useless . . . a thing which lends itself to criticism . . . so much lost time!" It is acceptable, she writes,

> to do what is strictly necessary for salvation, what entails a mediocre standard of religious observance, but that these religious duties should be fulfilled more out of love than fear . . . this is what the spirit of the world will not admit . . . will not tolerate. And how it takes revenge! With pity, with half-concealed smiles and discreet commiseration, society pronounces the word *dévot, dévote!* It accuses women of being "commonplace," going to church "without knowing why," frequenting the sacraments "by routine," or being "high-flown and mystical." There is no medium. Or else "*bigots* who believe only in their particular priest." Men are "weak minds led by their wives . . . people of limited capacity," etc.[76]

She concludes with this: "In the end, they are unable to . . . understand how the devout have such bad taste as to find God more amiable than the world, and such a narrow mind as to be content with the Infinite."[77]

Mathilde was told by Jesus that she would have great crosses; she felt a certain fear "not precisely because I myself shall have to suffer, but because I shall have to suffer in others or to see them suffer on account of my crosses." Precisely what these crosses would be, or when to expect them, he did not tell her. (In fact, they would begin in less than a year. She would try very hard, but unsuccessfully, to hide her pain from her family.) Meanwhile, her education continued. On Christmas Day, Jesus gave her a rule for doing good to others. She writes, "In order to gain souls to God, it is necessary to prove to them that God loves them, and in order to prove to them that God loves them, I am to love them."[78]

The role of suffering as it was commonly understood during Mathilde's lifetime was characterized by two important elements. The first was a conviction that whatever befell a person in life, whatever the pain it might occasion, was a function of divine will. The second was a belief that suffering in the human world reduced the experience of purgatory after death. Illustrating these points, Nevin writes,

> Zélie [the mother of St. Thérèse of Lisieux] had lived with discomfort in her breast for many years. The cancer set a new and rapid course which even therapy as we know it might not arrest…[Nevertheless, Zélie's] helplessness was not conditioned by fearful procrastination; it was essentially a function of her faith. At no time did she give up the certainty which had guided her entire life, that its course was determined by God. If it was the divine will that she live, then she would live. If it was her time to die, she knew that Marie was old enough to replace her as caretaker of the children.
>
> In tandem with such acceptance ran the belief that suffering in this life would advance the soul's purification and thus reduce the amount of time it would have to spend in purgatory. . . . Suffering was a way of settling accounts for one's failings in life, a reduction of debits which implicitly stored up credits for the next world. This bookkeeping mentality . . . informed Catholicism then as to a degree it still does.[79]

In brief, suffering was both beyond the capacity of a human being to regulate, and a difficult means toward a desirable end.

The beginning of the New Year was a time of special family gatherings. Mathilde wrote of a jumble of impressions: the delight of the children which brought smiles to the faces of the adults, regret for those absent and those grieving, private grudges all the more painful when one recalled earlier expressions of affection. What made it especially sad for her was when Jesus hid himself, as he sometimes did.[80] At a gathering later in January, she had been asked to play. She wrote that it was the first time she had not been nervous while playing for others "because I did not desire to play either better or worse than my Beloved wished me to." She always found such gatherings boring and tiring, but she was obliged to go and join in the conversation.

In February 1884, she was asked to play at another gathering. In the middle of her performance, she stopped suddenly and could not recover herself. This surprised everyone because they all knew her to be a gifted pianist, and it had never happened before. She was not perturbed by it; she thought it good for her to be "at least somewhat despised and held in contempt."[81] In contrast, when others noticed that she was a good example, she attributed this to the novenas which holy persons were making for her eyes. God must have granted their requests in a different way, since she would never have been able to attain this degree of calm and charity on her own.[82] Jesus taught Mathilde that the saints were able to perform such mighty works because of their purity of intention. They willed only one thing—to fulfill God's will no matter what they were doing. Hence they rested in the midst of action and worked more fruitfully, rather than being consumed by different motivations and enthusiasm in carrying out different tasks, which wearies people.[83]

Jesus was teaching Mathilde in other ways as well. For a fortnight, he allowed her to endure suffering and worry without any sense of his presence. She saw only her sins and became extremely fearful of having offended God. It seemed to her that everything in her was evil—except her will, which clung firmly to him. She had lost the remembrance of his graces and felt at the same time a strong repugnance to writing her journal, even to rereading it. She did reread a few pages out of obedience, however, as her director had counseled her in a similar situation earlier. She believed herself to be as rigid and insensible as a corpse, and she felt that nothing would ever be any different. From time to time, brief reappearances of grace revived her, but the darkness returned immediately. She ended the passage with this: "I have felt during these times that I have become altogether indifferent to the state in which God sets me." Her spiritual director added a comment: "So much the better!"[84]

Mathilde was urged by "a special mercy" to mention her recent failings. She had a servant whom she described as a good person, very estimable and trustworthy . . .

> who, I think, has a rather sleepy brain, or perhaps she has not learned to use it, for she regularly misplaces everything. Well, this accumulation of stupidity and negligence, to which I ought to be pretty well accustomed, became to me, on a . . . day on which I was badly disposed physically and morally, a source of perpetual annoyance. . . . I confess it to my shame, that in putting each thing back into its place . . . I grumbled to myself against the poor culprit at each fresh stupidity, and mentally accredited her with qualifications anything but flattering. I do not know how it happened; I was regretting it even while I did it. Yet I still did it, because, at first, reflection did not come in time to cut short the first word.[85]

She knew it was wrong, and though Jesus forgave her at Communion, she confessed it with many regrets. After she received absolution, Jesus showed her the ugliness of the fault. In that illumination, she realized the greatness of the so-called little faults; she felt a strong resolution forming within her to be ever patient and charitable with her associates.[86] Mathilde adds that Jesus' voice *never* distresses her, even when he reprimands her. Rather, it relieves and consoles her. "If the sorrow I feel over my faults is bitter, it is when I speak of them to myself. But when I speak of them to Jesus, and above all, when he speaks to me, everything is different. His presence alone is enough to reassure me."[87]

Again, early in March, Mathilde was ill and confined to bed for eight days, deprived of the Eucharist, and in too much discomfort to be able to do much praying. At her usual time of prayer, feeling a little better, she adored Our Lord; suddenly she was flooded with his light. The practical and immediate result was that she went with much joy to listen to her children's lessons in spite of her fatigue, so that she could maintain their usual daily schedule. She felt herself sustained by physical energy which her condition could not account for.[88]

Mathilde recalled her reaction, during catechism class, to first hearing about sin. As she was beginning to understand what was meant, she "felt an indescribable fear." Her devout mother had increased her daughter's insight by pointing out the way in which some Christians think nothing of deliberate sins, so long as they are not mortal, and thus do not expose them to the possibility of eternal damnation. Mathilde was horrified at the thought of God's love being so insulted, and immediately resolved "*never* to commit a voluntary and deliberate fault, however small it might appear . . . to be." She did not think she had ever broken this resolution.[89] (In fact, her spiritual director had told her that she had never, to his knowledge, committed a deliberate sin; to her great joy, Jesus had confirmed this.)[90] She added a prayer in gratitude for mothers who know how to be God's spokesperson for their children.[91]

In her usual modest fashion, Mathilde added that God must have accompanied her mother's words with a very powerful grace since she had felt it her whole life, and turned to him in prayer and thanksgiving. How could she have been protected from her weakness and illusions, from all her miseries; how could she have preserved an unshakable resolution in her heart unless God, in his incomparable love, had been watching over her? She prayed, "Ah, Lord, if this barren soil has borne fruit, it is [due to] all your graces."[92]

Not all Mathilde's insights were given to her by God. Regarding human interaction, her natural astuteness was quite sufficient. Here is an example:

> One must never tell people that they are unreasonable as if they themselves were blind to the fact. This is to be *too blunt*; self-love is mounted guard at the door and no one passes that sentinel. It is wiser to . . . creep in by some narrow passage . . . making oneself as small as possible. No one stops you . . . so one can reach the heart of the citadel. . . . Once there, one can cleverly awaken good thoughts which slumber in a corner of the conscience or the judgment; this thought has only to show itself for its proprietor to realize that . . . if he were not so weak and if it were not for this or that . . . he would much prefer to follow the path of common sense than to feel he is positively turning his back on it. This done, the first point is gained, for his eyes are now open to the light without seeing who holds the torch, and none ever appeal from the tribunal of their own justice.[93]

For Mathilde, keeping a record of everything—given the limited time at her disposal and "all the graces which are multiplying themselves"—was difficult. This was also true of all the instructions she was continually receiving from Jesus. She did set down one important fact: any advice that had come to her, "whether in spiritual direction or in a sermon or in my reading," had always been given to her by God beforehand. "Direction afterwards confirms and develops the teaching which I received from God; there is an admirable conformity between these exterior and interior helps; the conformity of truth."[94]

Toward the end of May, Mathilde was ill again. For six days, she was unable to leave the house and found it difficult to concentrate on prayer. This worried her, as she wondered how she would manage when she grew old, when her head would be unsteady and her thoughts dim. It was one thing to see old age as "next door to eternity," but she would find it very hard to feel her heart hardened and her spirit empty before God. Therefore she brought her concern to Jesus, fearing that such worry was an imperfection. He replied that if old age were to weaken her, the graces she had received would remain. Furthermore, she had no way of knowing what condition she would be in if she lived to grow old. She said no more; she humbled herself and entrusted everything else to God.[95]

We may see here a similarity to the doctrine of Thérèse of Lisieux, a younger contemporary, also in Normandy, but of whom Mathilde could not have heard. Mathilde learns the importance of spiritual childhood directly from Jesus: "to be like a child who does not know even what its father is going to do with it, and who entrusts itself without seeking to know this." She is always to ask him to do for her all that she is unable to do for herself.[96]

Having been told by Jesus that he wins souls by love, and that he longs for a relationship with them so much that he throws down every obstacle between the divine greatness and human unworthiness, and empties himself to attract them, Mathilde determined to do likewise herself.[97] She made two resolutions: first, to overlook and forgive the failings of others, and second, to seek all opportunities to go out of her way for others.[98]

She also made use of every opportunity for prayer or adoration her duties allowed. In July 1884, while accompanying her children to the Casino to hear a band, she made a supplementary adoration while listening, rather than saying her rosary privately. The concert, held from four to five, precluded her from being at the church from five to six, as she was accustomed to doing. And she was required to be home by six, although she had nothing to do until dinnertime. "If I were alone without the children, it would be the time spent at the Casino which would be shortened. Indeed, I probably would not go there at all." But since she was there, she adored

Jesus for all those present, most of whom probably did not think of him at all, at least not there or then.[99] Again, a few days later, she wrote of having [only] a few moments between dinner and the concert in which to pray.[100] The very active social life expected of an upper-middle-class matron must have been a real trial to her!

Early in 1884, Melanie Bellanger sold her house in Meulan and purchased one in Le Tréport. At the beginning of the summer, Thomas joined her there to help with the renovations. He lent a hand to the work himself, as he wrote his daughter: "We are in the midst of masons and bricklayers, which leaves me neither the time nor the place to write. Just now I am working on your little room, which will be a beauty. I am working like a real plasterer, but when you come, everything will be in order."[101]

On July 2, Mme. Bellanger also wrote to her goddaughter, Melanie. The granddaughter must have sent some roses, for which her godmother thanked her. She expressed regret that Mathilde had been ill, and hoped to hear soon that she had completely recovered: "The air at Le Tréport will undoubtedly be good for her." She complained that things were not moving as quickly as she wished; the workers slowed down when she was not there. The lovely ivy had to be removed from around the window of Melanie's bedroom because it would attract flies and spiders, but through that window, one could see the cliffs. And Melanie's father was painting a panel in the dining room. Thomas added that they were awaiting the arrival of the entire family with impatience.[102]

The family arrived for the vacation in July; Thomas's foster mother was then in Paris. She wrote from there to her goddaughter that she was happy to know the arrangement of the latter's room had pleased her. She had been shopping with Sarah (Thomas's sister) for various items, especially a statue of the Blessed Virgin, and wanted the advice of Henriette's husband, since he sold religious objects as well as printed holy cards.[103]

Mathilde, their two daughters, and Eugène, their youngest son, were no sooner settled at Le Tréport than Thomas, Albert, Adolphe and Mme. Bellanger took off for London. This was not in order to seek his father's family; he made no such effort. Rather, the group behaved like typical tourists, seeing the sights and staying in a French hotel near Regent Street, which he described to his eldest daughter as the loveliest street in London. It had many things to admire, but none to compare with Paris. The two boys, however, "were as happy as little kings." He concluded with warm, good wishes from her godmother, and he embraced all of them across the distance which separated them.[104]

Mathilde's journal suggests that she and those who stayed with her remained at Le Tréport for six weeks. She also wrote that leaving the sea was not as hard as when she was younger: "It used to seem as if I were saying farewell to a person. . . . But now, as I see only God in it and since God does not leave me, I no longer have this regret."[105] While the other family members were away, she tried to encourage the three children's spiritual growth, commenting that childbirth was nothing compared to the responsibility and challenge of bringing children up properly. She begged God that they might become worthy of him, might become what he willed for them. When she offered to him her anxieties regarding them, he, in turn, showed her that if we offer to him those whom he has given us, we find them again in him.[106]

The return trip took nearly a whole day. One traveler found the journey insipid and boring. Mathilde did not; she was united to God the entire time. Nevertheless, she found the trip tiring and could make only a brief prayer when she arrived home. As she had previously observed in the astonishment of recognition, however, God often provides the essence of a longer prayer in the space of a few minutes.[107]

Mathilde at the time
of her marriage: 1865.

Thomas at the time of
her marriage: 1865.

Mathilde at fifty, typing.

Mathilde knitting, undated.

Mathilde with grandson,
Jean Le Touzé, 1894.

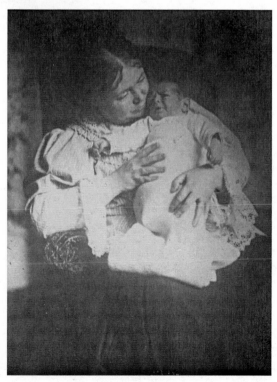

Mathilde with crying
grandchild, undated.

Elisabeth, her daughter
who died at 14 ½.

Family grave
in Vernon.

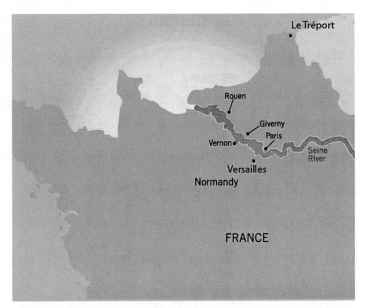

A map of northwest France, showing Paris and Normandy
to the English Channel

Chapelle de l'Adoration Réparatrice
Paris, 36 Rue d'Ulm

The sisters' convent and garden.

Motherhouse Community with author in 2002.

CHAPTER EIGHT:
A BATTERED WIFE, 1885

I n view of the time that Thomas, Melanie, and their two older boys had spent in London, one would not expect anyone to raise an objection to Mathilde's going, with her mother and elder daughter, on a pilgrimage to Lourdes. The trip was long in miles, to be sure, but Mathilde was to be only a brief time away from home. And indeed, that is how it seemed at first. In the middle of August, she could write, with obvious emotion, "I am going to Lourdes. I am taking my mother and my daughter. It is a great spiritual joy!" She hadn't had the slightest idea that it would be possible; it had occurred to her suddenly after Communion, and she was convinced that this project would not be hindered.[1] This may have been a parish pilgrimage, led by Father Grieu, since his eulogy credits him with leading such pilgrimages often.

On August 20, she noted that when she spoke of her desire, "not a single difficulty was even raised." Thomas agreed wholeheartedly, and Mathilde attributed his goodwill to a grace given him by Jesus and Mary.[2] At the beginning of September, her only regret regarding the pilgrimage was all the things the pilgrims had to pack. She wished it were possible to leave the body and its needs at home. But the only experience which resembles such a state here below is one in which the soul is habitually united with God, while its faculties retain enough freedom to apply themselves to necessary activities. She noted that she had indeed read of such a state three years earlier, in the writings of St. Teresa, but had not understood it then. She had not dared to ask for this, or even to desire it. But now Our Lord was presenting it as if she needed to reach it. She asked, "When will my soul be sufficiently purified? Is it possible that your love for such a poor creature is this great?"[3]

Soon after, her eye problems worsened. Before the entry for September 11, she stated that the following notes from her journal were written with her eyes closed because of their diseased condition. She wasn't "seeing" much of Jesus either, only a few brief visits in ten days. Aside from these moments of relief, she dwelt in hardship and obscurity, deprived even of the resource of rereading her notes, which no one else could read to her. In spite of it all, she had an inner quiet which was devoid of all feeling. St. Francis de Sales had described such a condition in his *Treatise on the Love of God*:

> But the state of tranquility where the will's sole activity is simply a consent to God's permissive will—content at prayer merely to be in God's sight, if he cares to look—is the best tranquility of all. It is free from all self-seeking. The soul's faculties find no satisfaction there—not even the will, except in its highest point, where it is content to be contented with having no contentment out of love for the contentment of God's permissive will in which it rests. The peak of love's ecstasy, after all, is to long for God's contentment, not our own; is to gratify, not our wishes, but God's.[4]

As if this were not enough, on the next day, Albert had some sort of accident, though not as serious as his earlier illness. For this reason, she did not know if she could go to Lourdes, although it had seemed to her that it was God's will and desire that she go.[5] Yet she was at peace: "Unexpected sorrow no longer takes me by surprise. . . . My soul finds [in suffering] both food and a deep peace, although nature feels the pain of it acutely, above all [when it affects] others. No doubt it is the supernatural satisfaction which God gives me in suffering which prevents my soul from losing her peace, even under a sudden blow."[6] Victor Frankl was convinced that the one thing we need in order to endure even great suffering without breaking under it is to be able to find meaning in it.[7] By identifying with Jesus in his passion, and especially through Jesus' reassurance, Mathilde could remain steadfast without the support of any of the medical, social, and legal services available to women today.

All the same, the situation was wearying: darkness without and, for the most part, within, so that she was tempted to lose confidence. She still could not reread her journal, and her mother was helping her to care for Albert, so Mathilde was deprived of having her read St. Teresa to her. Other adults, she writes, would not enjoy this book.[8] Just at this point, there came an unexpected confirmation: "What Our Lord predicted last year is beginning to come true. Those who used to speak against me, I am told, are now on my side. Humanly speaking, it is perhaps too late. Perhaps, on the contrary, God wishes to make use of them. . . . May it be just as he wills. I pray for all and feel I have grown very indifferent to these changes of opinion, unless the glory of God and the good of souls gain by them."[9]

That same evening, while praying for the pilgrimage to Lourdes, "Our Lord invited me to pray especially that he would purify the souls of those taking part in it." The next morning, he explained further. She writes, "All grace is an infusion of God in us. . . . The obstacles to grace generally come from sins and imperfections which sully the soul, also [from its being] so full of all created things. Thus God cannot impress himself on that tarnished mirror nor flow into that vase which is already so full." As God had invited, Mathilde prayed most of the day for the grace of perfect purification for herself and all the pilgrims.[10] Yet it seemed to her unfortunate to be going to Lourdes, given both the condition of her eyes and her physical fatigue.[11] This fatigue may have resulted from the extra work of caring for her sick son.

Eight days before the pilgrims were to leave, the storm broke. Mathilde believed either that the devil was furious that she was going to Lourdes or, more likely, that God wished to prepare her for her pilgrimage by an increase of suffering. "What a tempest was raised against the poor pilgrimage, at first agreed to with such a good heart and without any difficulty! I will pray there for those who unleashed this torment against me." Her great-grandson suggests that one can readily imagine Thomas having originally approved of his wife's plan. If that were so, it seems likely that Melanie had determined against it, and had brought Thomas to her view.[12] She got a grudging consent from both only when she suggested that it might help her eyes.[13]

The pilgrims left on the September 22, arriving the next day; Mathilde was very moved to see the grotto where Mary Immaculate chose to appear on French soil, and especially to hear eight thousand pilgrims praising Mary in song. She was united with both Jesus and Mary throughout her stay there. She prayed for everyone: the French Church, children, the sick, her parish, families, her son Albert, the conversion of Protestants, vocations, students, peace in her home, and her own life if it were for God's glory and useful to others. At her director's suggestion, she had written out all her petitions on a slip of paper beforehand; this she left in the grotto. She bathed her eyes and prayed for her sight out of obedience. She would not have done so otherwise, wanting to ask nothing from God except his love and his will for her. It hurt her to see how sad her mother was over her daughter's failing sight without knowing of the joy and spiritual support with which God was sustaining her. Mathilde offered to him her mother's prayers, too.[14]

The group returned by night on September 25. During the pilgrimage itself, Mathilde had had no opportunity to make any notes; this she did on the train the next morning. Before leaving, she had had a vision in which Mary had shown Mathilde her desire to save France, but the French had to respond with greater faith and prayer.[15] Jesus also told her that it was because of his love for France that he had given the latter his own dear Mother.[16]

Only after Mathilde's return do we get any hint of the problem which had embittered the more recent years of her life with her husband. Thomas had sworn that if her eyes benefited from her visit to Lourdes, he would mend his ways. She was able to say truthfully that there had been a positive improvement in the condition of her eyes.[17] But what ways he needed to amend she did not specify. She did write that on October 7 (in the month dedicated to devotion to the rosary) she was unable to be present for its public recitation in the church owing to having a visitor; she adored Jesus from afar, and experienced a union with Him "just as if my body had not been detained in the drawing room at home." This lasted until her evening prayer at ten, at which time the Father reassured her regarding "the painful and terrifying realities of [her] present life."[18]

Alain Le Touzé, reading between the lines of a letter Melanie Bellanger wrote to her goddaughter, surmised that Thomas's problem was alcoholism, which was not recognized as a disease, but was seen as a moral failure at that time. There were no treatment programs.[19] Melanie wrote, "I wish you a good day tomorrow. I have urged your father to make dinner pleasant through one of his informal conversations, of which he is very capable [instead of] being unpleasant or controversial."[20]

Apparently, when Thomas had had too much to drink, the aggressive side of his personality asserted itself, although this would have been carefully hidden from those outside the family. Nor would the official Church have offered any advice to the unfortunate wife other than prayer, patience, and good example. Given her own gentle spirit, Mathilde must have suffered greatly. Melanie, too, must have been suffering because of Thomas's behavior, but there is no record of her feelings beyond that one letter in which she stated that she had "urged" him to behave himself at dinner. From what little we know of her temperament, it was probably closer to lecturing than urging, and thus to little avail.

Perhaps because of the ordeal and the fatigue it induced, Mathilde was more vulnerable to temptations to self-doubt: "Poor soul, you are worthless. What are you doing? Comparing yourself to the saints? How can you believe that God has given you such favors? You deceive yourself and deceive others!" These are the thoughts which attacked her whenever she tried to pray; sometimes, at the very end of her prayer time, Jesus' glance restored her peace and security, but it was never more than a temporary respite.[21]

Still, she did have evidence, had she not been too tormented to notice it, that grace was working through her. In an entry dated October 27, 1884, Mathilde wrote, "Oh! What a sweet moment when that dear soul who has blamed me all through her life came to tell me that she will approach the sacraments...and that it is my doing! And yet I had never said a word to her on that subject."[22] The person to whom she was referring is not named; Alain le Touzé believes it might have been Thomas's eldest sister, Marie.

No wonder Mathilde wrote, at the beginning of November,

> For the past two months, except for a few graces, the habitual state of my soul has been that of privation of the Divine Presence accompanied by darkness, temptations of fear, anxiety, sadness, want of trust in God's grace, harrowing mental fluctuations . . . even when God kept my will united to his.
>
> At the actual moment of receiving graces and insights, it was impossible for me to doubt that they came from him, but afterward, when the shadows returned, I lost even the memory of the graces I had received and I no longer saw or felt anything but my sins and my unworthiness. I have had temptations concerning my spiritual life, temptations to discouragement and fears concerning my salvation. Then I would throw myself into the arms of God, telling him that at least I would love and serve him, against and in spite of all, in this world, begging him to do with me what he chose, now and hereafter.[23]

On the Feast of All Souls, Mathilde wrote that whatever reminded her of death was dear to her: "I know . . . that there is a purgatory . . . that without God my [spiritual] poverty would cast me into hell . . . but God is there. I think only of him and am not at liberty . . . to have any personal fear, any more than I can pray or act with a view to my own interest. . . . I ask nothing of God but to do his Will, yet I long for the moment fixed by him for my death."[24]

The annual retreat at the convent in Paris was later in November. There, Mathilde was warned, she does not say by whom, that her cross was going to get heavier and heavier. She accepted God's will with love, and placed all those whom she loved, as well as her concern for their spiritual well-being, in God's hands. She observed that surrendering those she loved into his hands cost her more than her own total gift of self. That she was here referring to conditions at home is indicated by her regret that those she loved would also suffer. Mathilde's own suffering would be thereby correspondingly increased. She also noted that she had not experienced, in this retreat, the calm she would usually have found. There was peace in the superior part of her soul, but otherwise it was as if she were not on retreat at all.[25]

Only near the end of the retreat did Jesus' presence flood her soul. He told her how much joy it gave him that he always found her the same towards Him, regardless of "whether [she was] in desolation or consolation."

"But where was love, where was faith, if I did not always . . . will to serve him to the best of my ability even when all seems to be lost? And if I did not guess his presence and adore the Beloved even when it pleases him to hide himself from my broken heart?"[26] She prayed especially for the children—exposed to anti-Catholic indoctrination in secular schools— "these children, the future French people. What will France be in twenty years, in ten years?" The gift of the retreat was an even greater love of the cross.[27]

Distractions during prayer are too much a part of human experience for most people to stress over; the usual advice today is to bring the concern into one's prayer. Apparently, such distractions were seen as a lack of devotion in the nineteenth century. Mathilde reports feeling "very ashamed" of thinking over some news she had just received from her children (probably her older sons, as the girls and Eugène would have been with her) during Mass. Jesus' "revenge" was to tenderly take from her the children who were filling her thoughts and enclose them, along with her, in his heart. Then she saw and loved them in him, and her "tenderness for them melted . . . in the . . . love with which the presence of Jesus inspired me."[28]

Despite the interior darkness and exterior troubles, Mathilde's will was unwavering; her sentiments during Midnight Mass on Christmas, 1884 make this very clear:

> I have brought to this Christmas Feast a great desire to be, to do, and to suffer in all things all that God wills. I have prayed ardently to Jesus to be born in me in whatever way he chooses, because his love desires all to resemble him, but not in the same manner. He manifests himself differently in Doctors, Apostles, Martyrs, priests, religious, and the simple faithful. Each has a different character, but Jesus is in all of them.
>
> All that matters is that he should be born in us, that he should grow in us without hindrance, that he should be in each of us that which he wishes to be. This is what I have asked him for myself and for all.[29]

In these few words, she sums up the whole of the spiritual life.

While praying in the church, Mathilde liked to be able to see the altar and the tabernacle, a childish preference, she acknowledged, since most of the time she prayed with her eyes closed. On December 28, two persons knelt in front of her, closing off her view completely. She continued praying. When they stood up and moved apart, she suddenly saw the Host very distinctly, which usually did not happen at that distance from the altar, and it appeared much larger than normal. It was, she writes, the first time that she had seen anything extraordinary with her bodily eyes. "I confess that I have some prejudices against this kind of sight, knowing it to be much less reliable than the others. In intellectual and imaginative visions, the soul is obliged to distrust herself, and this is no small difficulty. But here, over and above that, one has to distrust the medium of the body, which in the other cases does not exist." Once the priest set the ostensorium back on the altar after the blessing, she saw the large host once more, but after a few minutes, she saw it with its usual dimensions. It was, however, more distinct than she ordinarily saw it, due to the veil covering her eyes to protect them from the light. From this detail we learn that, even if her sight was better, there were still problems.[30]

Mathilde had longed to spend the last few days of 1884 in a year-end retreat, "in spite of the great and persistent troubles coming from outside." Jesus told her that the place of her retreat would be the Blessed Sacrament; that was where she should live, recollected in Him. This grace so reassured her that for two days thereafter, she was in deep peace, with a stronger and clearer view of the value attached to suffering like Jesus and with Jesus in her miniscule proportion. The large Host which she had seen with her bodily eyes seemed to have been impressed on her soul as a mark shining with Jesus' love, a confirmation of her choice, in spite of her weakness and natural sensitivities, to share in his sufferings and scorn, especially the disregard, by so many, of his Eucharistic presence.[31]

On New Year's Day, 1885, she asked in prayer, "Where will Love lead me [this year]? What will Love ask of me? I do not know, and I do not even wish to ask. *Fiat in all things* . . . praise to you!" Several weeks later, on a day during which she had "suffered extremely from more than one sorrow," she was ending her evening prayer as usual by offering her whole being to God, extending her arms in the form of a cross. Suddenly, Jesus manifested himself to her interiorly, and drawing her into a close union, filled her, not with consolation, but with a profound peace, a grace which left her with a special renewal of peace and strength with which to face the suffering which, each day, assumed greater proportions.[32]

Humanly speaking, she lived in apprehension: "I feel great troubles are in store . . . the future appears menacing. . . . And yet in the center of my soul there is peace. It seems as though it reposes in God, dominating all the fears and bitterness which terrify nature. At other times, no doubt, I shall fall under the cross . . . like my God on the Via Dolorosa. Each time . . . I shall try to rise again like him and with him." A week later, she wrote that Our Lord has ways *of his own* to refresh and rest her tormented spirit: "This morning at Holy Communion I had for a short while forgotten everything in the joy of him alone."[33] Jesus had taught her that our heartaches become part of the sufferings which complete in us the sorrows of his passion.[34]

February 12, 1885 was her forty-first birthday; she was given a vision of the light of heaven, which, she explains, "is God himself." Later that same day, she received a vision of Jesus offering himself to her as her spouse; that evening, she was obliged to go to the theatre. "The occasion revealed to me how much the grace of God has rendered me indifferent to all exterior glamour. I had no more trouble to remain recollected and united to God in the theatre than . . . in any other place. How sweet and yet how bitter it is to pray to him . . . there where one knows him to be so offended!"[35]

Thomas had not forgotten his promise to mend his ways, and whether as an act of penitence or a petition for the grace of transformation, had chosen to make a pilgrimage to the Holy Land, departing on March 13. Mathilde and their daughters went to Paris to see Thomas off. The train which they were to take back to Vernon was to leave just before the time for Eucharistic adoration. Mathilde complained to Jesus that it was not good of him to have allowed this, and thus he owed her something. The train schedule had changed on March 12, however, and was to leave an hour later. Thus they were able to spend the time in a church in which there was adoration.[36] While she prayed there, Jesus gave her some practical advice: "Love best what God loves best, what he allows, whatever it may be. It is not enough to accept, to will, what is painful; one must *love it better* than anything else, because *it is what God loves best.* That is now my sweet rule, for the present and the future." It seemed to her that this had increased her capacity for loving.[37]

The pilgrims traveled by boat, by train, and on horseback, a journey more time-consuming and much less convenient and comfortable than traveling by air today. Thomas wrote to the family regularly, giving an account of his experiences and his feelings about them. In a letter to his youngest son, Eugène, he described the voyage: "Tempests, hurricanes, thunderstorms, we lacked none of them. We were 120 hours on the Mediterranean without setting foot on land. Only today [they were off the coast of Greece] we are enjoying a little rest. There was no Mass on Sunday because of the lurching and pitching; two nasty beasts which followed us since we left Marseille."

On the other hand, they were well provided for with respect to meals. It was the middle of Lent, yet—dispensed by the bishop of Marseille because the sea air made them so hungry—they were served six meals daily. Without refrigeration, they had to bring all their meat on board alive—lambs, goats, pigeons, ducks, and chickens—to be slaughtered as needed. In spite of lack of sleep, Thomas was not seasick at all, unlike most of his companions, who had had "to pay tribute to Neptune, a nasty god! We awoke this morning to brilliant sunshine; the sea was beautiful and so blue that it restored the reputation it had lost during our difficult voyage." Their chaplain had celebrated Mass that morning along with five Franciscans returning to the Holy Land and five Canadian priests—pilgrims, bound, like himself, for Jerusalem. They were again out at sea, headed for Alexandria, which they expected to reach on the next evening. Thomas looked forward to returning to all his dear ones, after such a long absence.[38]

In a letter to Mathilde, he spoke of the beauty of the natural environment, which moved him deeply. Leaving Naples "on a somber night which promised nothing good," he was standing on the ship's bridge with the chaplain, watching Vesuvius emitting "its sinister red glimmers" in the distance. As together they beheld this imposing spectacle, Thomas was inspired to ask the chaplain to hear his confession. He commented that he didn't believe many Christians would have had the opportunity to fulfill their religious duties in such a solemn setting.[39]

Passing through the Straits of Messina, between the mountains of Sicily and Calabria, he wrote that those covered with snow sparkled like diamonds in the sunlight, and that the water was like an indigo lake, emphasizing the yellow shoreline, covered with what he thought must be olive trees. He did not see Charybdis and Scylla, however, "which existed only in Virgil's imagination." On the Ionian Sea, the water was phosphorescent, the sky full of stars: "[Standing] on the bridge, one was moved to pray." He mentioned having sent his travel diary to Melanie; perhaps she could make a "fair copy" for Mathilde to serve as an outline of all he wanted to share with her when he returned. Although the diary has not been found, the warmth and spontaneity of his letters, which even yet make his experiences vividly present, more than make up for its loss.[40] They also show him as a loving husband, at least when apart from Melanie.

On March 25, the pilgrims had reached Jerusalem. Thomas wrote to his wife that he had a lot to tell her about the city, but that all of his fellow travelers had been saddened by what they saw: a city situated in a cursed and desolate countryside, with ugly houses and high bare mountains, covered in places with scrubby vegetation. On Good Friday, they made the Way of the Cross, but he found the many different religious services at the Church of the Holy Sepulcher the next day very disturbing, especially that of the Greek Orthodox Church, whose rituals he found overly elaborate and lengthy. In the evening, the group visited the Dome of the Rock, which he found startlingly beautiful, especially when compared with the ugly basilica erected over Christ's tomb.[41]

On the very same day, back in Paris, Mathilde wrote in her journal, "For some weeks a strange intuition has often been given to me during prayer. I feel that some important change is going to take place in my life. I do not know the designs of God . . . but I have, as it were, an inner certitude that the conditions of my life will no longer be what they have been for the last twenty years. . . . I feel that an epoch is ending. *I am unable to chase this thought away.*" The next day, she noted that God was hiding himself in her soul, and leaving her without any felt consolation; her response was "Blessed be God." She added that she was continually repeating acts of abandonment and her loving preference for God's will, renewing with her whole heart her religious consecration.[42]

Mathilde's presentiment of an important change about to occur was verified three days later, with Melanie's sudden and unexpected death.

> Death has laid its hand on us. . . . What a sudden blow! My soul is more overwhelmed and absorbed by it than she could wish. My continual presence and prayers at that deathbed left me free, however, to go to Mass and Holy Communion without prejudice to anyone, but that was all I could do. . . . I pray all day long and a part of the night as well, in the midst of those interior and exterior desolations, those painful conversations which never cease and which weary the soul so intensely when she would prefer to speak only to God of her sorrow.
>
> God sustains me greatly through Holy Communion, when his presence illuminates the soul and carries her forcibly away for a short time from all things and from all thoughts. This morning, my soul in God breathed Eternal Life. . . . My wearied heart and mind revived again in that Being *where death is not*. I lived by that admirable light. Plunged in God, I saw, I felt, nothing else. I came away . . . altogether renewed and fortified.[43]

Thomas, of course, knew nothing of this immediately. On April 12, still in Jerusalem, he wrote Mathilde an affectionate letter thanking her for hers to him, which he had just received. He added that it had been a consolation to him; he had wept earlier because he had not had a letter from his mother since the one she had written on March 28. He had been to the Dead Sea, to Jericho and Bethany, three days on horseback over horrible roads. "Mme. Bellanger can tell you all the details." He was bringing home many souvenirs of the region; the Patriarch had given him some relics for her also. Altogether, he had about a dozen.[44] Mathilde made no mention of this letter in her journal, but the irony of it must have increased her grief and concern for Thomas.

What Mathilde did write about was how Jesus, during Holy Week, reassured her about Melanie: "*I am Mercy.* And then in an ineffable clarity He revealed himself to me as Mercy. . . . I saw the treasures of that infinite Mercy invading souls." The union of her soul with God in Holy Communion became more intimate and luminous: "God allows himself to be seen, to be handled, to be grasped. . . . My . . . soul embraces him without being able to say what it is that [she embraces], except that it is God!"[45]

Not until April 18 did Thomas learn of Melanie's death, under very poignant circumstances: "It was in the grotto of the Agony at Gethsemane that I learned of the dreadful misfortune, [which caused me such deep grief]. I was going to leave for Nazareth after receiving Communion at Calvary, when the chaplain took me in his arms and told me that I also was going to Calvary." In the grotto were written two quotes from Luke: "Here his perspiration flowed like drops of blood trickling onto the ground" and "Father, let this cup pass from me, but your will be done!" His fellow pilgrims and the local church officials did all they could to console him. The Patriarch sent him some precious relics, and all the religious superiors said Masses for his mother at the Savior's tomb. He also prayed a lot for her and for Mathilde, assuming that her grief must be no less than his own. Indeed, she felt grief, but perhaps more for Thomas than for Melanie, whom she believed was now with God.

In Jaffa, the pilgrims had visited a forest of orange and palm trees. If his mother had been there, she would have been speechless with admiration. "If God grants us life, we will all return to this beautiful region together." But this positive hope was much weaker than Thomas's feelings of loss: "What a joyful homecoming I had dreamed of! What a sad thing for me to return to my native land under a heavy veil of mourning! Today everyone on board is happy; the children are . . . prattling like the birds in our trees at Vernon." From this general happiness, he alone was excluded. His agony grew as the distance decreased. "All is painted in black in my troubled imagination. These terrible happenings come to grab me by the throat at the very moment when I would have been so glad to live tranquilly with you." He closed with a sign of concern for Mathilde, who must have written that she would come to Marseille to meet him. He asked her not to come, as the trip would be very tiring for her.[46]

We do not know the cause of Melanie's death, except that it was indeed without warning. She had written to Thomas and mailed the letter, on the very day she died. According to the Gazette of Vernon, April 4, 1885, she had died in Paris, but it was the poor of Vernon who would miss her most: "Her purse was always open to the unfortunate. Practicing her religion like a true Christian, she made use of her large fortune for good works. . . . Many weep for her and all regret her loss. Her beautiful soul in Heaven has already received the recompense for her good . . . deeds, but she leaves empty a large place among the living. Her foster son had the sorrow of learning of her death when in Jerusalem, and of being unable to close her eyes; he had at least the severe consolation of praying for her at the Savior's tomb."[47]

Mathilde did go to Marseille to meet her husband; together they went to the Sainte Beaume, a place of pilgrimage which tradition held to be where St. Mary Magdalene retired to do penance after Jesus' Ascension. There, Mathilde renewed again her act of total abandonment to God's will: ". . . to suffer, if he wills, this heartrending bitterness, what martyrdom! I will do it, but my soul shudders at it and yesterday I said to him, 'O Lord, what am I to do to enable me to bear such an ill?' He answered me with great sweetness, 'I bear it too!' and I . . . felt that mystery of love, of divine patience, which waits on sinners and suffers them, and [I] felt greatly comforted by it.[48] The next morning, she was able to attend Mass there, then she and Thomas climbed to the top of the rock together. She ended her journal entry with this: "It seems to me that the sun of truth rises higher in my soul, and gives her a clearer insight into the nothingness of all things."[49]

One might have expected that after Melanie's death things would be easier for Mathilde; alas, they only got worse. It was a true way of the cross for her. On June 9, she wrote, "My soul suffers, and has suffered greatly for the last few months, under the weight of crosses which restrict the [mental and emotional] freedom [I] need to think of God. I have to live in a state of worry which has become habitual. . . . This is the cry of . . . human nature at bay. Nevertheless, peace in God predominates over all." She added that if we carry our sorrows alone, we are crushed by them. But if we cast them into the immensity of God, it is we who, together with our sorrows, are carried in his mercy.[50]

Unable to deal with his grief in any better way, Thomas turned for solace to the one "tranquilizer" available: alcohol. In view of the symptoms he developed, Alain Le Touzé believes that the beverage he chose was a particularly pernicious alcoholic drink known as "the Green Fairy"; or absinthe, which became the most popular aperitif among upper-middle-class French drinkers after the Franco-Prussian War. A preparation of wormwood steeped in alcohol (initially wine, but after plant lice attacked French vineyards in the 1870s, causing a wine shortage, grain alcohol was substituted) to which were added anise and other flavorings, the final product was a clear green liqueur, which could be 70 to 90 percent alcohol.

A reporter in the *New York Times* of October 14, 1879, described its effects: "At first there is very little reaction from it; it quickens the mental faculties, lends a glow to the health and spirits . . . A regular absinthe drinker seldom perceives that he is dominated by its baleful influence until it is too late. All of a sudden he breaks down; his nervous system is destroyed; his brain is inoperative; his will is paralyzed . . . there is no hope for his recovery."[51] An article which appeared in the May 1915 issue of *Literary Digest* is even more graphic: "In the early stages, [absinthe] produces an agreeable feeling of intoxication. By its continued employment, the character becomes changed. To the brightness and gaiety of the first effects, succeeds a somber brutishness . . . nervous agitation, insomnia, nightmares . . . hallucinations . . . and profound mental troubles. Paranoia is also common, and it ends in insanity.[52]

Despite these frequently reported dire consequences, absinthe's initial effect was euphoria; it was a mood elevator and lifted depression. No doubt it seemed to Thomas a way to overcome his anguish at Melanie's death. But the addiction is powerful and fatal; the mental deterioration, once begun, is irreversible. Thomas became subject to bursts of violence, during which he was physically abusive to Mathilde. She tried, unsuccessfully, to hide the bruises from her family to spare them pain. Nevertheless, she spent many nights trying to calm him while he suffered from nightmares, hallucinations, and delirium.

Chapter Nine:
Illness and Death of Thomas, 1885–1887

L ife at Vernon became hellish for Mathilde and the children. Thomas's repeated episodes of violence made them, at times, fear the worst. His fits were the source of enormous worry, and although Mathilde does not describe them in detail, it is clear that managing Thomas's care was becoming incredibly difficult. Moreover, it became essential that she take over the family's financial matters to save them from disaster.[1] Given the lack of any legal status for women at the time, this undertaking proved a huge challenge. Mathilde had almost no time to keep her journal. She explains, "That's how it has been, more or less, due to matters demanding attention, for most of the last five months."[2] Nevertheless, on July 1 she could write this: "I see the difficulties and dangers clearly, but experience no fear, God having given me new arms for the fight. A part of my soul, having been drawn into him, finds itself above all [these] miseries, and all fear. This state is not always *felt*, but even when I do not feel it, it persists with . . . strength and security. . . . At the same time, he adds whatever I need in order to confront the difficulties of my task."[3]

Jesus communicated to her, without words, that he would hold her by the hand along the path of suffering, although his help would not always be *felt*. He invited her to climb that spiritual Calvary by placing her feet in his bloodstained footprints. Mathilde writes of longing to unite the blood of her heart, her emotional sufferings, to the blood of the heart of Jesus. She notes in herself a great contrast—she is able to suffer acutely, even to the point of heartbreak, at some occurrence, and yet, at the same time, will it calmly and without hesitation because she recognizes it as God's will:

> This, no doubt, is why, for many years past, every time a cross is foretold, I have a feeling of very great peace, while my soul shudders inwardly at the thought of certain particular crosses which wound the souls of those dear to me. It seems as if the prediction of a life full of trials harmonizes with a truth I hear interiorly, and at the same time nothing can give me greater

peace and strength in the midst of crosses than the thought that they are the express and special will of God in regard to my soul.[4]

After communion on July 21, Mathilde had a vision of God's wisdom. She expresses her understanding in words that one need not be a visionary to appreciate—the wisdom of God rules all things admirably,

> particularly . . . those human difficulties which seem inextricable to us. . . . His thoughts are not our thoughts, nor his ways, our ways. He often leads us, by a way which we think is conducting us to [a specific] goal, to an exactly opposite one, or to one more excellent which his will has ordained for us. [At times], it pleases him to deliver us from some apparently inextricable embarrassment by suddenly showing us a way out, which we had not even suspected. . . . This is why we should never be astonished or disquieted by God's dealings, whether with us or with others, but remain in peace and confidence, even when everything seems to thwart the accomplishment of works legitimately desirable in themselves.[5]

She added that this teaching "leaves the soul less susceptible to human agitations."[6] She was unable to write anything further for another ten days. She later explained, "Duty compelled me to fetch my children, and I yesterday made the thirteenth journey this year."[7]

Anyone who takes a faith commitment seriously, especially if family and close associates do not share it, wonders how to communicate it to them. Mathilde's desire to bring others to know and love God was intense, and Jesus showed her the best way to accomplish this.

> Jesus, our model, teaches us by his conduct towards us how we ought to behave towards others. Let us no longer try to improve [or] change our neighbor simply by our advice, but let us imitate our Good Shepherd [learning from] him that the only way in which we can do any real good to others is by the gift of self by example. . . . Let us, like him, apply our charity to those who have none . . . our forgiveness to the vindictive; in short, may the plenitude of divine love which fills us through [our] Communion with the Body and Blood of the God–Man overflow from our soul upon the souls of others.

> Every prayer, and especially every supernatural prayer, pro-
> duces acts in its own good time, as every seed produces a plant
> which shoots out of the earth in due season.[8]

None of this, however, alleviated in the least the chaos of her daily life: "I try to discern what must be done and what must not, what must be said and must not be said. This confusion is like the air I breathe in every day. Humanly speaking, it is a kind of martyrdom. Nevertheless, I am willing to suffer it until death if through it I can entice even a single soul to make one more act of love for God."[9] If peace and trouble were of equal merit, and God allowed her to choose between them, she desired to pick the one which would most enable her to resemble Jesus. Still, the distress was so constant and so powerful that she felt it was only her union with God which gave her the strength and calm she needed.[10]

The first sign in Mathilde's journal of Thomas's decline is dated August 31, 1885. She writes, "Yesterday my poor husband was at death's door, and we were expecting him to breathe his last. . . . All I asked of God was his glory and [what was good for my husband's soul]."[11] The next day, a vision of Jesus crucified strengthened her to suffer. On September 3, as the crisis continued, she wrote of "agonies worse than those of death for this poor dear person."[12] Mathilde saw what she was enduring as an act of reparation for human sinfulness, and thus part of the mission of Adoration Réparatrice. She had learned from Jesus that the principal way to do this was by the sacrifice of one's own will. Since it is tainted by original sin, we cannot conform our human nature, our will—without its immolation— to God's will. Suffering, therefore, is the essential part of reparation.[13]

Thomas's crisis apparently passed, though there would be many more, increasing in severity, until his death ended them. Lacking his medical records, we can only guess why this was so. We may suspect that alcohol poisoning, along with liver damage, were at the root of his worsening condition. Eventually, the liver would be damaged beyond repair, causing death. If, as his great-grandson believes, Thomas was drinking not just wine but absinthe,[14] the damage would have been much greater. "Most absinthe was between 120 and 180 proof; tolerance of that level of alcohol intoxication destroys brain cells, and quickly begins harming the liver. The drinking is usually interrupted frequently. With good nutrition, the brain damage clears somewhat . . . and the liver, even though insulted, resumes its function as best it can. . . . The brain damage is less forgiving, but neither really repairs."[15] Thomas's decline took two years and four months, a very long ordeal for the entire family.

In spite of her many personal difficulties, Mathilde continued to pray for France and for its spiritual health: "Poor country, in danger of losing its God! Can any Christian, seeing in her country so much evil, have a minute of rest and joy?"[16] This entry was written at the beginning of October, right before the legislative elections, in which, as it turned out, groups supporting Catholic concerns made great gains.[17]

Mathilde's time was mostly devoured by her family responsibilities, and she noted that it was with great difficulty that she could escape from them for half an hour to go to the church to pray. Once there, God quieted all the turmoil in her soul and assured her that, in spite of all her inevitable preoccupations, her union with him remained.[18] Mathilde did all she could to maintain at least the semblance of a normal home for the children. There was a family gathering on October 23, and after Communion the next morning, she had an intellectual vision during which Jesus said to her, "If others afflict you, I console you. If others despise you, I honor you. If others will not, or cannot, protect you, I protect you. . . . I am all things to you. Never seek anything outside me. This is not an order, but tenderness and mercy."[19]

One of the promises made by the *agrégées* of Adoration Réparatrice was to devote one day each month to Eucharistic adoration in a spirit of reparation, preferably in the convent chapel in Paris. Even during this difficult period, Mathilde seemed to have been able to be present at least some of the time. She was there at the end of October and prayed for all who suffer without love. With this intention, she lovingly ratified the acceptance of God's will for her, irrespective of its concrete manifestation at any particular time.[20]

There were some respites. On November 5, Mathilde recorded two days of improvement in her husband's condition, and a little bit of cheerfulness returned to their home. This relaxation was so necessary for her poor daughters, whom she did not wish to become too gloomy. During the lull, she was astonished at the absence of any corporeal suffering, since she had endured this almost constantly during her husband's illness. (She writes nothing directly about Thomas's being physically abusive toward her, but there are hints that he was.) Mathilde became aware of the beauty of nature, always a delight to her, which she had not noticed when her heart had been paralyzed in agony, and she thanked God for it.[21]

To add to her misery, unnamed persons sent her husband slander-ous letters, prodding him to cause a division between Mathilde and her mother. She was not at all distressed, but maintained peace and charity in the midst of such attacks, having endured so much heartache already that they seemed like nothing. She prayed that the perpetrators might be brought back to justice and charity.[22] Later in November, another wicked letter came to her husband against both Mathilde and her mother. She regretted that it had caused her some interior indignation, but embraced this cross, too, with love. Sometimes, when her distress or preoccupations were very powerful, her soul was carried into God's sovereign peace. This gave her the strength to continue the struggle.[23]

Surely one of the most distressing aspects of Thomas's condition was its unpredictability. Mathilde never knew ahead of time what to expect. On November 28, she could write, "What a peaceful meal! What a relief to see my poor dear somewhat calm! The little girls regained their cheer-fulness like daisies opening their petals in the morning. It's my constant preoccupation not to allow these poor children to become too despondent." In the midst of this welcome lull, however, her husband was still receiving letters denouncing her, one worse than the other. The letters aroused his in-dignation at the writers and did him a lot of harm. Thus, even as his wife worked constantly to instill an environment of peace, others applied them-selves to exciting and exasperating Thomas. Mathilde prayed that God would give such people the charity and justice they lacked, and questioned whether people with such a false tongue and so filled with animosity could really have the Holy Spirit in their hearts.[24]

It was some consolation for Mathilde that another person "who had been badly influenced" came to her; they were able to see and speak to each other. This otherwise unidentified woman told Mathilde that her ex-ample had done her good. Mathilde blessed God for allowing her to trans-mit the good which comes only from him,[25] but described her spirit as being one moment encouraged and then falling back into great uneasiness the next.

During this period, Mathilde was forced to act and breathe, against her preference, within an atmosphere poisoned by questions about financial matters. Unassisted by the presence of any experienced family members (Mme. Bellanger was deceased, Thomas incapacitated, and the Bertrands, her parents, elderly), Mathilde writes that even "in the presence of malice and shrewdness," as long as God allowed her to see her way clearly and do her work energetically, she did not hate the solitude which withdrew her from even legitimate human support, allowing her to endure her difficulties alone with God.[26]

Human support was not entirely lacking. Father Grieu added encouraging or confirmatory notes very often on the pages of her journal. And there was also the Superior at the convent in Paris, the spiritual director for all the *agrégées*. In early December, amidst "great temptations to despondency" as well as spiritual darkness, Mathilde again struggled with the fear that she might be prey to error and illusions, "mistaken myself and deceiving others. This temptation is the most terrible of all." She found solace in the memory of a tangible fact: "During the two days I spent in Paris [October 27–29], while I was giving the Superior of the convent an account of the union of my soul with Jesus in that morning's Communion, the good Mother answered me: 'Indeed, I noticed it; I did not know this morning that you were in Paris, but I felt that there was in the chapel a soul deeply united to God. . . . Lifting my eyes, I caught sight of you, and said to myself: "It is she."'"[27]

The servants had had the children's portraits drawn, and on the eve of the Feast of the Immaculate Conception, showed them to the family. The artist was not very skillful; their hair resembled baked earth and their faces were dark. But the servants took this misfortune with a good heart, and everyone was amused by the "masterpieces." To Mathilde's astonishment, she was able to laugh. It meant a lot to her to see how heartily her children laughed.[28] Her habitual attitude, however, was sadness and suffering.

The doctors' predictions of worse to come were heartbreaking for her. She expressed to God her willingness to suffer even more, if through this she might shorten her husband's purgatory. She also tried to suggest the same attitude to her older daughter, whose blood was boiling as she rebelled against the situation so painful to her mother. Nonetheless, Mathilde was confident that, through this cruel trial, God would strengthen the devotion already so strongly rooted in her daughter's soul.[29]

Christmas was far from festive for Mathilde, although she did her best to keep up appearances for the sake of the children. She writes of being very happy to see her daughters enjoying themselves a little with their brothers, "each according to her age and preferred tastes. However, even as their sweet gaiety touched my heart, I felt a sob tightening my throat. I quickly repressed it, fearing to destroy their joy, and appeared joyful myself, swallowing my tears. It is very rare for me to cry."[30]

Later in January, she elaborated on this: "It is a very small thing to suffer oneself. It is suffering in the hearts of others that is hard and bitter. . . . To see [my daughter's] face gloomy, a downcast expression replacing the bloom of her natural vivacity; to feel my beloved mother, already so much tried in her life, weighed down and broken under my anguish; my dear sister, all who love me, suffering cruelly at this time; this is what is infinitely saddening. Solitary suffering would not be suffering."[31]

Mathilde was very appreciative of the love of those close to her. She wondered whether God, who was giving her loved ones a share of her cross, would not also give them grace to bear it. Answering her own question, Mathilde concluded that if God had given her so much, with no merit on her part, surely he would do the same for them. She further reflected that it is not suffering that is evil; it is sin which separates one from God. Mathilde ended this entry by offering her suffering for those so separated.[32]

The first period of delirium occurred near the end of February. Thomas's hallucinations still left him sufficient awareness to recognize them as illusory, and it was possible to console him. Mathilde spent an entire night at his side, and he was able to pray Lauds with her "in his poor voice, totally changed." The crisis had begun two days earlier, and only that morning had they received the doctor's reassurance that this time it would not be fatal. The news gave her no comfort. "What reassurance! To know that we will begin again the same lamentable life, until, sooner or later, another relapse, no matter how many, [one of] which will inevitably cause his death!" Yet, "in the midst of all these upheavals, my soul is in deep peace."[33]

Caring for a person in such a state was both demanding and exhausting: "Day and night one must be up to prevent [Thomas] from breaking things, or injuring himself. It's impossible to say all the things that haunt his poor imagination, all that he sees as frightening or dangerous. Not a minute of rest for two days." Mathilde wrote that she felt like an orange that had been squeezed dry, and her health had been so affected that she had been unable to go to Mass, even on Sunday. Her only relief was her mother's presence.[34] She felt that her soul was in full rebellion, not against God, but against sorrow. Yet she continued to say *fiat*.[35]

Before the latest crisis, Mathilde had been concerned for Melanie's future. She was nineteen, old enough to marry, but any such arrangements would have been extremely difficult to make, given the situation into which the family had been plunged. Mathilde hoped to put their finances in good order, as well as to comfort all who loved her and suffered with her, especially her parents, whose old age was saddened by her ordeal. She took refuge in God's will, and "closed her eyes in order not to see the future, entrusting both the matter of finding a suitable husband for Melanie and her concern for her elderly parents to him." She did not write anything further for more than a week, "for want of time, and the absolute necessity of resting my eyes."[36]

In between crises, Thomas appears to have been still active in his usual fashion, even if he was no longer the man he once was. He seems to have grown milder, "apart from certain hours." Mathilde wrote that he went to church daily, prayed with great seriousness, and was preoccupied with his soul. He even trusted her with financial matters, although she had to act "behind the scenes" rather than with full authority. She had to concern herself with every detail, but without appearing to be concerned with anything. This entailed three or four times as much work, consuming so much time that other things had to be omitted.[37]

That she could assume so much responsibility for her family's practical affairs is remarkable since neither her upbringing nor her personal interests would otherwise have led her in this direction. Moreover, exercising financial stewardship for the family posed a genuine trial for Mathilde, as it required much time and energy that her whole being longed to use in contemplative prayer. Nevertheless, since these tasks were now "the duties of her state," she turned her attention to them with her characteristic wholeheartedness as God's will for her. Mathilde accepted monetary oversight as a great cross, and although fearing being inattentive to God, still wrote in her journal that her will was united with God more than ever.[38]

In the middle of April, Thomas was in better humor, and life became much smoother for a little while. The relationship between Mathilde and Thomas grew stronger, so much so that Mathilde wrote that their relationship had grown more in one year than in the previous twenty years of their marriage. "How different our life might have been, had I been allowed to behave this way toward him without hindrance from the beginning." The depth of her love and forgiveness manifests itself in her suggestion that "that soul [Melanie] who is now before God also sees it now, and without doubt is assisting us with her prayers."[39]

The worst was yet to come, though, as Mathilde well knew. Without telling Thomas, she had seen the doctor, who verified her fear that they were merely in a lull until the next relapse, the timing of which was unpredictable, and that a series of terrible crises would ensue. Her immediate concern was for Elisabeth, their youngest child, about to make her First Communion. She prayed that God would not permit anything to harm this child, "my sweet marigold, so many times offered to Jesus and Mary before her birth, and so drawn to them since!"[40]

The evil that Mathilde was enduring at this time, however, seemed almost nothing to her in comparison with the evils committed against God in France. The efforts of republicans to secularize France continued, and Mathilde grieved for the souls Satan was snatching through state interference with their visible supports. Even in the midst of her personal trials she expressed concern about the state of her country. "Isn't it right to be distressed by that?" she asks.[41]

According to local custom, the Palm Sunday procession went to the cemetery, carrying the blessed branches to the tombs. Mathilde comments, "It is sweet to pray for [those who] have gone first!" After being interrupted, she continued this line of thought in her journal the following day. She writes that, finding herself in the cemetery, she felt a sense of deliverance and lightness. It was clear to her that, although thinking of the end of life in this world is sad, it also marks the beginning of a new life because of the promise of the resurrection. Mathilde writes of wishing that there were some way to include the joy of the deceased in returning to God alongside the expressions of sorrow on their tombstones. Her entry broke off in mid sentence, not to be continued until Easter Friday, seventeen days later.[42]

Picking up where she had left off, Mathilde reflects on the words reportedly inscribed on tombs of the martyrs in the catacombs of Rome. In these, supernatural joy dominates expressions of sorrow. Mathilde asks herself whether, in a century which arrogantly calls itself one of progress and light, hearts greater than death might no longer be found, whether "faithful souls can no longer raise themselves to teach others to joyfully shake off the dust of exile when at last they reach the border of their native land?"[43] She was only forty-two, but looked forward to the unimpeded communion with God offered by death.

Mathilde did not make any further entries in her journal for over two weeks, primarily because of Elisabeth's First Communion and Confirmation. She then described with joy how recollected Elisabeth had been, both at home and at church, glowing with love for God. Elizabeth had told her mother that she would never forget "this day," and Mathilde prayed that it would determine the rest of the child's life, grounding her in holiness. A second reason Mathilde notes for delay in writing was that she had not felt well, due to exhaustion. Still, there is no indication that Thomas's behavior dampened the celebration of Elisabeth's Communion and Confirmation.[44]

Like any other mother, Mathilde experienced anxiety regarding the future careers of her sons. We know from a letter Elisabeth wrote to her brother Albert that Eugène, too, was now in Paris.[45] Mathilde was making an earnest effort to let go of her maternal preoccupations for their futures. She was leaving the matter in God's hands, as he had asked. At the same time, she was more than ever obliged to be vigilant for their spiritual welfare;[46] they were well supervised in their boarding schools, but Paris was full of temptations.

God sustained her through such anxieties. Later in May, she experienced him as a pure act: "I saw God acting eternally by one single act without going out of himself, without change, unmoved, willing all he wills by one single and eternal act of his will—his will and his act being one and the same . . . one pure act . . . as St. Thomas Aquinas has so excellently said."[47] Clearly, she had read Aquinas, but she gives us no clue as to where or when. Mathilde saw this grace as having further practical significance, "to substitute in all things his will for our will, and therefore to have one will with him."

Contemplating God as eternal act, she could remain centered in peace and love, which influenced her entire day, even one that might be stormy and busy:

> From early morning, a tempest of difficulties and trials within and without. I had to prevent my husband with great difficulty from taking a step which would have been gravely imprudent on his part. Then I had to write six pages to my lawyer in Paris, and send him another note in the evening. Through all this tumult . . . the reflection of the divine light lingered, and still lingers, in the depth of my soul, sustaining [me] amidst the conflicting activities. In fact, human events no longer make the same impression on me as formerly.[48]

One might expect that with so many personal trials, Mathilde would lose sight of other matters. In fact, she did no such thing. At the beginning of June, she was praying to the Sacred Heart of Jesus, "Save the poor France which You love." And thoughts of her personal unworthiness still troubled her: "My soul seems a desert, incapable of producing anything; it is often prey to the cruel fear of being ungrateful to the God it loves. . . . It is sweet to me to abase myself before God. . . . I would like to become holy for him whom I love, but the more I aspire to perfection, the more I see myself imperfect in everything; it even seems that there are in-surmountable barriers between a holy life and me.[49]

Mathilde felt an ardent thirst to do more for God, to fulfill even more the concept of *victim soul*, which served as a model for the spirituality of her time. But she did not know how to satisfy her desire to undertake its practices of penance and austerity. On the one hand, she had been forbidden to practice corporal penances; on the other, her health was affected by what she was suffering. The only form of voluntary mortification thus open to her was never to take or to do anything for pleasure. Fr. Grieu commented that this was an excellent penance.[50]

In the middle of June, Mathilde was in Paris, where she had to take care of some business matters before being able to spend three days at the convent. She offered her efforts to Jesus as best she could, and was filled with the thought of dying to herself completely in order that Jesus alone would live in her. Thus she accepted in advance "all through which he would purify me in this life, praying to receive all of it as a single act of love." This prayer of acceptance of the future had become habitual for her.[51] "Our Lord" had taught her that all the practical details of renunciation that follow upon inspirations of grace from moment to moment ought to result in an interior effort by which one becomes a *stranger to oneself*.[52]

Mathilde would have liked to stay at the convent longer; the days before the Feast of Corpus Christi were days of special prayer. But that was not possible. She had to continue her retreat as well as she could in Vernon. On Trinity Sunday, she renewed her self-offering, and on June 23, her day of reparation with which she ended her little retreat, she renewed her con-secration as an *agrégée*, offering her entire self—"the absolute gift of my whole being, of my *me* [ego]"—that is, to die to herself, in order that God alone would live in her, and she would live only in him.[53]

Mathilde's life continued: always her concern for Thomas, always the necessity of attending to multiple responsibilities which in other times would have been taken care of by Mme. Bellanger or Thomas, always the fear of Thomas's next crisis. On July 5, Mathilde was unable to go to church "because my poor invalid needed my care." This occasioned two observa-tions. First, while she could easily pray while responding to matters needing her immediate action, when she tried to finish an urgent letter, she was un-able to do so. She understood then that God did not wish her to write at the time she usually spent in prayer. Secondly, prayers made while going and coming, amidst obligatory external occupations, were as sweet as if she had been able to pray before the Tabernacle. She sensed that suffering was better than joy, and that grace made it possible for her to find a greater and purer pleasure in being deprived of the sacramental presence of her Beloved, through his will, made so clear to her. Father Grieu added, "Perfect. The best prayer is assuredly that made through fulfilling [one's] duty."[54]

On the Feast of Our Lady of Mount Carmel, a feast which had special significance to Mathilde, she was strengthened by experiencing the mercy and compassion of God: "My soul knew with inexpressible sweetness the compassion of Jesus for my sufferings, which continue during sleep. . . . [Words cannot express] the power, delicacy, and charm [of] divine compassion, nor how it suddenly cures the soul. . . . [Compassion] was shown to me [like] a great bowl holding us all, and I saw that no one would be able to . . . escape without a very pronounced and rooted evil will." This image of divine kindness filled her heart with charity for all who suffer.[55]

Thomas had another relapse in late July. Mathilde counted it his twentieth, and noted that it was quite bad. A few days earlier, when she had been in the midst of complications and incessant worries, Jesus had said to her as she was praying, "Are we not *two* in your difficulties and perplexities?" These words were so true, so evident and tangible in both important and trivial events, that her heart was filled with love remembering them. So often he pointed out a way of resolving what had seemed to her an impossible situation. No wonder the author of *The Imitation of Christ* called Jesus "among all friends the [most] faithful." The doctors found, as she had expected, that Thomas's condition had grown worse. Even if he pulled through, these terrible relapses would leave him disabled. Mathilde prayed that, through his love and mercy, God would look after the soul of his poor child.[56]

August was no better. Mathilde's time was "minced fine by a quantity of details resulting from many important matters, and also by the daily concern for everyone, quite demanding at this time." All her children were home for the summer vacation. This left her almost no chance to write, and even less to pray as she would have liked. But even a moment of solitude with God strengthened her.[57] Mathilde notes that her husband was faithful to daily Mass, which pleased her a great deal. At least occasionally the children were with her as well. One morning after Mass, they took the opportunity to go for a walk before the midday meal, stopping to visit a number of churches. She writes that these short visits were like water refreshing her thirsty soul; she longed to rest at Jesus' feet and left each church regretfully. In response, Jesus united her to himself in a very simple and consoling union which lasted during their walk and their return by carriage.[58] She found this union especially precious, since her family occasionally seemed as insensitive as stones in the presence of the Blessed Sacrament. She knows that "'the Spirit blows where it will' and as it pleases him, and all that pleases him is good for me." Nevertheless, being sensibly embraced by him was fortifying.[59] Here we also see Mathilde's ingenuity in devising ways both to spend time with her family and create an opportunity for spiritual refreshment

On the Feast of the Assumption, Mathilde, Thomas, and their five children attended Mass together, and all received Communion. After the sacrament, Mathilde "offered to God, with everything of which my heart was capable, my five children, who had joined me in Communion." She prayed "that God might strengthen them so that each could perfectly accomplish his most beloved will." Mathilde further entrusted to God with particular love "the poor, dear father of this family, he who stops me, nonetheless, from worrying about stones thrown into my garden of pious practices." She then adds a cryptic comment that "it is nevertheless evident that, at bottom, Thomas does not think what he speaks." Under the circumstances, this appears to be an observation that his illness had progressed to the point that he was unaware of what he was saying.[60]

In view of the stress which the whole family was enduring, it is not surprising that tempers flared. Still she would not allow the children—in this case, Melanie (nineteen) and Albert (seventeen)—to misbehave: "I sent my two eldest children to their rooms because they had answered me rudely. I will not tolerate that at any age. The Fourth Commandment exists to be kept. But . . . I prayed fervently to God that my own imperfections may not do any harm to my children. I must say they submit at once when I make my authority felt.[61]

More troubling for her was the occasion when she sensed that one of her children had not told her the truth and would not admit it. This brought her to tears. She prayed and told God that she would willingly suffer everything else, but would not accept seeing evil in her children. Moved, as she said, by grace, the child came back to her and, seeing her sad, admitted what he had denied. God inspired her to speak words that would be good for him to hear, and she was greatly comforted by his confession.[62]

As Mathilde struggled to balance her multiple responsibilities to her family and to God, Jesus reassured her that her suffering and activity were increasing her aptitude for contemplation. Such a union, which exists primarily in the will, rather than in the consciousness, is extended by Jesus to his friends. He offers intimacy through the sharing of his suffering, but finds few who are willing to share it. Jesus told Mathilde to set her heart on him in a spirit of adoration, like the Sanctuary Lamp that consumes itself before the altar.[63]

The boys returned to school in October; Mathilde wrote that the vacation had been strenuous in every way. She hoped that it had been a benefit for them, that she had been God's instrument in doing them good. She also noted that in the year just past, it had seemed to her that God had given her an additional ability to understand the hearts of her sons.[64]

Trying to keep up with all she had to do was a physical strain, and Mathilde was ill for five days in the middle of October. After "a terrible day," at the end of which her ill husband had mentioned Blessed Marie Alacoque, Jesus reminded her of all she had heard about devotion to the Sacred Heart, inviting her to offer all her suffering to him under this title. She did so with joy. Nevertheless, she sometimes felt that the unrelieved stress would be more than she could endure were it not for the way in which Jesus was constantly supporting her.[65]

Because of the numerous demands on her time, Mathilde was prevented from writing anything from the middle of October until the middle of November, when she at last was able to spend a few days of retreat at the convent. Receiving Communion, she was united to Jesus as light, and felt that this true light would rectify human deficiency in all things, if we would submit ourselves to it, instead of first running after so many false lights. She, who had "been born with a devouring thirst for knowledge," recognized that in comparison with the eternal light, all created knowledge is as nothing.[66]

Mathilde received a letter from an unnamed person expressing hatred for her. Alain Le Touzé believes it was Thomas's sister Marie, who no doubt blamed her sister-in-law for the state in which she found her brother. Mathilde's response was to ask pardon "for that poor soul who hates me, and hates you in me." She was happy to have a share in his experience of hatred during his own life on earth.[67] Nevertheless, the letter upset her. She believed she saw a need to respond to one point in it, but recalled her confessor's advice to offer no reply. Mathilde was beginning to find joy in suffering, and peace in agitation and worry, because she knew them to be

God's will for her.[68] She sensed that God was at work in her soul constantly, and so, each day, she was more indifferent than the previous one to whatever occurred. Her most ardent desire was to accept her sufferings simply out of love for God.[69]

Marguerite, Mathilde's cousin, defended her against the many criticisms leveled at her, some of them apparently vitriolic. She pointed out that Thomas's foster mother had agreed to his abandoning studies toward a legal career early in the marriage, thus countenancing an "act of rash imprudence [that] was the ruin of young Thomas, and made Mme. Bellanger responsible for his sad future." Mathilde, who had deplored this decision at the time of its making, had been forced to keep silent about her apprehensions. Her influence, even then, had been no match for that of her mother-in-law.

Concerning Mathilde's conduct within her family during Thomas's illness, Marguerite states, "God alone knows what Mathilde suffered, not only from the violence of the one to whom she had vowed such pure affection, but also in watching the progressive deterioration of the intelligence and good qualities of her husband. From that time [the onset of Thomas's illness], she became a true martyr, the object of humiliations and violence which she kept totally secret."[70] Mathilde's mother, spending part of the summer with her, became the unhappy witness of her daughter's suffering.[71]

Christmas, 1886, was sad for them all. The children, even the youngest, were burdened by sorrow; they had hardly any respite. December 27 was a day of anguish. Mathilde did not dare to go to Mass because of the discomfort she saw Thomas experiencing, and she did not know whether the health of her husband would permit her to go out on December 31.[72] She was able to get to Mass on January 1, however, after which she wrote, "*Sit nomen Domini benedictum* [Blessed be the name of the Lord (as uttered by Job)]. This is my motto for this year, whatever it may bring. I intend to repeat it on every occasion." Jesus confirmed the peace he had given to her earlier, telling her that God is peace because he is order, and neither agitation nor chaos can disturb it. He showed her how to keep her peace in God in spite of everything.[73]

Occasionally, there were better moments. In the middle of January, on a day that found Mathilde very busy with tiresome correspondence, as well as with two visits that had left her no time to pray, her spirit was lifted by the conversation, "innocent and Christian," during dinner with her family. It brought back the sweetness of her brief morning prayer, which had guided all her activity. She likened that prayer to "a heavenly dewdrop at the bottom of each day's chalice, sweetening all bitterness."[74]

But this was rare. Only a few days later she wrote of the agony all of them were suffering. Always and above all, she worried about the grief experienced by her children over the condition of their father, and "as [her] good confessor reminded [her]," struggled to sustain their spirits under such traumatic conditions.[75] On January 24, Mathilde wrote that maintaining a sense of serenity in family life had been almost impossible owing to Thomas's condition for the previous three days—seven dreadful meals, and it wasn't over. She wrote that, had she alone been the one suffering, it would have been easier to bear, but her daughters were suffering, too. Humanly speaking, it was too much to endure. Mathilde wrote that the strength supplied by God, and perceived only in retrospect, had sustained her through the previous six months.[76]

That February, with Thomas still in crisis, Mathilde continued to seek to unite herself with Jesus in his agony. She wrote that she had to postpone her confession a week, and that she spoke of the turmoil at home when finally able to go. Although her confessor's response sustained her courage, Mathilde did not dare to speak of her interior suffering for fear of bursting into sobs in the confessional. Afterwards, hiding herself in the little Marian chapel, she cried for a long time, submitting to the Father's will along with Jesus, even though her nature cried out.[77]

Toward the end of the month, Mathilde received very bad news concerning the family's finances; she had to act immediately to avert many problems. The situation rendered her habitual burden yet heavier, further complicated by financial worries as well as its subsequent distress on those who loved her, particularly her mother and her daughters.[78]

On the first Friday of Lent (February 25), Mathilde was given a powerful insight into the passion of Jesus: "The sufferings of the God–Man appeared to me in a light in which I had never before either seen or understood them . . . and before me stood that unknown and terrifying sorrow, as deep and as immense as the heart of God, knowing no other measure than that of the divine will, and the power of suffering of a God Incarnate!"[79]

Seeing the parallel of her own sufferings with those of Christ comforted Mathilde. Beginning March 4, however, Thomas had another relapse, which Mathilde describes as serious and painful. She had no time to note it in her journal until March 6, but then noted that she felt remarkably free and serene in dealing with this new trial. She writes, "of course I attributed this only to grace." While experiencing the horror and suffering of her situation, as well as uncertainty concerning its outcome, Mathilde's will was so identified with God's will that any other desire was extinguished in her soul.

On the previous day, she had been able to leave the house long enough to attend Mass for the first time in several days. Mathilde had not been feeling well even before her husband's setback. But on March 4, which was a Sunday, there was no way for her to leave Thomas. The scene is vivid: "I write these notes in the middle of a thousand interruptions, of my poor deliriant's hallucinations, fits of rage and rambling speech." Nevertheless, her union with Jesus after Communion the previous day had rested and fortified her for this crisis, which grew twice as violent by the following evening.[80]

On the fourth day of Thomas's delirium, Mathilde writes that nothing could be so grievous as the habitual state of her poor invalid and his prospect of repeated relapses. She spent the entire evening reciting the rosary in an effort to calm Thomas, with whom there was little that could be said. He had become very quiet, somber, and bewitched by his relentless visions. She had to send for the doctor to get him to go to bed. His persistent silence frightened her, and without saying anything to each other, she and her mother both asked themselves if he was losing his mind altogether.[81]

The crisis ended on March 8, but as the doctor had warned her earlier, the abatement provided no real relief. Thomas no longer knew himself or others, a prospect more frightening for him and the family than even his death would have been. They could not prevent themselves from feeling it; Mathilde's mother and her daughter felt it no less than she. But they also believed that if God had reconnected the nearly broken thread of his life so many times, it was so that his dear soul would be able to draw from this existence some spiritual good that they were unable to see. Mathilde prayed that Our Lady of Lourdes and St. Joseph might bring relief, and some easing of the pain which her mother, daughters, and younger sister were experiencing. She trusted that it would bring them blessings during the year.[82]

Mathilde suffered physically from the strain of her life. She developed a severe headache which prevented her from leaving the house, and she was ill for several weeks. On Holy Saturday, she was in bed, writing her notes in pencil. She was too weary to think, almost too weary to pray, but nothing troubled the deep union of her soul with God. She writes that during the month in which she had been deprived of Communion, her long-ing, as strong as ever, had been so absorbed by her love for the divine will that, without being destroyed, her desire was transformed.[83]

At the end of April, Mathilde added eight pages, expanding her prayer experiences during the two previous months, when she had had so little time to write. She notes that before her husband's most recent relapse, she had felt drawn to make a private retreat, but its first day coincided ex-actly with the onset of Thomas's attack. During the entire time she was suf-fering with and caring for him, Mathilde followed the inspiration of the Holy Spirit as well as she could. She was, of course, unable to spend any time in church as she would have liked, but reflected prayerfully on her re-sponsibilities, especially on the business letters, which devoured a major part of her time.

Mathilde then made a resolution to write less, and to entrust to Providence all the difficulties regarding the state of her poor husband, as well as the aggressive bad will of certain others. Father Grieu observes in Mathilde's journal that it is good to entrust all to God, but comments that this trust does not absolve her of the responsibility to pay attention to her family's business matters.[84] Mathilde's inclination toward a retreat thus pre-pared her to draw on spiritual resources in managing the crisis of health at hand, as well as, in the midst of this crisis, to look after her family's tem-poral affairs.

By the beginning of May, Mathilde was able to go to church for the first time in a month. She was wholly absorbed in Jesus in a union of profound simplicity. She compared her soul to a plot of ground which had been dried and cracked by the heat, now silently drinking the water of heaven, penetrating her and restoring her life. She writes that, during this time, Jesus showed her that he was using her persecutors as a means of uniting her more closely to him in a willing acceptance of an ordeal allowed by God.[85] She often came to Mass weary and distracted, however, because of all the matters to which she had to attend. She told Jesus that he must find her soul in as much disorder as she sometimes found Elisabeth's room. Just as she replaced all her daughter's little treasures, so his hand restored order in her soul, bringing all to an unspeakable peace. Not until after his visit did she discover the good order into which he had put her faculties, and which she, like her little daughter, tried to maintain as long as possi-ble.[86]

Although Mathilde had no *felt* sense of union with God, it re-mained, as Jesus had predicted, profound and complete. She was receiving constant counsel from Our Lord regarding her spiritual life. Jesus called her to an even deeper conversion. As she tried to be faithful to the inspiration, Mathilde noted on a piece of paper that could always be kept with her the practical matters that she believed she was being invited to reform. First, she was not to spend time on useless thoughts and reflections, not to dwell even on the biggest problems. Second, in the presence of anyone unjust, impious, or who outraged God and persecuted the Church, Mathilde was to moderate the very lively indignation which gripped her.[87] No doubt, such persons were those she was forced to encounter socially; it is unlikely that she would have sought them out of her own accord!

These were good resolutions, to be sure, but even Mathilde sometimes found them hard to keep. At the beginning of June, she begged God to forgive her for having replied heatedly to someone, perhaps a guest, who had been exonerating Freemasonry, "meaning no harm, it is true, but it was said at table, in front of the servant." Mathilde was concerned on the servant's account, because she felt a responsibility for the religious, moral, and intellectual good of those who served her family. "Nevertheless," she adds, "I should not have discussed Freemasonry with so much fire."[88]

Mathilde's heatedness would today appear as fanaticism. After all, Freemasonry had presented itself in the eighteenth century as a "religion of humanity."[89] But leading freemasons soon argued for "a cosmopolitan conception of brotherhood under the cloak of a deism so vague that the papacy . . . came to consider it incompatible with . . . the teaching of the Catholic Church."[90] The religious background of this fraternal order was gradually replaced by positivism, so that after 1865, such traditional religious beliefs as the existence of God and the immortality of the soul were excluded as incompatible with freedom of thought.[91] Leading freemasons of the time, seeing themselves as "the educators of modern France," became convinced that what was needed was to restore a secular understanding of society. In their view, the destruction of Catholicism was an essential prelude to renovation.[92] "After the war of 1870, most of the leading republicans were also freemasons."[93] No wonder that Mathilde saw it as dangerous, and stated her opposition strongly!

To her anxiety for Thomas was now added worry over her father, who was apparently becoming more confused as he aged, and concern for the effect of her father's condition on her mother. Even so, when she turned to God in prayer, she found that she had not lost her union with Him in the depths of her soul.[94] "The plenitude of sorrow loses itself in the plenitude of love, because love, stronger than death, is stronger than sorrow." She remembered how, two years earlier, her father had received Communion with them in Vernon. Now he did not even know one year from another, and they felt the contrast keenly.[95]

By July 13, 1887, it had become evident that her father would have to be institutionalized. It fell to Mathilde to make this sad fact clear to her mother. She wished that she could have suffered her mother's grief in her stead, and for the first time, she was unable to sleep. As she lay awake, she was tormented by the fear of being an unnatural daughter, acting badly towards her father, putting away one to whom she owed her life. At last, worn out, she fell into a deep sleep and awakened with the certitude that she was following the right path.[96] But this did not ease her heart. It was, after all, she on whom it fell to take the initiative, to convince and sustain her mother in making this necessary sacrifice, to be the agent of their separation.[97] Returning home to Vernon, she was so tormented by a sense of having violated the sacred bond of affection between father and child that she fell ill, but God strengthened her.

At the end of the month, Mathilde described her state: "Between these three beloved persons, my father whom I have lost, my mother, plunged into sorrow, and my poor husband, slipping further and further down a fatal slope, I feel such anguish that I can hardly breathe."[98] Yet she recognized more than ever the distance between the evils affecting her personally and the more public evils, especially all the offenses committed against God. She feared that, in spite of themselves, others might be affected by this secular spirit, this hatred of God, a sort of Hell, of exile. Concern for the safety of the little ones whom Hell was seeking to take away from God was a major anxiety, and she prayed that at least the suffering which each devout person offered to God might be able to avert such a misfortune.[99] This concern shows a deep, perhaps unconscious, appreciation of mysticism as taking responsibility for the world, an account of which is fully developed only long after her death—for instance, in the work of Karl Rahner.[100]

Mathilde was able to get to Mass and Holy Communion for the Feast of the Assumption, and to take a brief time for prayer in the evening, when she was greatly strengthened by a vision of the glory of Mary in God. She saw Mary wearing a long blue mantle, spread out over the earth, including France, and again prayed that it would protect her country.[101] On August 30, she noted that two years earlier her poor husband was at the point of death, and that, although the last fifteen days had been especially difficult, she herself, for the three previous days, had succeeded in not looking at her suffering, resting instead in silent adoration of God and resignation to his will, a state which had become habitual, thanks to grace. But this took a physical toll on her. She was not able to go to Communion or to concentrate on God, and her mind was full of dark thoughts, especially the fear of being damned. Seeking God, she could not experience his loving presence. Nevertheless, she persevered in her *fiat*.[102]

At the beginning of October, another cruel letter arrived. This one said, among other things, that every kindness which Mathilde had shown to one of her sisters-in-law was "pure ostentation." Every good that she had done in support of this woman—and, by extension, her actions in general—were portrayed as evil. At least in this instance, Mathilde had some family support. "My husband and my three sons returned the letter to its sad and brutal author with their [calling] cards." Her personal reaction was to pray that God might at last bring those who wished to create dissension in her home to justice and peace.[103]

Thomas's little niece Caroline Louise Fourcault, daughter of his eldest sister, Marie, was, like all the other cousins, accustomed to spending her vacation in Vernon. She was the same age as Elisabeth, and had, like Elisabeth, just made her First Communion. While there, she was taken ill and died on October 11. Mathilde prayed that God might receive her innocent and devout soul, and sympathized profoundly with her sister-in-law, in spite of the fact that this woman had told Mathilde that she hated her. "Poor soul," Mathilde wrote, "to lose her only child! What sorrow! What human being could console her? Only God can heal such a wound."[104]

This tragic event did not lessen her union with God. On the contrary, she wrote, only three days later, her understanding of the prayer of passivity:

> The prayer of passivity is not only *the silence of the soul* before God, it is also very truly the *answer of God* to the soul . . . a language without words. . . . God takes possession of the whole being by His all-powerful embrace! In such happy moments, it is no longer *I* that am there, it is *he*. I see myself no longer, I see only Jesus. I am not destroyed, but his life takes possession of me, dominates and absorbs me. . . . I know myself no longer. . . . I adore him, but the divine action penetrates and transforms my adoration; the Divine Being thinks, lives, and loves in me. I live no longer except through him, as the Apostle said, "It is no longer I who live; it is Jesus Christ who lives in me."[105]

Poulain adds a footnote: "These are the characteristics of the transforming union."

In spite of her deep union with God, Mathilde could not help feeling inadequate. A few days later, after Communion, Jesus reassured her: "I am the one who knows, you do not; never seek to know anything . . . by your own judgment."[106] This gave Mathilde immense peace and joy. It is perhaps not insignificant that at about the same time, in a little town just over fifty miles east, a teen-age girl was preparing to enter the Carmelite monastery. In the few years before her death in 1897, Thérèse of Lisieux would come to a similar insight, and find great peace and joy in what she would call "the way of spiritual childhood."[107] Although their temporal vocations were very diverse, and neither knew of the other's existence, both were led, again in different ways (for Thérèse was no visionary), to the great spiritual insight that all we have to do is to allow ourselves to be loved by God. We must learn to die to "our egoism, self-determination, and self-achieving, [letting God] recreate us in love in a way that only God can do."[108]

There are not many entries covering the next two months; nearly all are concerned with Mathilde's prayer. The exception is that of November 10, in which she writes of her joy in her father's return to some degree of self-awareness, which enabled him to pray. This was a great consolation to her. "Nevertheless," she adds, "these four months have been unforgettable." This was above all because of her mother's anguish, prayerfully accepted, which, she was convinced, had brought this relief to her esteemed father. On November 13, she was in Paris at the convent; she felt herself united with God like a drop of water mixed with the wine in the chalice.[109] Apparently her time there was brief, but her mother must have accompanied her, because she was able to stay until the end of the retreat on November 16.[110]

On the same day, Mathilde's father received absolution. Mathilde, who seems not to have been present, prayed that his holy life might be crowned by an easy and tranquil death.[111] She continued to be concerned for her sons' spiritual welfare, and how to communicate her own love of labor for God to her daughter, who seems to have been pleading with her mother to give herself some rest.[112]

Her confessor had recommended that she not omit, in her notebook, her external activities, so she made an effort to comply. She reports that, for the previous thirteen days, in addition to her usual routine, she had been very involved with letters, telegrams, and consultations about some important business affairs. She had obtained her husband's agreement in this cause, which would never have happened without God's help. The matter was not a simple one. It concerned removing furniture from one house and installing it in another, at some distance from Vernon, which Thomas had seen, but to which she was not able to go. A lease was involved, and Mathilde did not know how to conduct the transactions. Thus she had the additional effort of locating a distant lawyer, who should not have had to occupy himself with it, to handle it for her. All these difficulties, however, seemed to her merely to strengthen her habitual union with God.[113]

At the end of November, after Communion, Jesus comforted her: "It is *I* who is suffering in you. Through you, I continue to suffer the sorrows of my Passion and offer them to my Father." This consoled her a great deal, and she thanked Jesus for having given her a taste of his own chalice.[114] Yet she had not forgotten her concern for her country. In a long reflection on the loss of devotion among her countrymen, she entreated Jesus, a few days later, to "save the dying world anew, [to] save France."[115]

Mathilde was in Paris on December 12, but did not record for how long, merely that it was her first moment of solitude.[116] On December 22, she wrote of her prayers for Eugène, her youngest son, nourishing the hope that he might become a priest and asking that he be granted the virtues he would need. The next entry is dated December 31; Thomas had entered his final crisis on Saturday, December 23. Mathilde had been beside him constantly, and though she had made a few notes, had neither the time nor heart to write in any detail. Retrospectively, she described Thomas's last agony and death.[117] Although she had experienced profound grief, Mathilde's spirit did not dwell in it. "Underneath all feeling, my soul remained tranquil, united with God."[118]

Mathilde spent Christmas Eve beside her husband as he lay in pain and delirium, writing, "My spirit, although in the grasp of terrible anguish, retains its liberty by the grace of God."[119] On Christmas Day, she was able to get to a low Mass at noon. But she writes that it would have been impossible for her to have done anything more. God had strengthened her with "a short . . . union with the *Word made flesh*; my soul was flooded with the splendor of the Divine Person, One, and yet having two Natures." The violent delirium, which, she wrote, had begun at 6:00 PM on Saturday, continued without respite. "My poor husband is crushed in extremity. *My soul is crushed.*"[120]

On Monday, December 26, Mathilde was able to attend Mass and receive Holy Communion "at last." God took possession of her whole being. Worn out by her sorrowful vigil, she became frightened at the possibility that, instead of death, what awaited Thomas was permanent insanity.[121] Raising her soul to God, she expressed herself ready "to accept anything, *no matter how painful*, if it be to his glory and the best for the soul of my poor suffering one."[122] God's response was to enfold her in his love and peace.[123]

The family sought repeatedly to reach out to Thomas, to make him aware of his condition. Mathilde writes that, before nightfall, certain fleeting signs gave them the hope that he had understood, and that he joined himself interiorly to the Sacraments [Last Rites] of the Church. He was given absolution. Then, "the three holy priests beside him, and all of us on our knees, his childhood friend [a priest] and spiritual brother in God administered Extreme Unction. . . . How I blessed God for having given us, through the mouth of my good Director, the advice not to postpone the Sacraments, even in the hope that he might recover a little more awareness and be able to speak! Later, it would have been too late!"[124]

Yet Mathilde reports that she remained anxious for him. At midnight, she spoke to him of God, and brought a small crucifix to his lips. To her joy, he kissed it. Then they considered that a few of them might take a little rest. She herself could not rest; she could only pray. A little later the [unnamed] person who had been keeping vigil beside Thomas came to find them, and she hastened to Thomas's side. Kneeling close to him, with her mother and daughter beside her, she repeated the holy names of Jesus and Mary. Shortly, at about 3:00 in the morning, he died peacefully, with his eyes closed, his expression calm, and the trace of a smile on his lips.[125]

Mathilde remained beside him on her knees for a long time; her grief was completely dominated by the thought of the judgment of God. "My soul was really present there trying to help that soul so dear to me and to second his guardian angel with my prayers. I confided [him] into God's Hands with full confidence and love, and . . . felt the divine mercy receiving into its arms that soul who had always fought so valiantly and ardently for God's cause and led a Christian life without any fear of human respect." Her family insisted that she rest for a few hours. Once in her room, she knelt and renewed her religious consecration, entrusted her children "my poor dear orphans" to God and implored the Holy Spirit's inspiration in her new life, asking for his guidance in the accomplishment of all her duties. "After this, I prayed for *him*."[126] She adds, "Naturally, I could not sleep."[127]

January 3 was the next opportunity which Mathilde had for writing. She stated that she had ended New Year's Eve and had begun New Year's Day in prayer for the whole world, but especially for her new life.[128] She had been unable to sleep because of her concern over Thomas's suffering in purgatory. "I pray for him habitually, almost continually, without its hindering the divine union." On the previous day, she had regained some calm, reflecting that the divine action was purifying the soul of her beloved husband, bringing him ever nearer to God, that he would be "accepting his sufferings and aspiring to that closer union." She joined herself by prayer to all the Masses being said for him, and had the consolation of feeling that her husband was at peace. She added that, although she did not draw any absolute conclusions from such feelings, they did ease her heart a little.[129]

The Feast of the Epiphany fell on the first Friday of January, Mathilde's day of reparation as an *agrégée*. Accordingly, she set aside her own sorrow to think only of the outrages committed against God, and to offer herself to him in reparation. Jesus, coming to her in Communion, enabled her to understand that he was the only one capable of offering reparation; she was just a poor little instrument which he was using to restore the glory of his Father.[130] She consecrated her widowhood to God, abandoning herself solely and entirely to his holy will.

Two days later, she wrote that she had already met the soul of her dear departed in God. The first time it was with the feeling that he was at peace, and the second, with a feeling of great sweetness.

> These impressions come suddenly, and with great force, in the midst of that prayer which suspends all the powers in God. I can neither avoid them nor doubt them when they occur; yet in my ordinary life and my normal state my soul still fears purgatory. I do not clearly know whether [my husband] is in Heaven. How I wish I knew! Nevertheless, if it were possible for me to know more than God permits, I would certainly not desire it. I continue to [pray to God on his behalf], and also to have many Masses said in many sanctuaries for that soul so dear to me and so full of faith and zeal.[131]

Most of us, especially many women, might well find Mathilde's attitude odd, in view of all the suffering Thomas had caused her and his entire family. Certainly, no social worker or priest today would encourage a woman to endure twenty-eight months of such a nightmare. We might even wonder how God could have encouraged her to endure it! At this distance, there is a great deal which we cannot know. What we do know is that she would have had no real alternatives. She had no independent means, and no social services were available to her. Even with divorce newly legal, it would not have been an option for a devout Catholic of the late nineteenth century.

In those days of propriety and the conventional distance between husband and wife, spouses could easily live "alongside" one another without ever really getting to know each other.[132] A psychologist might conclude that, in view of her lack of social contact with a variety of men (other than those of her exemplary family) before her marriage, she had projected on Thomas her own inner ideal male, patterned on her father, and never got to know him as he really was. Clearly, Thomas did have many endearing qualities; even Marguerite gave him credit for these. And Mathilde would not have been the first woman in history to have loved a man who was not all she believed him to be. Marguerite lays the blame on his foster mother; let us rather follow the example of their great-grandson and "abstain absolutely from passing any judgment on the different actors in this drama."[133]

CHAPTER TEN:
THE HARVEST YEARS, 1888–1894

Mathilde was now a widow, and the full responsibility for her family's well-being—physical, financial, and spiritual—fell on her shoulders. She resolved to maintain a peace of spirit, setting aside all worldly concerns, except those which God willed for her for the good of her children. She felt a natural sorrow at the loss of Thomas: "I miss that poor dear absent one so much." Yet "the word *widow* strikes [Mathilde's] ear with a spiritual lightness," which she describes in words very familiar to the great mystics: emptiness, nothingness, human insignificance.[1] It suggests a humility which cries out to God, an emptiness as deep as God's great full love.

January 23, 1888, found Mathilde in Paris, at Adoration Réparatrice. She notes that January 27 would mark one month after her husband's death. She writes of a vision of Jesus in a robe of dazzling whiteness, which seems to her to symbolize his separation from all worldly desires. Once again, he tells her to make his good pleasure the center of her life, "alone with the Alone," at every moment in everything. The Superior at the convent gave her joy by speaking to her about making a formal vow of chastity; this she had wanted with all her heart. Mathilde, who mentions St. Jean of Ruysbroeck on the subject,[2] felt that, after her husband's death, God wished in this way to transform her natural affections. Human practical considerations might have suggested that she seek a second marriage, but Mathilde did not see a vow of chastity as an obstacle to fulfilling her responsibilities to her children. Rather, she found the idea of remarriage repugnant; she preferred to remain a widow for the rest of her life.[3] Mathilde wrote that she was glad not to be an old widow (she was forty-three) for the greater honor to God her consecration poses "while . . . still somewhat young."[4] Moreover, she did not reject the state of marriage as such, and notes, on February 1, that it was the twenty-third anniversary of her marriage.[5]

It was possible for Mathilde to stay at the convent in Paris more frequently, but this, too, had a downside. It was a grief to return to Vernon and not find her husband there, as he had always previously been.[6] She still had very vivid memories of the horrible and painful crises which she had witnessed during Thomas's last illness and the trauma of his crises. Mathilde had been helpless to alleviate the crises, and during severe episodes, she endured attacks on her own person. A contemporary reader would thus find it reasonable to expect that Mathilde would have experienced post-traumatic stress disorder, including such symptoms, for example, as detachment or estrangement from others, outbursts of anger, as well as distress or impairment in social, occupational, or other important arenas of function.[7] But Mathilde describes only the vivid memories of her husband's crises, what we might call "flashbacks." In any case, had she experienced further symptoms, no therapy would have been available for her.

The only protection Mathilde had available to her was her relationship with Jesus; he met her needs by revealing his beauty to her. She writes that Jesus taught her "that what I had suffered under those circumstances had been to purify my soul from her natural love of ideal created beauty, and that, in exchange for those terrible and heartbreaking scenes, a clearer vision of the beauty of God would be given to her.[8] The kind of understanding that Mathilde here expresses is consistent with the spirituality of her time; ours would require a different articulation of her experience. What we do know to be true is that God always brings good out of evil for those who love him.[9]

Meanwhile, Mathilde had much to attend to. In fact, the family's financial situation was reasonably secure. At the time of her husband's death, Thomas's real estate holdings were not insignificant. Besides the property in Vernon—the large house in which they lived, a smaller one for a caretaker, and an adjoining one which had belonged to Melanie Bellanger—there was a country house; a farm; a large piece of property at Le Tréport, with residences, offices, stores, a house which overlooked the Channel; and a hotel in Paris.[10] Quite a lot to deal with!

All financial matters were now in her hands, although she was dependent on lawyers to carry out her decisions. On one occasion, she had no time at all to pray until late at night. The entire day had been spent attending to financial matters and writing letters. On top of all this, the lawyer for whom she had sent, who lived out of town, arrived in the evening. Apprised of his arrival, "I made an exclamation of annoyance, which, I fear, was not at all edifying."[11] Maybe not, but very human!

Mathilde's first concern was always for her children. She prayed for them constantly, and worried about their futures, anxious that no spiritual harm should come to them. Jesus told her, with great tenderness, "I will never leave you." She realized then that all she needed to do was trust in God, and she felt ashamed of her anxiety.[12] It seemed to her that Our Lord had been working to supernaturalize her love for her children. She, too, desired this. She blessed him for the consolation he gave her through them, and prayed that neither her concern for them nor preoccupation regarding their future would interfere with her union with God.[13]

Toward the end of February, Mathilde asked Father Grieu for permission to make a vow of chastity. Happily, she found he was willing to allow her to do so, although he wanted her to make it provisionally at first. Immediately, she knelt before the Blessed Sacrament, to vow chastity provisionally until Holy Thursday. She chose that day to make the vow formally, because, besides the significance of the day itself, it was during the month of St. Joseph and within the octave of the Feast of the Annunciation.[14] She praised God for his mercy to her: "There was great joy between Jesus and my soul." Not knowing "how one makes this vow," she said simply, "Beloved, I vow chastity for your love."[15]

Her vow notwithstanding, the well-being of her children was no less important to Mathilde than it had ever been. She spent five days in pain because she feared a serious failing on the part of one of them, although, as it turned out, this had not occurred. (The child in question was probably one of her boys, away at school, else the matter would have been more quickly clarified.) Often she had to omit her customary prayer periods in order to attend to the children's needs, and on February 27, two months to the day after Thomas had died, she spent the whole day with her daughters, comforting their grief for their father by her presence.[16]

Exactly a month later, Father Grieu gave her permission to make a perpetual vow of chastity.[17] Her soul was "inflamed with love and gratitude, but hardly had I left the confessional when a tempest of desolation, of fear of unworthiness, panic, false reasonings" swept over her soul. Mathilde interpreted this as an effort by the powers of darkness to dissuade her from taking this step; the tumult lasted until the evening of the following day. Then the Lord calmed her, and Mathilde could look forward to the morrow "that beautiful day of Holy Thursday on which Jesus 'loved us until the end,' and on which I was going to consecrate my whole being to him."[18] Father Grieu's comment in her journal was that these temptations were a further proof of God's will, which the devil was trying to thwart.[19]

The following morning, March 29, 1888, she pronounced her vow

at the elevation of the Host in the Mass. Having forgotten to ask her confessor for a formula to use in making her vow, she used the words of her
consecration as an *agrégée*: "In the presence of the Holy Trinity, united to
Our Lord Jesus Christ. . . I, Sister Marie Aimée of Jesus, vow perpetual
chastity for the glory and the love of God." Father Grieu wrote that this
was quite sufficient; there was no reason for her to be troubled about it.[20]
Of course, it was a private vow, without any outward sign; were permission
granted for such a vow even as recently as the early twentieth century, it
would have been given on the condition that only the person's confessor
would know of it.

Because of his infirmity, Felix Bertrand had not yet been informed
of his son-in-law's death. When Mathilde visited him in Paris and told him,
he wept. She prayed for guidance in making some decisions preoccupying
her with respect to her poor father's condition: "I want absolutely to do
God's will, and to be preoccupied only as much as he wills about them."
She writes of her husband and her father as "the two arms of her cross,"
but Jesus, "my royal spouse, is in the middle," giving strength and rest.[21]

She increasingly shared Jesus' concern for the world and especially
for France. He asked her to pray that those who were offending God would
receive mercy rather than justice. Her apostolate was to be kind to everyone, in imitation of his infinite mercy, "because that is what is most lacking
in the world." In fact, he frequently mentioned the failure of love, the lack
of an interior life among so many, even among priests. Accordingly, making
up for and defeating spiritual evil occupied a greater place in her prayers
and in her life as a "victim soul" united to Jesus.[22]

Although this term, suggesting neurosis, is uncongenial today, the
attitude which it describes has a long history in spirituality. We find it already in the ninth chapter of the Book of Daniel,[23] in which he identifies
himself with the Israelites who had been unfaithful to the Covenant, praying
in fasting and sackcloth for forgiveness. The definition given in the *Modern
Catholic Dictionary* is this: "A person specially chosen by God to suffer
more than most people during life, who generously accepts the suffering
in union with the Savior and after the example of Christ's own Passion and
Death. The motive of a victim soul is a great love of God and the desire to
make reparation for the sins of mankind."[24]

We may question today whether Mathilde's suffering was "specially chosen by God," but we cannot deny that she suffered greatly during
her married life, quite apart from trials of illness and anxiety for the physical and spiritual safety of loved ones that are common to all loving and

devout parents. Personal motives and behavior are what separate the concepts of "victim soul" and neurotic suffering. Mathilde's resilience and focus on the well-being of others and her warm relationships with them are evidence that neurosis was not involved. Mathilde was especially concerned for the salvation of her countrymen; repeatedly she prayed for France. But she no longer prayed for herself alone; in fact, she was beginning to pray, as well, not just for her children, but for all children.[25]

On April 25, 1888, the fifteenth anniversary of Mathilde's first supernatural grace, she looked back over those years and wrote that the motto, "God alone," had truly been the beginning of a new life, "so impregnated and saturated with grace that my weak nature could not resist them." She added that she would never forget them.[26] On May 3, Mathilde was in Paris; it was First Communion Day at St. Thomas d'Aquin. Remembering her own First Communion in that same church, thirty-three years earlier, she was moved to tears at seeing the little ones dressed in white for the occasion, especially one whose garments were of inferior quality—a child of the poor "clad in the garments . . . of charity . . . one whom the world does not even notice. . . . My soul is lost in the love of Jesus for that little disinherited child of earth."[27]

From May 19 to May 23, Mathilde was at the Adoration Réparatrice convent. While there, Jesus asked her to "be [his] channel to carry [his] graces to others. . . . The channel contains and encloses what is entrusted to it . . . and only overflows where it is meant to overflow. He added, "I am the channel; unite yourself to me and you will give me to others."[28]

Later, while still in Paris, Mathilde attended a Mass offered for Thomas at the church attached to the minor seminary he had attended. After the service, the priest showed her the classrooms and the dormitory, all of which made her heart ache.[29] Returning to Vernon, she had to sort her late husband's belongings, a sorrowful task. Among them, she found a box in which he had carefully kept a scrap of her wedding veil, a dried flower from the bouquet she had carried, his white cravat, the pen with which they had signed their marriage contract, and a wedding announcement. She commented, "What power a little faded thing has to move the human heart!"[30] She, and her daughter after her, kept these tokens. Her great-grandson has added that, when family members found them after Léon Le Touzé's death—and 130 years after Mathilde and Thomas's marriage—they were just as moved.[31]

Adolphe, the second of Thomas and Mathilde's three boys, had hoped after finishing his preliminary studies to be accepted into the naval academy. Alas, it was not to be. Mathilde did not record what happened, except to write that it was not his fault. Adolphe was disappointed, and she felt it with him.[32] This refusal did not preclude a military career entirely, however. He was accepted into the army's academy[33] and was killed in the First World War. Mathilde's eldest son, Albert, had successfully passed his examinations and was admitted to the School of Fine Arts. Eugène, her youngest boy, was having trouble with his eyes and had surgery in mid July. Mathilde had had hopes that he would become a priest, but did not ask this grace for him alone. She prayed rather that God "choose brave apostles from among all young Christians."[34] Eugène never did become a priest. He, too, died in the First World War, which Mathilde did not live to see.

Charles de Cabanoux, Mathilde's maternal cousin, was installed as pastor of Our Lady of the Fields in Paris in the middle of July. It was his first assignment as pastor. Mathilde united her prayers with those of her paternal cousins Emmanuel and René Delaperche, both priests, that his ministry would be fruitful. Their shared faith was a joy to her.[35] Charles ended his career as the pastor of St. Thomas d'Aquin, one of the most important churches in Paris. A wise and humble man, he was a great support to Mathilde throughout her life.

Mathilde's eyesight continued to be limited. In August, she wrote that she could only write with a pencil, and could not see what she was writing.[36] Her eyes continued to grow worse until she could hardly see at all. No doubt, this made her periods of aridity in prayer even harder, since she could not then find comfort in rereading what she had written during times when she felt God's loving presence more strongly. She accepted this lovingly, reflecting that it was only just that she would suffer a little after having been consoled so often. "Isn't it fair," she asks, "that when it pleases him, God hides himself from one whom he had visited so much?"[37]

In the middle of October, Mathilde moved with her mother to an apartment at 6, Cité Vaneau, Paris, not far from where her parents had lived earlier.[38] She writes that this move, made to assist her mother (given the hospitalization of her father), was made with relative calm. She prayed that God would bless and sanctify them in their new dwelling.[39] The move did not immediately involve the entire family; Elisabeth wrote to her sister Melanie from Vernon, asking for a complete account of all the details of "our nest" in Paris and begging her to hurry back to Vernon. The husband of Mathilde's sister, Elisabeth's Uncle Charles—as well as trusted servants—stayed with Elisabeth. She reported that he was very gracious.[40] Excellent train service allowed Mathilde to travel between Paris and Vernon frequently, in less than a two-hour trip each way. Nevertheless, the move did complicate her life a bit more, and she writes of a multiplicity of concerns and business matters in which she tried not to be any more absorbed than God wished.[41]

By mid November, both daughters were with Mathilde in Paris. She notes that she was making her retreat at the convent, but was not staying there overnight on account of her girls.[42] She preserved her interior recollection by speaking little and with circumspection, repeating little of what she has heard, not dwelling on external matters and not showing her feelings.[43] On January 1, 1889, she consecrated the new year to the Blessed Trinity. She writes that she felt embraced by Jesus' love, and understood that she was "to live in the Holy Trinity by that life from on high, which lends itself to every duty, but surrenders itself only to God." In a vision "more rapid than lightning," she apprehended "all the voices of the world dying and ending in a song of immortality. . . . All will be appeased, all will be silenced; all will one day give place to the eternal alleluia which my soul heard today."[44]

On Monday afternoon each week, Mathilde had an "open house" for family and friends; this allowed her more solitude during the rest of the week. During all the conversation, she was able to remain recollected, letting the others talk and saying little herself, except insofar as charity required it.[45] She also had to visit others. She records a miserable evening during which "it was necessary to admire the flower baskets, to partake of the buffet lest one be ungracious, and to make polite conversation." In spite of this, good came of it. She met again some childhood friends with whom she reconnected for the sake of her children.[46]

Her union with God continued to grow. She writes that when God takes possession of her soul, it "no longer knows how to distinguish herself from him whom she loves; nothing remains but God alone; . . . it is beatitude begun."[47] None of these graces led to an inflated opinion of herself. Echoing the emptiness described by other mystics, she writes, "I see myself before God as one who *is nothing, knows nothing, can do nothing*. Each day I see these truths more clearly."[48]

As her father was not improving in the hospital, Mathilde was anxious to bring him home. For reasons she does not explain, this was very difficult to arrange; each attempt ended in failure.[49] At last, the persuasion of her entire family proved successful. She counted this a great blessing, since her father "surrendered his beautiful soul to God" only a few weeks later, on March 9, 1889, surrounded by his family, "with all the consolations of the faith." It was her cousin Charles, his nephew, who administered the Last Rites and committed him to God. The day after the funeral, Mathilde went to the convent with her mother. It appears that this was for her mother's sake, because Mathilde writes that she was so tired that she had to fight against sleep the whole day, but managed to hide it.[50] The family did not return to Vernon immediately. In late March, while walking with her daughters, she noted how much "the Champs Elysées makes me regret the absence of our woods."[51]

Being in Paris during Holy Week afforded Mathilde an opportunity to visit the Altar of Repose in more than one church on Holy Thursday. Visiting seven churches on this day was a pious custom prior to Vatican II, of which she took full advantage.[52] At other times, when Mathilde's fragile health prevented her from going out, even for Mass (she seems to have suffered from frequent headaches and fatigue), she offered this sacrifice for the spiritual good of others.[53] Of one such occasion, she writes, "Always a recluse, . . . but I am learning to recognize the action of God in all these states."[54] This did not exclude times when she felt tempted to sadness and impatience, but resisted them with the help of grace.[55]

Marking the sixteenth anniversary of her initial mystical experience on April 25, Mathilde wrote that, in view of all the graces with which God had "loaded" her, in spite of her inadequacy, to have refused God anything, great or small, would have been monstrous on her part.[56] Shortly afterward, on May 21, her cousin, Charles de Cabanoux, celebrated the twenty-fifth anniversary of his ordination with a Mass at the convent. Mathilde prayed for him and her whole family, asking that their descendants continue to love and serve God, as well as give him priests and religious until the end of time. After the festivities, the family returned to Vernon, where Mathilde's duties left her little opportunity for prayer.[57] In fact, she was unable to write more than a few pages for the next month.[58]

Many, the Catholic hierarchy especially, deemed France's defeat by Prussia and the experience of the Paris Commune in the previous decade to have been "the consequence of moral failure on a national scale."[59] This led devout Catholic laymen, as well as some bishops, to conclude that "salvation would come through the Sacré-Coeur."[60] They further believed that a public act of repentance was called for, and that the form it should take was to dedicate Paris, and by extension all France, to the Sacred Heart. To symbolize public repentance, they suggested erecting in Paris a church dedicated to Jesus under this title. This project would require not only the support of the archbishop of Paris,[61] but also that of the government.

Archbishop Guibert, successor to the murdered Archbishop Darboy, saw such a project as an act of reparation by France both for the excesses of the revolution and for "the terrible year" after the end of the Franco-Prussian War. He was anxious to have the proposed Basilica built on Montmartre, the highest point in Paris, both to counter the spiritual vacuum among Parisians and to rekindle devotion through a change in the city's spiritual landscape in harmony with civic changes brought about by Haussmann. But securing the site required a vote by the National Assembly to acquire the property by right of eminent domain.[62]

The Archbishop's hope was naturally shared by Mathilde, and she had expended great energy in asking those who could do so to use their influence to persuade the delegates to support the request.[63] The National Assembly passed the needed legislation in the summer of 1873, and a provisional chapel was built to encourage pilgrimages while the basilica itself was under construction. The work itself proceeded in fits and starts, however, so that the provisional chapel would not be closed until 1891.[64]

At the beginning of August 1889, the family went to Le Tréport. Mathilde's sons, having passed their examinations, were with her. She felt a natural pride in them, and resisted the temptation to "show them off" by taking them with her on a little trip.[65] Nevertheless, Mathilde spent much of the vacation planning activities for them. Early in September, they went to vespers at a church some distance away. She noted afterwards, "My sons rode there on horseback, and thanked me heartily for the day's pleasure. It seems that I am considered very ingenious at organizing holidays. I am very pleased, because I want my children to enjoy themselves within proper limits, for two reasons: 1. Because I owe it to them when they have worked well. 2. Because, having the honor of representing piety to them, I do not want ever to be the reason for their finding it boring."[66] They all enjoyed the natural beauty of the sea, the sky, and the cliffs; Mathilde meditated on the splendor of God's creation.[67] She liked to spend the first two hours of the morning in silence beside the sea. It was a penance to her to keep silence only intermittently because she had to pay attention to the children while they were swimming. Understanding that others had no such attraction, she did not wish to impose it on them; instead she writes that she "ought to imitate their virtues."[68]

There were also therapeutic baths in Le Tréport; Mathilde inquired about them for one of the servants. There, however, she "was aroused to disgust and anger by certain innovations which bore witness to a complete forgetfulness of human and Christian dignity," and she told them so in no uncertain terms. In her notebook, she comments that she did not regret this in the least.[69]

That September, the family returned to Paris, but in the hurly-burly of the city, Mathilde missed the little country churches.[70] Paris was bustling with crowds coming to the Exposition, exhibiting new technology and architecture as a way of trying to restore Paris's pre-1870 standing as a world leader. Electricity, the phonograph, the telephone, the first automobiles, moving pictures, faster trains, a new and vastly improved sewer system brought greater comfort to the city dwellers. The crown of the Exposition was the Eiffel Tower.[71] The family all went to see the marvels exhibited "so far as is suitable to my children," and Mathilde found some interest in them herself. Nevertheless, she writes, "This interest remains on the surface of my soul. The works of men hardly touch me anymore; they are too far remote from God."

Further on, she explains the contrast she is making; among the works exhibited were reproductions of some parts of the most beautiful churches of France, works inspired by faith. The family had begun their viewing with these. Mathilde comments, "Our artists of today are clever, but they will not have known how to reveal God to man with that same energy and grandeur. . . . Oh, my ancestors of stone, when I saw you there yesterday I said to myself that my century ought to blush . . . for its little faith, for its cowardly materialism which stifles the sap of inspiration, arrests the elevation of the mind towards the ideal, and dries up the noblest sources of genius and of art!"[72]

Their vacation over, the boys returned to their schools. Albert was desolate at having to leave home, and wrote a sad letter to his mother. Mathilde was glad that he had such positive feelings about being with the family; she missed him too. But it was her duty to require that the boys return to their studies. It was better for them, and important for their future. She hoped her reply would cheer him up and restore his usual good humor.[73]

Her children were a real consolation to her, and she blessed God for this. Above all, she was grateful that God "*is in the depths of all our souls,* mother, children, sister, and this is why we form a *really united* family. I esteem this the greatest good, after the faith, I can leave my children, because it is the characteristic of a truly Christian family." Her aunt Caroline (Charles's mother), who shared these same ideals, said that she liked to stay at Vernon, because "it is 'the house of peace.'" Poulain adds that the servants felt the atmosphere of virtue as well, and used to say, "Madame and her mother are two little saints."[74]

Mathilde's own interior state was not always so peaceful. She was not immune to experiences of darkness and anguish of heart. "I feel myself burning with impatience, without any motive, against people whom I love the most. I want to break something. I feel displeasure, involuntary but full of bitterness, against others, against myself, against everything. I am even tempted against God, although this is only a passing feeling. I go on praying as usual, and I think grace prevents anyone from noticing my interior state." Father Grieu's comment is that she should not torment herself about such occurrences for they happen to everyone.[75]

As her vision continued to deteriorate, Mathilde wrote of a mist continually before her eyes, which prevented her from reading or writing. Poulain believes that this was occasioned by conjunctivitis. Whatever the condition, it obliged her to write in pencil without seeing what she was doing.[76] From October 21 on, Mathilde wrote notes as she could, and Mother Anne at the convent copied them into her notebook for her. She continued to accept everything with love, desiring that God's will be perfectly accomplished everywhere.[77]

Aside from her vision problems, Mathilde seems to have enjoyed a brief period of serenity. In late October, she recorded that, after twenty years of being tested by humiliation and "martyrdom of the heart," she was being tested, especially in the year just past, by the happiness of real family life, the abundance of God's blessings, and the praise in which she has found herself surrounded, much to her astonishment. She fears these blessings might make her proud: "It is difficult to be humble in directing and correcting others, and as it is often my duty to do this, I should [include humility in] my examination of conscience."

She further comments that it was now necessary for her to live in the midst of everything with a certain degree of detachment, something that she found herself better able to do than had earlier been the case. Father Grieu added a reminder: "But happiness in this world is not permanent. Great joy is nearly always the beginning of great sorrows, alas!"[78] In November, the family returned to Paris for the winter.[79] During her evening prayer on November 26, Mathilde was inspired by God "to make an act of immense desire that his will be perfectly accomplished everywhere."[80]

Father Grieu's warning was prescient: Elisabeth, Mathilde's fourteen-and-a-half-year-old daughter, became ill the next evening, on November 27, 1889. She had a high fever and was delirious. The doctor was not worried, thinking it only bronchitis. Mathilde, however, feared it was more serious. She was right; in a mere five days Elisabeth was dead. This huge grief to the entire family was sudden and unexpected. Mathilde writes that, during this brief illness, Elisabeth had "prayed as in the years of her robust health, and everything that her confessor in Paris and the little cousins her own age tell me confirms me in the opinion . . . I held myself as to the serious development of piety which in these last months had taken place within her."[81]

"When I saw that dear little one fall into her last peaceful sleep, I gathered up all my strength in order to give her to God with my whole heart and to accompany her little soul to him. . . . I was bringing her up for him, and my only desire was to see him call her entirely to himself in the religious life. . . . His grace sustains me and gives me, together with the bitterness of the chalice, the spiritual joy of suffering.[82] Mathilde of course experienced "some transports of natural sorrow," particularly upon return to Vernon, "where everything reminds us of her short life."

Elisabeth was laid to rest beside her father in the family plot in Vernon in brilliant sunshine. Mathilde comments, "Nature does not go into mourning for angels." She adds, "My heart has adored even while it broke because it recognized the will of God. With grace, nothing is simpler."[83] Many of her associates came to offer condolences; Mathilde focused on a single insight. "It is to love the holy will of God even more than my child. . . . Thus there is peace and love in sorrow."[84]

On the Feast of the Immaculate Conception (December 8), Mathilde remembered how, a year earlier, Elisabeth had gone back to Vernon with her sister for the feast, the anniversary of her having been received into the Children of Mary. On the same feast, seven years earlier, Mathilde herself had become an *agrégée* of Adoration Réparatrice: "What joy in my heart, and what confusion over my unworthiness!" Thirty-five years earlier, she had been so happy because the dogma of Mary's Immaculate Conception had been proclaimed. Now her little angel was in Mary's arms.[85] Her response to these memories was to abandon herself to God's Will, accepting "the present cross and the crosses to come."[86]

Acceptance did not remove Mathilde's natural sorrow: "All through these days . . . I have neither sought nor fled from emotions of grief. I want to feel as much sorrow as God wishes me to, and when I feel

[it] ready to overwhelm me, I turn it quietly into an act of love." Passing by the door of her daughter's room, "which has remained closed," she knelt with arms outstretched in order to renew her sacrifice. "Immediately my soul was filled with great sweetness, I saw Jesus in Heaven and my child in him. . . . As long as this grace lasts, I feel as if I have never lost my child."[87]

On the day after Christmas, Mathilde came down with a fever and could neither read nor write for three weeks. Her account of those days was not written until January 13. For the first part of this period, her mother also was sick. So Mathilde had no one to read to her, as she would not ask her children to read the authors she would have chosen. She united her helplessness with that of the Divine Infant, and joined the sad year just ending with the New Year, 1890, in a single act of love.[88] Nevertheless, January 1, 1890, was sad, humanly speaking: "My soul was raised up in God . . . and in him my darling child wished me a happy and holy year through his divine love. . . . He showed me how happy he makes her through his love and this love overflows on the family left behind to mourn her on earth."[89]

On January 3, 1890, there was to be a dinner reuniting the grieving family, but because of her illness, Mathilde was unable to attend.[90] She was still not well enough to attend another family dinner on January 18—although her mother and children went. "And as I was taking my solitary meal I had no time to reflect on my loneliness, for Jesus and my little Elisabeth came and kept me company. . . . The feeling of the absence of my child was completely obliterated by her presence. . . . Yet how did I know of that presence, since I neither saw nor touched her? It was by that certitude of faith which surpasses the testimony of the senses." Seeing the love flowing between Jesus and her daughter, "I could only bless God for having taken my child for his glory, and for the happiness which he showers upon her."[91] What a clear expression of selfless love! Not until late January was she able to get to Mass again. She had felt that her soul had been "dying of hunger for the Eucharist."[92]

Yet it is apparent that Mathilde was steadily growing in peaceful acceptance of God's will, not only in this deprivation, but in her visual difficulties and—hardest of all—her increasingly frequent and prolonged experiences of God's absence.[93] She still felt Elisabeth's death keenly. Her vision having improved somewhat on January 21, she was able to study her little daughter's photograph—the blonde hair, the intelligent and innocent expression, "at first glance . . . it seemed to me that she was about to speak!" But, much as she missed her, Mathilde did not wish her back on earth, since that would deprive her of the joy of Heaven.[94] With respect to herself, Mathilde felt quite useless; she again offered God the loss of her vision, and even of her life, if he so willed. If, on the other hand, he willed that she continue to live, she prayed that it would be for him alone.[95]

The twenty-fifth anniversary of Thomas and Mathilde's wedding was February 1, 1890. She noted that it was also "two years and one month since the death of my husband, and two months since the death of my daughter. People keep their silver weddings according to the fashion of this world; they are also kept after a heavenly fashion." She had been too tired to go out to Mass: "Hardly had I begun my morning prayers than . . . my husband, whom I have several times felt in God since his death, appeared to me again and with him . . . my little angel. Together we renewed my sacrifice and offered to God this child, the last dear flower of our union . . . and we three were with [God] like one soul inflamed with his love."[96] Her living children, unaware of this mystical anniversary celebration, brought her bouquets of violets, since these were the flowers their father had brought her each year. She appreciated their affection.[97]

Elisabeth would have been fifteen that February 3. Mathilde had renewed her sacrifice, recalling that her daughter had often said she did not want to be fifteen. Even though it was a sorrow for her family, God had given her a blessed eternity in exchange. Mathilde found comfort in this.[98] But such experiences of consolation were brief. She described her ordinary state as "darkness of the soul accompanied by suffering of the body with my failing sight and the impossibility to read or write." Her spirit still did not waver: "I live in a very simple act, always the same, of entire conformity to the will of God."[99]

Melanie was now twenty-three. It was high time for her to be married, and finding a suitable spouse occupied most of Mathilde's time during the first half of 1890. She asked her daughter Elisabeth to pray for this intention as she considered possible candidates. The first she rejected as unsuitable; the second match, which appeared much better, beyond all their expectations at the time, fell apart "due to the unexpected and unusual behavior of an uncle who has something absolutely odd in his brain."[100] She found his intervention so bizarre that she believed his brain, after his death, ought to be studied by the researchers at the Academy of Medicine![101] Her great-grandson added that one would dearly love to know of whom she spoke. It is evident that she did not always keep her opinions to herself when evaluating family members.[102]

Fortunately, her cousin Charles had a suggestion: a young man from his parish, to whom he had taught catechism, and whom he knew to be intelligent, a true Christian, an industrious professional with a pleasant personality, named Léon Le Touzé.[103] Mathilde was delighted and the contacts were made. Both of Léon's parents were dead; a letter from Léon's mother, Leonie, written in 1885, before her early death, has been preserved in the "Little Family Chronicle": "I bless in advance she who will be the wife of my dear son. I would like her to be a well-brought-up, Christian young woman [who will be] a daughter to my husband and a sister to my daughter. From now on, I bless her and love her."[104] Léon had only an unmarried sister, Louise, ten years older than Melanie, and a bachelor uncle, Albert Lenfant. On May 20, Mathilde dictated a letter, which her mother wrote for her, to an unidentified friend, describing their first meeting: "Melanie found it very easy and pleasant to talk with Léon, and felt at once the understanding which exists between families having the same values. She was very attracted to him, and her mother was very positive about their future together, as were other members of her family.[105]

On May 30, she received the formal request for her daughter's hand.[106] A few days later, Louise and Leon were invited to join the Boutles at dinner. Mathilde's letter to Louise was very cordial, and asked the latter's help with planning the engagement dinner. Louise also helped to plan the wedding and was warmly welcomed into the family circle by Mathilde. The marriage contract was signed on July 3 at Mathilde's home in Paris. The civil marriage took place on July 5, and the religious ceremony on July 7, 1890. This last took place at the Church of St. Francis Xavier. Louise, Albert Lenfant, and a friend were the only ones whose signatures appear on Léon's side. On Mathilde's side, there were twenty-four signatures, all but the last two family members. Charles de Cabanoux was delegated to officiate at the wedding. His address to the young couple has survived; it was twenty-four pages long. It praised, as was customary, their good qualities as well as those of their family members. It was "a perfect example of the ecclesiastical eloquence of its day."[107]

Léon was a graduate of the Polytechnical School. At the time of their marriage he was a deputy inspector for the railroad and better off financially than his bride. He was also very generous. Their honeymoon trip took them through Austria, Germany, Switzerland, and Italy; it was very pleasant. He wrote to Louise that Melanie was always so amiable and cheerful that it was a joy to travel with her. He regretted that he had only a month for their trip. "Six weeks would have been much better." Melanie added a little note in which she proclaimed herself "happy beyond words with Léon."[108]

No doubt, Mathilde was profoundly grateful for their happiness. Not only had this marriage secured her daughter's financial future, but it also promised to offer Melanie the emotional security and peace of heart of which she had known little while growing up, and had not experienced in her parents' marriage. Nevertheless, it required an adjustment for Mathilde, who felt her daughter's absence.[109] After they returned from their honeymoon, the young couple lived mainly in Versailles. Mathilde could visit them, and she did, but, as any mother knows, the daily intimacy was gone. Mathilde's deep union with Jesus never protected her from normal human emotions, nor would she have wanted it to. Neither would she have been an interfering mother-in-law; she would have remembered too well what grief this could cause.

Mathilde's three sons still returned to her at every vacation, and spending time with them took priority even over keeping her journal. After Communion on March 20, 1891, she had seen the love between the Father and the Son, "so great, so tender, so ardent that a Person equal to themselves necessarily proceeds from it. God is love. The nature of love is to give itself."[110] Even though the charm of this vision remained with her—in fact, it increased during the next three days—she was unable to write further about it immediately. Palm Sunday was March 24; she notes that this day belongs to the family. "The divine light remained above everything, even when I was organizing the plans for their amusement and entertainment during the Easter vacation with my sons."[111]

Only then was Mathilde free to continue her meditation on the love uniting the three persons of the Trinity, and the way in which we are made able to share in this love. Because the Word of God could not give us his divine nature, he chose to share our nature. This made it possible for him to unite himself with each of us in the Eucharist, the greatest gift of his love, transforming us into himself. Having received this gift, we must, in turn, give it to others.[112] She writes, "In order to imitate God in his gift of love, we must love our neighbor to the very gift of self. There is no real love without the gift of self. But if we wish to imitate God better still, it is *God himself* that we must give. He gave himself to us without measure and forever; we should give him to our fellow creatures."[113] This insight, which Mathilde here expresses so clearly, is unique to Christianity. Louis Dupré, in his general introduction to *Light from Light: An Anthology of Christian*

Mysticism, comments that in Christianity Jesus is not merely a teacher of Enlightenment, as was the Buddha, nor was he a prophet like Mohammad or Elijah. "He himself becomes the object of mystical love" and it is this incarnational emphasis which accounts for "the earthy and humane quality" of Christian mysticism.[114] It is not just the person of Jesus which is an object of reverence: "The entire creation (in all its finite aspects) is virtually included in the incarnated Christ. . . . The love of all creatures in Christ implies more than loving them *as if they were Christ*. . . . Saints have always understood that the incarnation has united the Christian's love of God to the love of the creature."[115]

Mathilde still continued to pray as usual, whether in aridity or comforted by a sense of Jesus' presence.[116] When she asked him later how it was that he did not weary of one so insignificant, he replied, "I ask you only not to weary of yourself."[117] She visited the convent as her duties and health permitted, keeping the first Friday of each month as her day of prayer and reparation. In September she visited Melanie and Léon for a few days,[118] and later in the month, she was in Vernon.[119] This pattern would become quite regular. The family seems to have spent the winters in Paris and the summers in Vernon, except for the "dog days" of late summer, which they usually spent at Le Tréport, by the sea.

On the first anniversary of Elisabeth's death, November, 30, 1890, Mathilde had many affectionate visits from members of her family, but what strengthened her most was offering her beloved child to the Blessed Trinity. She felt Elisabeth as a radiant bond of union between herself and God in a singleness of love, and, as she had so often since her daughter's death, reaffirmed her *fiat*.[120] Jesus cheered and fortified her by showing her that our earthly affections are *only a beginning*. The truth is quite the opposite. In heaven they reach their true development. Those who *love in God* can already begin to love one another in this way while still in this world.[121]

Unlike those who believed God required radical asceticism, Mathilde made use of less dramatic practices. Her entry for February 3, 1891, includes this: "I have often refrained from making certain little observations to inferiors when they bore no necessary relation to their work. Their shortcomings are often excellent occasions for mortifying my own self-love and excessive sense of order. I have made a little progress in this respect."[122]

Her grown-up sons returned home as usual for the Easter vacation, and, again as usual, Mathilde arranged activities for their amusement. "I am in turn costumier, fitter, stage manager, impresario; I send out letters of invitation, and so forth."[123] In a footnote, Poulain added, "For several years she took the trouble to compose comedies herself, which people thought charming, and which she taught her children to act before relatives and friends. She took charge of everything, even the scenery."[124] She saw this as her duty, providing them and their friends with wholesome fun. Thus it did not lessen her union with God: "At the summit of my soul and above all this, there remains untouched a luminous zone . . . where love lives in a perpetual prayer."[125]

On May 19, 1891, the anniversary of the day on which the young couple had first met each other, they learned that Melanie was pregnant. Mathilde wrote with joy in her heart, "I recommend to heaven the dear baby which I hope will double your joy. . . . Your grandmother and brothers send warm regards."[126] Mathilde bought a baptismal robe, which has been kept and used by her family ever since, but this little one never wore it.[127] Born at home on August 11, the little girl lived only two days. Mathilde had the comfort of baptizing her ten minutes after she was born; she was named Elisabeth. As the newborn hovered between life and death, Mathilde prayed, "Whatever happens, blessed be God!"

The loss of Melanie's first child was a great sorrow to the whole family, but especially to the young couple. Mathilde wrote, "My heart is broken again because this time it is my children who are directly affected."[128] A later reflection put this heartache in perspective: "How could . . . the Father, who took his delight in his beloved Son . . . sacrifice that Son for the redemption of the world? It is a mystery of love. And what a lesson flows from [it] to enable our human hearts to accept the most difficult of all sufferings: that of seeing our children suffer."[129] Six months later, Jesus expressed his compassion for mothers: "If mothers knew how to seek, they would find in his heart a most powerful . . . tenderness ready to understand and console their heartbroken love."[130]

Mathilde was given more immediate comfort as well. The family's "second little Elisabeth" was rejoicing in eternity and celebrating there the Feast of Mary's Assumption. This gladdened her, in spite of her maternal distress.[131] Several weeks after this, Jesus "showed me that the relations of the Elect with one another are very diverse and that they are happy and glorious in proportion to the degree of spirituality they have acquired on earth. Filling my heart with great sweetness, he made me see how that little soul which I had the joy of baptizing will be [lovingly] attached to me in happiness for all eternity."[132]

The second anniversary of Elisabeth's death brought sadness, but at the same time adoration and praise. Mathilde dreamed that Elisabeth was beside her, that her child took her hand and embraced her, "weeping because of my sorrow. I returned her kisses through my sobs, and traced a triple cross on her breast, each time making an act of love, renewing my sacrifice." Elisabeth then returned to God. Mathilde's grief was calmed by perceiving her happiness and the love which God lavished on her. Father Grieu added, "All of this is possible; it is a consolation which you well deserve."[133]

Her own spiritual understanding continued to deepen. She asked her spouse how he had been able and willing to lavish himself on one who had never done anything to deserve it, and was told, with great tenderness, that *love has no reason but itself.*[134] "The Father gives Jesus as spouse to souls so that he may continue to live, in them and through them, that life which he wished to live personally on earth, and which is no longer in accordance with his now glorified state."[135]

On New Years Day, 1892, Mathilde had no time to write more than this: "May your kingdom, your love, increase on earth and in my soul." Her sons were home for vacation, and she had been ill at Christmas. Three weeks later, she had a high fever. Her doctor confirmed that if it were to last, it would be fatal. Mathilde's response was to offer her life to God with all her heart, if he wished to take it. She spent the long hours in prayer, offering herself for France, "poor France, so far from God!" She felt some regret that, at what might be the end of her life she was still so imperfect, in spite of all she had been given, but she let go of this, and even concern for her salvation, if it were his will to take her just as she was. The fever broke two days later, and she praised God for allowing her to continue serving him.[136]

Mathilde noted, as she did every year, that February 3 was Elisabeth's birthday. She would have been seventeen years old. "But I have felt that she is in the arms of God; blessed be he!"[137] Some time later that month, her daughter Melanie conceived again, a joy and anticipation which was tinged with a natural anxiety. The summer of 1892 turned out to be blisteringly hot, and Mathilde did her best, with great tenderness and maternal experience, to encourage her daughter and ease her fears. In mid August she wrote to Melanie from Vernon:

> How exhausted you must be by this heat! I have been bothered
> by it all day. This wearisome season must increase your discom-
> fort. Like you, I am in a hurry to see you relieved. . . . Assuredly

it will soon be better.

I will come on Tuesday as you wish. Above all, my poor darling, do not let yourself think that this discomfort and its approaching conclusion is other than completely normal. Not only is everything going very well, but the first time is always the hardest, even had your first time been totally ordinary, and you have a double reason not to prejudge the second by it. You are aware that not only are you better prepared for an easy delivery, but the little one is very active, no complications have occurred, . . . and your labor will be less difficult.

Believe this, my sweet, and do not worry uselessly. I will join your husband, whom I embrace tenderly, on the 5:55 PM [the commuter train which he took home regularly from his office in Paris] on Tuesday.[138]

Caring for her daughter did not interrupt her union with God. On August 31, she learned from Jesus why so few souls arrive at a permanent union with God. "So many only understand union with God accompanied by enjoyment, and know nothing of the pure union of will in suffering." Father Grieu added this later: "The union of the will with God in suffering is assuredly a good and holy thing and capable of prolonging and maintaining the union of the soul with God. It is easy to remain with him when one finds him in joy; it is less so when there is suffering."[139]

Melanie gave birth to her second child on September 18, 1892. Mathilde praised God for the safe delivery of a healthy baby, and prayed that this little boy, and all others in its generation, might live a life of faith, praising and loving God. He was named Charles Albert Felix; Albert after his godfather, Albert Lenfant, Charles after Léon's deceased father, and Felix after his recently deceased great-grandfather. Mathilde was his godmother.[140] It seemed to her that, during the weeks preceding his birth, she had had more peace and abandonment to God's will than previously, and this grace was a new spiritual benefit intended to sanctify each new loving relationship.[141]

In his "Little Family Chronicle," Charles's son has preserved a note from Mathilde's mother, Cécile Bertrand, who remained in Vernon, as well as a long letter from Melanie's brother Eugène, in which he expressed his joy. He added that the newborn would fail him as a nephew if he did not become a soldier. Albert, however, hoped he would become an artist. Charles did indeed become a soldier, and although he lost a leg, survived the First World War,[142] as his younger brother, Jean, born in 1894, did not.[143]

Mathilde returned to Vernon at the beginning of October, and both she and her mother were back in Paris in November.[144] On New Years Day, 1893, she spent the entire day contemplating Jesus' words, "My food is to do the will of him who sent me." She added that she did not have the leisure to write anything further.[145] Her mother, Melanie, and (during their vacations) her sons were with her. Her joy in them did not prevent her from seeing their faults, which troubled her. "It even seems to me that the more I love them, the more I see [their shortcomings] because I would like them to be perfect." It was above all their spiritual well-being that mattered to her, but Mathilde also appreciated the goodness, perseverance, and consolation which they gave her on earth. It was a special joy to take in her arms her little grandson, innocent and pure after his baptism.[146]

It was becoming increasingly difficult for Mathilde to see. This, in addition to the time it took to attend to the family's temporal affairs, limited the number of her journal entries. She described her condition as a cloud over her eyes. It seems to have been intermittent, periods of obscured vision alternating with others in which she could see what she was writing.[147] Between the weather and her poor vision, Mathilde led almost a cloistered life. In March 1893, she was unable to go to the convent, although her mother went. On her return, Mrs. Bertrand told her daughter that the sermon had been on death. The preacher had said that as soon as the soul leaves the body it finds itself in the presence of Jesus. Mathilde was deeply moved; she felt how sweet the moment when she fell into his arms would be.[148]

Marking, on April 25, the twentieth anniversary of her initial mystical experience, Mathilde wrote that she ought to have become a saint, and that her misery was a source of confusion to her. But she was untroubled by this; she placed her confidence in God's mercy. All he asked was that she would do what she could. She willed it only as much as he willed it.[149] On the Sunday within the octave of Corpus Christi in early June, she was given an intellectual vision of Jesus which filled her consciousness to the exclusion of every other consideration. It lasted throughout the service. She added that she could not recall at that moment everything which had occurred since her last "manifestation of conscience." "If it pleases God, I will write them and make my manifestation of conscience, which I am unable to do at this moment." She feared that she was abusing the charity of others by trying to write at all, "because I am unable to see even the point of my pen. I abandon everything to God."[150]

Therefore, it is not surprising that Cécile Bertrand wrote to

Melanie, who had invited her to visit them early in June 1893, that she would not be able to come right away because Mathilde had an appointment with the doctor regarding her eyes. If all went well, they would come later in the week on "Léon's train."[151] Mathilde herself wrote little that month: she noted that she was doing so without seeing clearly. "While I was feeling very afflicted at this state of mutilation and impotence to which I am reduced through the partial loss of my sight, Jesus suddenly appeared to me in all the splendor and integrity of his perfect human nature united with his divinity. This . . . made [me] forget all [my] miseries, which [I] bore afterwards with greater peace. Blessed be God!"[152]

Léon, having given his bride her first view of the mountains on their honeymoon, planned to take her, their two-year-old son and his wife's entire family on a "grand tour" of the Swiss and northern Italian mountains. It had to be postponed because Melanie came down with scarlet fever. The delay made it possible for Adolphe, who had just graduated from the military academy, and would have a month's furlough before reporting to his first assignment, to join them. It was a "grand tour" indeed—eight family members and two servants taking a month's vacation abroad! What made it especially enjoyable was their congeniality. Little Charles delighted them all with his spontaneous joy, and was much admired by those who met him.[153]

They traveled by first-class train from Paris, stopping first in Brunnen, Switzerland, then Lauterbrunnen, Grindelwald, Interlaken, through the Furka Pass to Lugano, and finally Milan. There they visited the cathedral, which contained the tomb of St. Charles Borromeo. He lay in a rock crystal coffin, and a fee was charged to view his relics. Melanie found this distasteful. Like her father eight years earlier, she was scandalized by such intrusive mercantilism. (Her mother was more tolerant.) The crypt was decorated "in the Italian fashion" and one forgot its ugliness in the presence of the frail remains of one who was universally venerated.[154] But Mathilde also found the trip tiring, especially as they were mostly in Protestant places. At Interlaken, she was moved to find a little Catholic chapel in which Mass could be celebrated by visiting priests. There she heard a very fine explanation of the gospel story concerning the paralytic given by a foreign priest fluent in several different languages.[155]

All the beauties of nature spoke to Mathilde of God: "I have seen a frail little streamlet leaping between jagged rocks . . . mock at the huge masses and terrific precipices, and reappear as . . . fresh as ever and so limpid that one could count the pebbles in its stony bed. This is an image of the soul guided by God in its journey through life.[156] She then remarks on her own moments of anxiousness during the family's experience within this nature: "One is outdoors from morning until night; it is good to pray among the mountains. We are surrounded with splendor. We often flirt with danger, but one cannot be afraid. We trust in God. I pray for everyone during a thunderstorm, but without anxiety that the lightning might strike me. Why, then, should I fear to cross a precipice on wooden planks, when everything depends on God's holy will in both cases?"[157] Mathilde adds that trust does not justify imprudence.[158] On the last page of the travel journal kept by her children, she wrote in her own hand, "May it please God that our little company come together again some day, and give us the joy of seeing these magnificent sights once more."[159] The travelers returned in the same way, and Mathilde was back in Vernon again on October 5.[160]

Thomas's sister Catherine went to God early in February 1894. Mathilde described her as simple, righteous, loving, and devout. She died piously and peacefully, without a lot of suffering. As she prayed for Catherine, Mathilde was given a vision of purgatory: "I see the suffering of these souls, not at all gloomy and oppressed, but active and fertile. . . . Each minute, they progress like a boat on the open sea, sped by the wind, with each wave driving it to port. They are not in the least like prisoners in a dark well, these . . . souls. If they do not yet see the divine sun of heaven, they receive it like dawn and twilight. Their suffering is peaceful, because they are assured of their entry into paradise."[161]

A further insight was given her in prayer two days later: "I saw the love which exists between [God] and those penitent souls. He possesses them by his grace and they possess him by a feeling of accomplished justice. They both love and will this justice. The look of love with which God envelops these souls is something great and sublime."[162]

The next few entries contain no details concerning the family or Mathilde's temporal affairs. Her prayer life continued to mature, but finding words to manifest this was becoming more and more challenging. "I seem to be always writing the same thing when I wish to speak of [the entrance of the divinity into the soul] and have written nothing [that does it justice]."[163] The limitation is not on her side; it is the nature of human language that is the problem. Words express concepts, and concepts are abstract, referring to a nature common to many things which share it. They cannot express what is not only concrete but unique, and nothing is more concrete and unique than mystical experience.

CHAPTER ELEVEN:
FROM DARKNESS TO LIGHT, 1894–1908

The last fifteen years of Mathilde Boutle's life were spent in managing an advancing blindness. Despite the limitations this imposed, she continued to contribute substantially to her children's lives, care for her mother, broaden her understanding of the meaning of fidelity in the concrete details of her life, and deepen her acceptance of God's holy will. As with many chronic illnesses, Mathilde's loss of sight was progressive, rendering her increasingly homebound as the winter of 1894–95 settled in: "The cold wind and the condition of my eyes, or rather the holy will of God, prevented me from going to the monastery due to the ice sheets which my eyes do not permit me to face. I am alone much of the time. But solitude with God refreshes the soul."[1] She further notes, "It seems to me as if [I] were getting more used to this suppression and that each day I love this will of God in my regard better and better."[2]

Her writing, however, continued, and she explains that Jesus continues to teach her interiorly:

> Those who do not sufficiently conform themselves to the will of God can paralyze the intentions of his grace regarding them. God in his mercy often abstains from sending us trials which he sees we are not prepared to bear properly, yet, if we could have born them, would have [brought] new graces for us. No doubt [this is why] it often happens that, after we have made an act of entire and generous abandonment to God, he sends us some sorrow, our prayer having . . . drawn down the cross, and at the same time, the grace to bear it with love.[3]

Mathilde's manner of understanding was consistent with the spirituality of her period, although today we might rather think that such an act of abandonment opens our eyes to noticing and accepting a painful reality already present. Indeed, Mathilde's *fiat* did not prevent her from oc-

casionally feeling overwhelmed by the obstacles created by her deteriorat-
ing eyesight. Her partial blindness made keeping a journal especially difficult, and consequently she wrote less frequently, sometimes only once a
month. Occasionally, what she wrote in this period was illegible.[4] Praying
about these concerns on January 1, 1896, she heard from Jesus these consoling words: "Nothing that I have willed can ever harm you."[5]

In addition to accounts of her prayer experiences, Mathilde provided details of her activities within the family, often interspersed with her
worries about France under the Third Republic. Her descriptions of day-
to-day interactions and visits with family, travels, and concerns arising in
her adult children's households remain vivid. Nor was she merely a chron-
icler in these later years; her notebooks give us insight into her continuing
engagement with her family. For example, we learn of her involvement in
planning and assisting with appropriate activities during a winter vacation,
for those with her but younger in years—including the plays for which she
had always been known: "The busy and absorbing course of private the-
atricals has just come to an end, but they have had . . . the advantage of af-
fording my young people healthy and literary occupation for several weeks.
This time I was able to exercise greater control over my mind, to lend myself to all that was necessary, and yet to remain occupied with [God] . . .
whether before or during the festivities.[6]

Adolphe was the commander of a fort near Modane in the Savoy;
Mathilde went to visit him in October 1895. The mountains always moved
her: "In God there is neither time nor place; his spirit blows where it will.
. . . While contemplating them . . . one adores the divine majesty revealed
on the crest of the mountains like a gigantic handwriting. . . . Snow has
fallen, and lies on the highest peaks. They float above the earth in a sky of
blue even purer [than they]. I leave my dear child commanding his fort
under the protection of St. Michael and the angels of these mountains. . . .
May they protect my child, from all harm!"[7]

At the end of July 1896, she wrote an account of the previous seven
months, explaining that she had written little because, in addition to her
lack of visual clarity, two of her sons, Adolphe and Eugène, had been married. Eugène had married on February 4, 1896, and Adolphe had married
on July 6.[8]

Mathilde had been petitioning God on behalf of Adolphe "so far
from me and exposed to [all the temptations of] army life. This winter has
been filled with my efforts regarding this, and God has blessed them be-

yond [my] hopes, bringing it about that I would find [the sort of person] my son needs, with other advantages which neither he nor I had sought."[9]

Marie Lorieux, his bride, came from a distinguished and well-to-do family.[10] She seems to have been a good wife and mother as well as a devout Christian. Eugène had married his first cousin, Alexandrine Pougny. She was Mathilde's sister Elisabeth's daughter, and so Mathilde's niece. They had spent many happy summers together growing up, which is probably why Mathilde wrote that it was "expected and very uncomplicated."[11] As Alain Le Touzé adds in his "Little Family Chronicle," the ease with which the marriage was brought about was, regrettably, not a promise of its survival.[12] Whatever their eventual futures, Mathilde clearly neglected no effort, consideration, or trouble to see that her children were socially well-established in life, financially secure, and, to the best of her ability, devout.

What the continuing support Mathilde provided to her family cost her was revealed only in her journal: "My spirit is quite weary, enduring a kind of continual violence since my duties have necessitated my living in Paris, resuming and increasing my relationships, leading a relatively active life with respect to my children, their careers, marriages, etc." Even living with the mother Mathilde loved dearly, and with whom she had so much in common, had its downside. Though she thanked God for her mother's presence, especially as her mother was a great help to her because of her limited vision, it was nevertheless true that her temperament was better suited to solitude than to sharing her life so closely with another person. She writes, "One is less alone with her mother than with a husband, because a man has different occupations than those of a woman. These differences do not exist between mother and daughter."[13]

Mathilde's resolution for the rest of the summer was to find God in her children and grandchildren—"my dear little cherubs"—to rejoice in "the affection which God gives me, but not to seek it. To be patient and peaceful in him." Mathilde asked that God bless this time, during which the family was all together again, and make it blossom in faith and love.[14] She left Vernon and returned to Paris in October.[15] In December she noted how difficult it was to be able to write there, with the shortened daylight and less privacy.[16] She longed "to do some good," and she regretted the infirmities that left her less able to be so. Jesus replied, "Charity is never lost. . . . You weep over the good which you see left undone, but I take care that you do another good which you do not see."[17]

More grandchildren were born: Jacques Boutle, son of Eugène and

Alexandrine on November 28, 1896, and in April 1897, Yvonne, daughter of Adolphe and Marie.[18] At the New Year, 1897, Mathilde wrote that she would have liked to live a more austere life, but she was not free to do so. Her mother lived with her and her children were around her, having returned home for the holidays. "What to do? Recollect in the silence of [my] heart that *he gives what he wishes*—the degree of renunciation which is possible [for me]—and he will do the rest. This is my resolution, this is my confidence."[19]

As usual, the entire family spent September 1897 together. Mathilde called it "a month of reunions." She first prays that God would use their time together to benefit them all: "I count on him to inspire what I ought to say and do on every occasion. To participate in everything, and maintain an interior silence—that's the rule [during] vacation. . . . In practice, this [means] to keep [recollected] as much as one's duties permit, and to avoid all unnecessary words and thoughts."[20]

Reflecting afterward, she wrote, "I have tried to do good [to all] around me, or at least not to scandalize others by my limitations. It seems to me that I have been, at the same time, more at the service of my family and more withdrawn [spiritually] with God."[21] Not until a month later was she able to resume her journal: "It has been impossible for me to write; everything is conspiring against it. Apparently, this is how God wants it."[22]

Greeting the New Year, 1898, Mathilde prayed that God would be present to her and to her compatriots: "As much as possible, every hour, every minute . . . make of me all that you wish me to be, and do through me all that you wish me to do. . . . Mercy, O my God, for the Church, for France, for poor sinners personified in your servant who implores you. Grace and mercy for all those hearts which you have given me. Do to them the good which I cannot sufficiently say or do."[23] A few pages later, Mathilde again fretted at the gap between what she desired to do and the limits set by her failing vision: "[I] accept this life of a mummy with greater peace and love. Yet how difficult nature finds this *impotence* in the hundred and one little things which go to make up our daily life."[24]

Nevertheless, Mathilde still found herself encumbered by social obligations, and again reminded herself that, where violation of principle is not a concern, she ought graciously to allow the preferences of others to take precedence: "Actually, the practical rule for me is to renounce my own way in every social contact, except those which relate to God."[25]

Adolphe was now stationed in Vitry with his wife Marie and little daughter Yvonne. In February, he had written to Melanie, inviting her and Léon to visit, promising that they would not be bored, and that he would not force his brother-in-law to join in the dancing. A letter which six-year-old Charles wrote to his mother during their absence, expressing the hope that when Adolphe retired from the military he and his family would come to Mathilde's home in Paris, suggests that Charles and his younger brother spent this time at Cité Vaneau with their grandmother and great-grandmother.

In June 1898, Mathilde and her mother went to Lourdes, probably as part of a group of pilgrims from her parish in Vernon.[26] The family has a barely legible letter from her to Melanie saying that her eyes were better, and that Adolphe and his family would be unable to come to Versailles and Vernon until September.[27]

Mathilde made no entries at all between June 22, 1898, and May 1900. In a footnote, Poulain states, "It is probable that, owing to the increasing loss of her sight during those two years, Lucie often labored under the illusion that she was writing, when in reality her uncertain pen made no mark at all. A good number of blank pages traced here and there with a few vague lines in ink are evidence of this."[28]

At some time during the early part of 1900, Mathilde's children bought her a typewriter. In the Archives of Adoration Réparatrice, a letter, dated July 20, 1900, and typed by Mathilde to her cousin, Marguerite, begins with an apology for Mathilde's return from Versailles to Vernon without seeing Marguerite. In addition, Mathilde apologizes for using "my little machine. It is precious to me in helping me not to tire my mother with all my [letter writing], and in not [having to] try the patience of my good pastor in Vernon with my illegible handwriting."

Marguerite's mother, Mathilde's Aunt Caroline, was with her in Vernon, as was her own mother, Cécile Bertrand. Mathilde states that "it is very pleasant for us to be together." She finds their presence strengthening: "Our family lacks nothing; [it is] so protected by God's grace! But the eighty-year-olds seem more blessed and enlightened by heaven, their hands filled with a harvest of virtues received during a long life of humble and pure faith."[29] She wonders how much longer she would have them with her. Their deaths would leave a void which only God could fill: "O, my dear Sister, if only he were all in all things to us, and in all [people]! If only he would transform into himself this poor heart which believes itself dead [to all else] and never is! Is it your prayers which help us and our children to walk in the footsteps of our dear mothers?"

Mathilde also inquired about the possibility of getting a replacement for the ring which was the symbol of her consecration as an *agrégée*, since the original one had broken: "It is true that I have worn it for eighteen years." In closing, she asks prayers for "our two new [little ones], Maurice (son of Melanie and Léon) and Germaine (daughter of Adolphe and Marie), and for the second child of Eugene and Alexandrine, with which the latter is pregnant, that it might be blessed like their first!" Mathilde typed the signature "your little sister Marie Aimée de Jesus," the name she had taken when she became an *agrégée*.

From that time on, Mathilde typed her entries, and Mother Anne, one of the nuns at the convent, copied them into Mathilde's journal.

Mathilde's journal states that she, and apparently other members of her family, made a trip to Germany, "necessary and willed by God, I believe," in the summer of 1900. She grieved that it was a Protestant country; the Blessed Sacrament was not reserved in its magnificent old churches, and it was seldom possible for her to get to Mass. On August 12, she was at Badenweiler in Wurttemberg, where she found a little Catholic chapel. It was very poor, but she was able to receive Communion at last. "I have prayed during this entire trip for this . . . country, so compromised by heresy. . . . If nature is beautiful and so beneficial for the body, the soul suffers [because] the King of Heaven is so unknown in a land which he has enriched with such beauty!" Along with her prayers, she offered the pain she felt: "This beautiful country is peopled for me by shadows. I can only see these somber mountains and giant firs of the Black Forest in a dim way. I express admiration of it all to spare others pain."[30]

> At times I have paroxysms of sorrow at being able to see the beauties of nature only through a veil. Perhaps formerly I loved too much and felt too vividly the poetry breathed by the earth . . . and all the world of living things. All this used to make me dream. It is true that I offered this created magnificence with my whole soul to God. When I was young, I made a prayer of it; now God wishes me to make a sacrifice of it. . . . I kiss his hand which gives me this suffering and that other, harder still, of not being able to see the features of those I love. May his grace be with me!"[31]

Mathilde found it a sorrow that none of her sons had been called to the priesthood, not even Eugène, for whom she had cherished such a hope earlier. So great was her longing that she shed tears over her disappointment in private: "It is [only] with God that I weep. Then, not wanting to yield to this very personal feeling, I extend my arms in a cross, and sobbing, say some 'Hail Mary's,' [offering] my suffering for the future priest." Father Grieu commented that offering one's suffering to God in prayer was always a very good thing, especially if the suffering was not sought, but endured out of love for God. Still, he did not see why she was upset by not having a priest in her immediate family. On December 23, 1900, he wrote, "Here, above all, it is necessary to accept and adore God's will."[32]

There is no record that any of her direct descendants ever did become a priest. God will not interfere with human freedom, even to answer the prayers of one as advanced in the unitive way as was Mathilde. God had taught her this lesson ten years earlier, when he showed her "with what love and what regard for his creature he ordained that the will of the [human being] should be *free*. For if [it] were not, . . . the gift [one] makes of it to God would not satisfy love. . . . God therefore made his creature free . . . because he loves her and . . . desires that she should be able to give herself to him by *a free return of love*."[33]

As a new century got underway, Mathilde felt a special need for prayer for her country, as well as for her family.[34] Religious practice was declining in most of France due to the republican anticlerical offensive. Perhaps for these reasons, Mathilde's resolutions for the New Year, 1901, were "to adore, to make reparation, [and] to intercede." Jesus told her that she had given him many souls: "I write these words quite simply, though I would be very embarrassed to explain them. Oh, may I give him souls, the souls of my family, the souls of France, souls throughout the world!"[35]

Mathilde's view is confirmed by the following description given by a social historian:

> Taking Easter Communion under the Third Republic was a much more affirmative, even courageous, act than it had been [earlier]; government employees who did so were unlikely to be promoted, and even ordinary people had to be prepared to carry the stigma of what was clearly perceived as an anti-Government act. Those who gave up the central practices of Catholicism were thus those whose faith had never been strong; the faith of those who persisted had been tried in the fire, and they came to constitute a nucleus perhaps more fervent than before."[36]

Mathilde feared that the Antichrist himself had appeared. But Jesus reminded her that neither diabolic nor human wickedness could go any further than God allowed. He does not wish the death of the sinner, but that he be converted and live. He respects human liberty even when it is used for evil. Father Grieu added, "These considerations are precious to sustain our courage in these sad times."[37]

The New Year brought a new sorrow to the whole family. Eugène and Alexandrine's second child, another little boy, whom they named William, was born on January 7, 1901, but lived less than twelve hours. Mathilde felt her children's affliction deeply, and prayed that God would give them all the graces they needed in their trial. But she was unable to join them: "At the very hour when [the body of] their dear little angel was laid to rest in the family plot, I was undergoing an operation on my eyes."[38] She had been promised that this operation would improve her vision, but it seems not to have done so. As if this were not enough, Jesus hid himself. For many weeks, she was without any experience of his presence. She made a strong effort to accept "this state completely lacking in any consolation with [unconditional] love and abandonment." This fortified her.[39]

Another New Year, 1902, dawned; Mathilde greeted it with "Confidence!" She had been unable to go to church for six weeks, so going on New Year's Day, 1902, was no small joy. "My soul, as it were, was carried into the arms of the all-powerful God above the stormy sea of this world. Confidence! In God above all!"[40] In periods of sickness and spiritual privation, she felt that she was doing nothing for God, while others were performing admirable works with love, zeal, and intelligence. "[I] am happy to see God so well served, but if [my] will were not attached to the will of God above all things, [I] would envy those generous Marthas of the active life."[41]

Mathilde made no further entries until May 25, 1902. "Looking back on that long trial of seven months of suffering, . . . Jesus said to [me], 'Do you not know me? Am I not always the same, however frequent or rare my visits may be? Or whatever the interior or exterior state in which you receive me may be?'"[42] When she had been unable to keep her journal regularly, Mathilde often gave an account of what had passed during the period in which she had not written. In June, she said that she had felt as if her soul had been like the seeds in the ground under the snow, waiting for the sun."[43]

Since, in spite of all the efforts made to improve it, Mathilde's sight was still clouded, she was deprived of the spiritual relief of the sacraments, the Mass, and the church. Her response to this physical suffering was the same as always. She offered it to God and placed everything in his hands.[44] Her response to interior suffering was the same: "Even when I see you no longer, I seek you. Even when you hide yourself, you are incapable of ever failing me! My soul says *fiat* and this fiat . . . is [my] . . . life." Nevertheless, she felt a very human desire for the grief to end: "A great longing to quit this life comes over me, to no longer have to witness evil and offense against God in myself and in others any more. But I only ask him to leave me in this world just as long as it pleases him, so as to reach the degree [of union] he wishes me to attain."[45]

At Christmas, 1902, a brief entry meditates on the vulnerability of the Child in the manger as the source of all true power and wisdom. In Mathilde's next entry, dated January 1903, she explains that it has been impossible to write more often: "My eyes and my health [make writing difficult] at this time of year. Happily, these are not any obstacle to prayer."[46] To her sorrow over the evils afflicting the Church, France, and individual human beings, as well as that caused by her physical limitation, was added her greatest personal trial—a sense of God's absence, of being separated from God, without knowing why. This experience endured, with varying degrees of intensity, for many weeks. It did not weaken Mathilde's *fiat*, however. Suddenly, without warning, God would again be present, and in an instant she would be at peace in God's will, content to accept what he permitted, and asking only that his will be accomplished fully in her and through her.[47]

May 21, 1903, was the Feast of the Ascension. Mathilde noted that it was the first time in six months that she had been able to attend Mass with her mother: "The [church] bells were pealing joyfully; I stifled a sob, thinking that perhaps soon their voices will be silenced and the doors of the church closed to the faithful. . . . Lord, save us. . . . Do not let the gates of Hell prevail against your churches!"[48] Mathilde spent the summer of 1903 in Vernon, as usual, and also as usual, other family members came, especially the grandchildren. Mathilde was greatly occupied with them— as well as with taking care of business, correspondence, and the house— so much so that at times she feared that she had sinned through an excess of activity.

She adds that these words would bring a smile to the lips of anyone who knew her in Paris, had they read them, since there she "seemed to live the life of a shellfish." By contrast, in Vernon, she had too little solitude, and thirsted for it. She offered everything for the health of the Church, of

France, and "our poor Vernon," where Father Grieu was struggling to maintain a private (Catholic) educational institution for the children.[49] Meditating on her self-offering at the end of August, Mathilde realized that it is not the quantity or intensity of sufferings that deepen union with God, but the wholeheartedness with which one offers them to him: "The more we give to God, the more God gives himself!"[50] Meditating on the Hypostatic Union, Mathilde shows a far greater reverence for the reality of our incarnate state than was prevalent in the spirituality of her society:

> I see God going out of himself, urged by his love! He calls the created element to him, the soul which he has made in his own likeness. But surely the body will stop him; that body fashioned from the slime of the earth, from all that is most material in the principle of all things? No, it will not stop him. Love, in its impetuous flight, forgetting to disdain it, will not turn back even on account of matter. Human nature, surprised and trembling, is even admitted to give its consent through the voice of Mary. Mary says yes, and it is done . . . Fiat! And the Word is made flesh, and from then on one and the same Being says: I am Man, I am God."[51]

The conflict between Church and State was intensifying, and Mathilde was understandably anxious. And hers was not an ungrounded anxiety. On October 20, 1902, a parliamentary commission to examine proposals for the separation of Church and State had been established.[52] The right of members of religious orders to teach, or even to exist as an order, was under attack by Emile Combes, the Prime Minister.[53] Mathilde complained to God, asking why he was not helping. The answer came that he was "waiting until the number of faithful persons who offer themselves to me with entire abandonment in this trial is complete."[54] Later, Mathilde wrote what she had been told: "God has designs completely unknown to men, according to which he can permit evil to a degree which astonishes, without the rising flood being able to reach the secrets of his mercy."[55]

Mathilde's prayer for the New Year, 1904, was to need nothing except God. She writes, "The earth can revolve and crumble, the soul can survive without the earth, but it cannot survive without God. God alone is stable and faithful. O God, have pity on us. May your kingdom come!"[56]

She continued to pray fervently for the Church and for France as the secularization of education and the seizure of the property belonging to the exiled religious orders continued. But the notebooks contain no fur-

ther entries until that summer, when Mathilde was in Vernon. In a long reflection on the evil times through which the Church in France was passing,
she notes the futility of all opposition to divine will. Commenting on this
concept, she observes that the will of those who use their freedom to do
evil "do God's work without knowing it. It is not divine authority that op-
presses human liberty. [Rather,] it is human will that follows, without even
knowing it, the direction of divine will, because it has received its very
essence from divine will, and returns to it, even if it prefers to be its contrary."[57]

What sustained Mathilde in all of this, and would do so in even
more painful trials to come, was her union with God: "This union forms
an extraordinary contrast with the atmosphere in which one lives. Across
this tempest flashes lightning. . . . It is the sovereign action of God, who,
in less time than it takes to say, has suspended all the powers of the soul
and holds them enfolded in his loving embrace. . . . The spirit is fortified
and pacified. . . . Praise be to God, and may he save us!!!"[58] At summer's
end, Father Grieu added that what Mathilde had written during 1904 was
superior to everything she had written before. He could see the progress
she had made in loving God, a love beneath the cross. He notes, "Evidently,
in this crisis of persecution, those who love the most are those who suffer
the most. This suffering and surrender to the will of God is the best [atti-
tude] for us."[59]

Back in Paris, Mathilde greeted the New Year, 1905, with only the
words which had appeared before her "inward spiritual eye"[60] at the time
of her first mystical experience, "God alone!"[61] A month later, Pope Pius
X granted the faithful the opportunity to gain a plenary indulgence at the
moment of death. Mathilde then wrote that she did not wish this for herself.
Instead, when she thought of death, her prayer was that, before leaving this
world, she would have reached the degree of virtue, or the correction of
her faults, or the union with God which he willed for her to attain here on
earth. She left all the rest to his mercy.[62]

There are no further entries until July 1905. Mathilde was in Vernon again, wishing that there was some way to communicate to others all
she had been shown of God's desire to give himself to us. "The man
[Descartes] who said 'I think, therefore I am' was applauded; Can I not
also say, 'God shows himself to my soul, therefore God is'?"[63]

Religious persecution intensified, and on December 11, the Law
of Separation of Church and State was promulgated.[64] Mathilde made an
act of contrition for herself and all who needed it, and a peace of ineffable

sweetness filled her heart, giving her a fortifying confidence in God which sustained and consoled her.[65]

Mathilde's anguish over the change in French law did not constitute her only sorrow. She writes as well of an intense personal one, which she does not identify. It is only from the "Little Family Chronicle" that we learn of the failure at this time of the marriage of Mathilde's son Eugène. This constituted a double grief for Mathilde, as her son was married to her niece. Eugène had been a law clerk, he and Alexandrine had moved to Vernon in 1896, and their son Jacques had been born there that same year. But Eugène, at some time thereafter, quit his job to live in idleness and to frequent cafés, which he nearly always left in a state of inebriation. Alain Le Touzé suggests that the death of the couple's second child in 1901 may have accelerated Eugène's degeneration. The latter would claim in court that his alcoholism was an "unhealthy and hereditary compulsion."

Although it is possible that the grounds for which Alexandrine would sue for divorce in 1907 were unknown to Mathilde, she could not have been unaware that the spouses were living apart.[66] Still, Mathilde greets the New Year, 1906, with this: "Glory to God in the highest heavens, and peace amid the sufferings of earth to [those] of good will. . . . In spite of all anguish, all sufferings, all fear, when [one] thinks of God, [one] feels that there is nothing between him and [oneself]. . . . Union with God is not separation from all exterior things. It consists in solitude of the spirit fixed in the divine will above everything which, even from the standpoint of duty, dominates, occupies, and overwhelms her."[67]

That winter brought the usual hardships. Mathilde was once more rather a recluse, with the same health problems and even more interruptions than usual. This was because, besides all the correspondence and business matters, the rest of the family was visiting much more often out of concern for her elderly mother. Mathilde's regular prayer periods were shortened, yet her spirit remained at peace. She was conforming herself to what God willed, and adoring him in everything: "I believe that I am no more united in adoration [when I am] in the church than when I am unable to go, because I adore him all day long. . . . Nothing in an active life prevents this. Jesus always returns to visit [me when I] am unable to go to seek him. . . . Oh, goodness and mystery of love! Some sense of your presence remains in our rooms, as in a little church. . . . You have indeed done well to stay with us, dear Lord. How else could we bear life, its persecutions and its horrors!"[68]

That July, Mathilde wrote of being distressed by the violence of the government's persecution and by the evils committed against God and souls. "What will be the future of the Church of France," she asks. "Is it condemned to die . . . like the early martyrs?"[69]

To Father Grieu she wrote that she was sometimes tempted to discouragement, seeing the triumph of evil and its threats for the future. "Is this wrong? Should I be upset by these troubles?" He wrote back that despair is never allowed, that one single thought sustains us: Nothing can happen in this world except by God's will, and God wishes only our good.[70] Father Grieu added that her feelings need not upset her, noting that if she did not have them, she might become proud on account of the high graces of prayer that she had been given. Thus, her feelings were keeping her humble. In September, Mathilde noted that in Holy Communion, when the powers of her soul are in abeyance, she lost all sense of physical suffering, and even of [psychic] suffering. "If only, remembering these infinite kindnesses, [I] could concern [myself] no longer with anything earthly…[except] what is absolutely necessary!"[71]

Trying to give an account of the state of her soul, Mathilde wrote that she felt, as we might say in English, "between a rock and a hard place." On the one hand, she noted external religious persecution and its effect on people, even in the countryside. On the other hand, she endured a more personal grief due to "certain errors and indifferences right in the midst of the family." It is this last, about which she was not more specific, that caused her the greater pain.

Mathilde's response was to throw herself into the arms of God, wanting only his will in all things. In her notebook, she remarks that her sorrows are detaching her still more from everything. Father Grieu commented beside these passages that submission to God's will during trials is certainly a form of obedience, and that the greater the trial and the harder the obedience, the greater the merit.[72]

Mathilde's entry for New Years Day, 1907, is very brief, just a prayer that the holy will of God be done in all creatures and in all things.[73] She recalled this act of self-surrender in a particularly poignant passage the following March: "The soul who has said her *fiat* to the God of love does not withdraw it, . . . but I did not know what that holy will was going to ask of me. The beautiful soul of my beloved mother went to heaven on February 21. On that very day, and ever since, I have never been able to pray for her without feeling her soul in God. . . . O blessed a thousandfold is the love which uplifts at times our poor hearts broken by the apparent separation of death!"[74]

Cécile Bertrand was ninety years old at the time of her death in February 1907 in Paris. Out of a loving desire to ease their mother's mourning at the loss of her own mother's presence, Mathilde's children took her back to Switzerland that summer.[75] Mathilde also moved from Cité Vaneau to an apartment shared with Melanie and her family at 31 Raspail Boulevard.[76]

The next journal entry, written in Engelberg on August 15, 1907, on the Feast of the Assumption, acknowledged the grief that Mathilde still felt. She writes, however, that the soul united to God loses sight of the earth, finding herself, she knows not how, higher than the highest mountain summits, so much that there is no comparison. "It is this which gives [one] the only true rest in sorrow."[77]

The family stayed in Engelberg for at least two weeks. Looking back over her life, Mathilde wrote at the end of August that when she was young, and especially after her first supernatural graces, she was enthusiastic about creation, and offered it on her heart as on an altar to the Creator. Walking with her children, she had tried to raise their little souls from the beauty of visible things and their childish joys to the goodness of their Author.[78] But now she could no longer see the splendor of things.

> I see them imperfectly even in that great handwriting of the divine majesty on the brow of the mountains. And if my eyes perceive for an instant the sun shining on the whiteness of their immaculate snows, I am obliged to close them, and I offer to God, together with these wonders, the sacrifice of not being able to see them. How much harder is the sacrifice of not being able to see beloved faces anymore, to be scarcely able to distinguish their features! All this is the will of him whom I love. I bless it; I love this holy will. How difficult it is to write about my soul here where I have to expend myself in writing such a multitude of sad and necessary letters. All this renders the pressure of a doubly great sorrow even heavier. It would crush me if God did not sustain my soul. From time to time, he [takes me in his arms] and, there, makes me breathe a celestial atmosphere, but how short are such moments!!! All the rest is night, anguish, impotence.[79]

The doubly great sorrow was the pending divorce. The initial judgment of December 1907 had given Alexandrine the custody of the couple's eleven-year-old son, Jacques, and required Eugène to pay alimony as well as child support. But the divorce had not been officially granted at the time of Mathilde's writing. Eugène had appealed the judgment, claiming that he was not responsible for his actions due to hereditary addiction, and declaring, on March 3, that his vice had disappeared after treatment. He stated that he was ready, and offered to resume life with Alexandrine under normal conditions. She was not convinced, nor was the court, which doubted the genuineness of Eugène's "cure." Even were the recovery real, the court determined that Alexandrine's earlier suffering was serious enough for the divorce to be granted on June 27, 1908.[80]

In the summer of 1907, however, the final decision was still in the future. Mathilde, who describes her abandonment to God as "holding on to him by a thread," willing only what he wills, and struggling, only as much as he wills, against the stream of difficulties and great human evils, prays: "Have pity on us, Lord; save France and all those who suffer in her! Use our tears to wash away the injuries committed against you, mix them with the blood of our Savior which cries to you for mercy!!" Father Grieu comments that her resignation is very Christian and very moving.[81]

Another New Year, 1908; it would be Mathilde's last on earth, but neither she nor her family had any reason to suspect this at the time. She greeted it with an act of complete abandonment: "O my God, O Father, I abandon to you this poor creature that I am. . . . I also abandon to your mercy all that I lack, that it may forgive me, all that weighs me down, in order that it may uphold me. I will all that you will, my God, my Father! You have not put me in this world to do my will, but yours!"[82] The final entry in Mathilde's notebook is dated February 8, four days before her sixty-fourth birthday. She explains that "the trials which afflict my soul likewise absorb all my time and the little strength I have. I have no leisure for writing, and all I can attempt is to summarize [the state of] my soul."[83]

Mathilde aspired to become simpler, freer to unite herself with the One who alone is necessary, as her duties grew "more and more complicated. I ask my director whether, in the midst of all these exhausting and necessary matters [she does not detail these, but we may assume that she was setting her financial affairs in order, seeing to it that her children and grandchildren would be provided for financially], the deprivation of the freedom and leisure to go to church and to [say my usual] prayers is not itself a prayer?"[84] Her question was never answered. She was in Paris at the time, it was winter, and more than likely there was a delay in getting the journal to Father Grieu in Vernon. In any case, this superb priest became seriously ill at the beginning of the month, and died on March 15. After Mathilde learned of his death, she made no further entries, since he could no longer read them. Her last manifestation of conscience must therefore stand as a summary of the state of her soul in the final weeks of her own life.

> In the midst of this storm, of this painful crisis which breaks my heart, of the overwhelming business, I am touched to see that as soon as [I] think of God . . . he is already present, more present to my heart than my heart itself, so that recollection and union need not be made afresh but subsist to a certain degree permanently underneath all the multiplicities, travail, and sorrows of life. Thus the faithful friend seems not to lose sight of this puny creature as if she were alone in creation.[85]

> This double life of continual effort to respond to all the obligations which God imposes [on me] with respect to creatures, of the effort to endure what seems beyond the heart's strength if it were not aided by God; and at the same time constantly being drawn more strongly to God than to creation; this duality is unified by a single intention: To want God, and, in him, all that he wills.[86]

Poulain quotes the final part of this entry: "When the soul is battered to the earth, broken, neither knowing nor seeing any longer where she is, for God sometimes wills that also, then she lives day by day as if each one were to be her last, committing all her care, all her preoccupations, to God and trying only to do his will from moment to moment. *Fiat voluntas tua!*"[87]

Poulain further reports that, before their deaths, Mathilde had told Father Grieu that "she would die during Holy Week, but she added that she did not know upon which day. The confessor vigorously rejected this idea, repeating again and again that her health was quite satisfactory. But Lucie persisted. On Monday in Holy Week [April 13], as she kept her bed, they sent for the doctor, who could discover no symptoms of any illness, but merely that she was suffering from exhaustion. She died very quietly, in a transport of love, on Good Friday, as she had desired."[88] Poulain does not state the source of his information. He was not there, and Father Grieu was already dead when Poulain read her journal. We may well question some of his details, nonetheless. Was he, like the sisters of Thérèse of Lisieux, projecting on Mathilde his own view of holiness? Her great-grandson was not there either, of course, so he quotes Poulain's description of Mathilde's death in the "Little Family Chronicle."

Alain Le Touzé also quotes a letter to Melanie from Henriette Alcan, Thomas's youngest sister, written on April 6, 1908, eleven days before Mathilde's death. In this letter, Henriette, who had remained close to her brother's family, expresses concern for Mathilde and asks about a doctor's visit on the previous day, agreeing with Melanie (who had been expected to visit their home in Vernon) that she should remain with her mother in Paris.

We also have independent verification from the letter of Mathilde's granddaughter, Yvonne (cited in the introduction), and from the "Little Family Chronicle" that Mathilde was unable to attend her granddaughter's birthday dinner on April 13.

In any case, the invitation to her funeral Mass at St. Thomas d'Aquin, preserved in the Archives of Adoration Réparatrice, states that Mathilde died on April 17. The Mass was celebrated by her cousin Charles on April 20, Easter Monday, and she was laid to rest in the family plot in Vernon with her husband and little daughter. Alain Le Touzé adds that, as Eugène's divorce was not yet final, he and Alexandrine were listed among the mourners as "Mr. and Mrs. Eugène Boutle."

Along with her will, Mathilde left written instructions regarding her funeral arrangements. They were to be as simple as possible, no more than the poorest could afford, and the difference between their cost and what was customary for persons of her class was to be given to the pastor. She requested that her children give the pastor in Vernon 200 francs for bread for the poor, and stated that if she were to die in Paris or elsewhere, and they wished to have a low Mass for her, there were to be neither flowers nor wreaths.[89]

What Mathilde felt about her death she had written many years earlier, on May 7, 1886, when she was forty-two: "Old age! Blessed old age, I greet you in advance! You are feared when you should be loved as life's happiest period, because you are its end . . . the dawn of the eternal day. When I see my temples growing white . . . a smile spreads over my face. When I am old, if I live to be old, I will console my children by telling them then (which I dare not say at present) with what joy I see each year disappear behind me, because it is one less between me and eternity.[90] She added that one still should not wish that the time of one's deliverance would be hastened, but rather wait lovingly for the time willed by God.[91]

Years later, in May 1901, with her sight fading, Mathilde commented on the character of this waiting: "[I] have seen [myself] surrounded by all sorts of natural and supernatural impotence; and Heaven was barred. But the soul can always say 'Lord, thy will be done!' and coming out of these steep and rough paths where she has thought . . . to have lost her way . . . to acknowledge with love that he whom she did not see was still upholding her."[92]

Though we have neither "last words," nor any eyewitness account of Mathilde's death, we have the greater witness of her life provided by her notebooks. Marguerite Savigny-Vesco comments that while Mathilde lived, "she gave God to her family through her affection, her musical ability, her kindness."[93] Her notebooks extend this testimony to all of us, and reveal the beauty of Mathilde's character—her wisdom, common sense, and loving concern for others. These qualities remain as evident as her wholehearted surrender to God through all the circumstances accompanying a dependable, resolute engagement with all the obligations of her daily life. Reading Mathilde's words, one regrets never having had the opportunity of meeting her, or of being a guest in her home, remembered by "her relations and friends" as "a center of peace."[94] What was long hidden from even those closest to her, however, can now inspire all who read her account of a life fully lived on both the human and mystical levels. Savigny-Vesco calls her "a mirror of the Holy Trinity."[95]One might prefer to see her as a window so clear as to be almost invisible, through which the light of Christ shines without hindrance.

AFTERWORD

Lucie Christine was a small woman, with dark, curly hair, usually covered by a hat in public—as was customary for women at the time. Very quiet and unassuming, she did nothing to call attention to herself. She appeared entirely unremarkable; if we were to see her in a group, we would be unlikely to notice her. Unless . . . unless we were to observe her at Mass, totally absorbed in prayer. Then we *might* wonder— an upper-middle-class matron, wife of a well-to-do "man about town" and mother of five, with servants to relieve her of all domestic duties, free to indulge her taste for fine clothes, art and artifacts, to socialize and gossip with other upper-middle-class matrons, praying with the devotion of a con- templative nun? Assuredly, this was *not* common then—nor is it now. We *might* be intrigued and interested to learn more about her. I was, when I first learned of her in Evelyn Underhill's *Mystics of the Church.*

Underhill sees her on the same level of mystical development as Teresa of Avila and Angela of Foligno, both of whom lived in the Middle Ages, and became religious women—the former, a cloistered Carmelite, and the latter, a Third Order Franciscan—after her husband's death.[1] But here was no medieval nun, rather a married woman only a little removed from us in time, facing most of the same situations and challenges that women, especially married women, still face today. Finding the book upon which Underhill's brief account was based—Lucie Christine's journal— was the first obstacle to my investigation, as it was not listed anywhere I could find in 1968.

On a hunch, I contacted a friend, at the time a student in the Jesuit theologate, who found and obtained a library copy for me to consult. As he handed it to me, he remarked, "I was reading this coming up on the train, and I can't imagine why you wanted it!" The reason might have been plain: I was myself a wife and mother, teaching philosophy on a tenure-track line, trying to write a doctoral dissertation, and longing for a deeper spiritual life. I wanted to learn how she had managed the *time* for her spiritual growth. After all, the woman called Lucie Christine had the same twenty- four hours we all have. But the book was a disappointment. Apart from

193

about a dozen and a half entries, there wasn't a thing in it that couldn't have been written by a medieval cloistered nun!

The editor and redactor of this text, Auguste Poulain, S.J., explained in his preface that he had decided to omit a great deal of the original, partly because of the journal's length (2,395 pages), and partly because there was so much repetition. Actually, the difficulty, for Lucie Christine, as for those of us who have wished to make her writings known, is the paucity of our language for expressing mystical experience. No matter how much the mystic's understanding deepens as she grows in grace, she must use the same few words to describe her prayer. But the major reason Poulain omitted practically everything I wanted to know was that Lucie Christine's family had prohibited the inclusion of any personal information—especially "the trials and joys of family life"! What had he been forced to leave out?

He called his edition *The Spiritual Journal of Lucie Christine*, (that is, "Light of Christ," the pseudonym given its author to honor her family's desire for anonymity). Regretfully, I tried to set aside any hope of learning more, and concentrated on my dissertation. Even after its completion and defense in 1975, I pursued other research topics, as I saw no way to discover the whereabouts of Lucie Christine's original notebooks.

Several years later, Rev. Theodore Cunnion, S.J., suggested that I check the *Dictionnaire de spiritualité ascetique et mystique*. To my surprise, there were almost two columns on her. I learned that her real name was Mathilde Bertrand Boutle, that the notebooks were owned by the religious order, Adoration Réparatrice, of which she had become an *agrégée* in 1882, and the order's address in Paris.[2] Therefore, when a good friend, Rev. Philip Sandstrom, was returning to Paris in September 1987 to complete his doctoral dissertation, I asked him to contact the nuns on my behalf. His letter of inquiry got a firm refusal. Only Poulain had the expertise, and "what has not been published must not be published!"[3] So I appealed to the Jesuit who had written the entry in the *Dictionnaire*. In his gracious reply of April 9, 1989, he stated that he had gotten all his information from the sisters, and that I should go to speak with them personally.

Time and financial constraints did not allow this until May 1998. At that time, I sent letters of recommendation, two published articles, and a paper I had twice delivered on "Lucie Christine," and asked for a meeting with the nuns. The fax agreeing to a meeting was waiting for me when I arrived in Paris. There had been changes in the leadership of the order, and the new Superior General, Sister Cecilia, originally from Ireland, was willing to give me access to the original notebooks. Even more helpfully, she had contacted Lucie Christine's great-grandson, Alain Le Touzé, who also was willing to meet with me before I left. Rev. Sandstrom, who is entirely fluent in French, accompanied me to both meetings. Since Alain Le Touzé had not read what I had sent to the nuns, he wanted to do that and then consult with the family.

Several months later, I received a package from him stating that the family had decided, as had the nuns, that I could be trusted. Therefore, he was sending me portions of his "Little Family Chronicle," which included many details concerning his great-grandmother that were not in her spiritual journal. He even arranged, when I came to Paris on a small research grant in 2000, to take me to visit many of the places connected with her life, which gave me the opportunity to photograph them.

A research grant from Fordham enabled me to spend the summer of 2002 photographing every page of Lucie Christine's journal. But not until I was granted a Faculty Fellowship for the academic year 2006–2007, assisted by the generous bequest of Jacqueline Aron, was I able to give the story written by the woman herself the undivided attention required to allow her writings to present their own account. As I began work, reading each page she had written, I was amazed at how much more difficult the life reflected in Mathilde's journal had been than that which was reflected in Poulain's book. Truly, it seemed a miracle that she had not broken under the strain of what we would today consider trauma—from chronic verbal abuse to the death of a young child.

Nevertheless, Mathilde continued to look after her family, to dissuade her alcoholic husband from engaging in highly imprudent financial ventures (a task for which she had neither training nor legal authority), and to care for him with love and devotion until his early death, even though, as he deteriorated mentally, he became physically abusive. There were no shelters for battered women; divorce, although legal again, would have been unthinkable for a devout Catholic like Mathilde; and as long as her husband lived, she had no direct access to anything the family owned.

How did she manage all this? Mathilde's only support was her faith, and after 1870, her mystical experience. By 1882, she had some human support as well—both through a wise confessor and through the Superior General of Adoration Réparatrice, of which she had become an *agrégée* at the suggestion of her first cousin, who had become an Adoration Réparatrice nun. Each gave her the reassurance that her religious experiences were not deceptive and could be trusted.

How Mathilde managed so many difficulties, while continuing to be the anchor of her family's well-being, was her confessor's question also. It was he who asked her to keep a journal detailing her struggles, endurance, and support. At his request, she included a retrospective account of the first twelve years of her mystical experiences. Thus, covering a total of thirty-eight years, Mathilde's journals provide us with both a description of her spiritual development and a record of what Poulain calls a growth in grace from simple piety to transforming union, the highest level of mystical prayer.

I know of almost no other account written by a married woman about her own visionary experiences. Until quite recently, most women were illiterate, and even literate nuns were only rarely encouraged to document their spiritual journeys. Women's writings were seldom considered important enough to preserve, unless they were nuns who had founded an order, or gained the support of a male religious. Margery Kempe, who lived in fourteenth-century England, is the sole exception. Not only is Margery more distant from us historically, but she became a public, even controversial figure in ways that contemporary wives and mothers might not feel drawn to emulate.[4]

Lucie Christine, on the other hand, remained within her religious, family, and social situation, influencing others primarily by practicing a ministry of kindness. She reached transforming union through her fidelity to grace and by fulfilling her responsibilities to her husband and children, without explicitly challenging the patriarchal assumptions of either society or the Church regarding women. She just "outgrew" these constraints, perhaps without even realizing it, as her focus lay entirely beyond their province. In his review of Romano Guardini's German translation of Poulain's work, published in *Theologische Revue*,[5] J. Zahn states, "Of the many spiritual diaries which, over the years, I have been able to examine, none can compare with the volume under discussion." He describes Lucie Christine as "a woman of unusual giftedness and deep cultivation . . . situated directly in a busy life . . . a woman of valiant, sound judgment and tender feminine judiciousness [who] presents us with information concerning the history of her religious longing."[6]

We owe the preservation of her spiritual journal to her eldest daughter, Melanie Le Touzé, who kept it (despite reservations about its contents), and to Adoration Réparatrice, the order to which Melanie delivered the notebooks after her mother's death, as a note attached to them by her mother earlier had requested. The nuns were allowed to read the notebooks, but they were asked not to share them with any family member, probably because of all the tragedy and pain recorded therein. No one in the family even knew of the notebooks' existence until Lucie Christine's son-in-law, Léon Le Touzé, died in 1942. A reference to them was found in a case of family mementos kept by Melanie and Léon. Then four of Mathilde's descendents asked the nuns for permission to read the notebooks in order to complete a family history. With the passage of time, the nuns judged that there was no longer so great a need to maintain the requested secrecy, and permission was given.[7]

Although Lucie Christine had no formal schooling, since this was not considered necessary for girls at that time, she describes her experiences with astonishing precision and clarity, using homely similes to explain her experiences. Her spirituality is remarkably solid, characterized by devotion to Jesus, especially in the Blessed Sacrament, and to Mary, his mother. She was an accomplished pianist, and writes simply, but with a sure sense of phrasing and prosody. And she is humble. Many of the self-referential passages express her regret for her occasional distractions in prayer, or for having to omit prayer time to fulfill her duties as wife and mother; in none of them does she regard herself as other than an instrument chosen by God because of her insignificance.

While we may not imitate her mystical experience (indeed, some of us would prefer not to be visionaries!), we all can learn much from her fidelity to her responsibilities and the growth it occasioned in the context of prayer. We can admire her wisdom and even enjoy her humor. She accepted her human feelings without judging them. Nor did she set herself above others—or feel incapable of issuing a reproof! In instances when she believed that a person or policy was deliberately creating a problem—offending truth or proper respect for the body—she expressed righteous anger, later regretting her vehemence without feeling guilty about the anger itself.

All our greatest teachers down through the ages, whether spiritual guides or philosophers, have insisted that the only way to a deeper, richer, more serene life is to wake up and live in the real world in one's own time and place. Bookstores are filled with accounts of how to achieve this. But before there were abstract analyses of our malaise, there were stories. And for most of us, the concrete example of a life well lived is more motivating than any theory. Might not the witness of Mathilde's life, a life full of challenges that could easily have broken her spirit, serve to awaken us to the possibilities in our own situations? It is because I believe that she can still inspire us today, whatever our spiritual tradition, that I was moved to write her story.

Notes

Preface
[1] Underhill, E. (1911) *Mysticism*. New York, E.P. Dutton and Company.
[2] Matthew, I. (1995) *The Immpace of God: Soundings from St. John of the Cross*. London, Hodder and Stoughton.

A Note on the Translation
[1] O'Brien, "Lucie Christine."
[2] Grom, "Ich sprach zu dir, ohn' alle worte."
[3] Guardini, *Lucie Christine, Geistliches Tagebuch*.

Introduction
[1] Letter from Alain Le Touzé, 23 January 2003, in the possession of the author.
[2] Letter from Yvonne Le Touzé, in the archives of Adoration Reparatrice.
[3] Parry and Girard, *France since 1800*, 14.
[4] Ibid., 18.
[5] Ibid., 109.

Chapter One: A Parisian Childhood, 1844–1865
[1] Horne, *Seven Ages of Paris*, 162.
[2] Strayer et al., *The Mainstream of Civilization*, 552.
[3] Horne, *Seven Ages of Paris*, 169–70.
[4] Ibid., 166.
[5] Parry and Girard, *France since 1800*, 13.
[6] Horne, *Seven Ages of Paris*, 184.
[7] Ibid., 179.
[8] Ibid., 166.
[9] Ibid., 170.
[10] Ibid., 171.

[11] Ibid., 221.

[12] Devèze, *A Brief Guide to French History*, 66.

[13] Parry and Girard, *France since 1800*, 34.

[14] Horne, *Seven Ages of Paris*, 226–27.

[15] Parry and Girard, 11.

[16] A. Le Touzé, *Petite Chronique Familiale*, V: 77, 79.

[17] Ibid., 66.

[18] Ibid., 46.

[19] *Une Mère Chrétienne*, 13.

[20.] Ibid., 15.

[21] A. Le Touzé, *Petite Chronique Familiale*, V: 59.

[22] Letter from Yvonne Le Touzé, in the archives of Adoration Reparatrice.

[23] A. Le Touzé, *Petite Chronique Familiale*, V: 54–56, 58.

[24] Demolombe, *Traité de l'adoption*, 11.

[25] A. Le Touzé, *Petite Chronique Familiale*, V: 64.

[26] Gibson, *A Social History of French Catholicism*, 123.

[27] A. Le Touzé, *Petite Chronique Familiale*, V: 65.

[28] Poulain, *The Spiritual Journal of Lucie Christine*, xii, 20.

[29] A. Le Touzé, *Petite Chronique Familiale*, V: 76.

[30] Boutle, *Journal Spirituel*, 42; 2364; Poulain, *Journal Spirituel de Lucie Christine*, 463.

[31] Poulain, *Journal Spirituel*, 27, 57.

[32] Boutle, *Journal Spirituel*, 197; Poulain, *Journal Spirituel*, 154.

[33] Boutle, *Journal Spirituel*, 30; Poulain, *Journal Spirituel*, 30.

[34] Nevin, *Thérèse of Lisieux, God's Gentle Warrior*, 73.

[35] Poulain, *Journal Spirituel*, 20.

[36] Ibid., 20–21.

[37] *Une Mère Chrétienne*, 6.

[38] A. Le Touzé, email to Astrid O'Brien, 2008.

[39] Sr. Cecilia, A.R., pers. comm., 2008.

[40] Poulain, *Journal Spirituel*, 18–19.

[41] Ibid., 17–18.

[42] *Une Mère Chrétienne*, 7–8.

[43] Parry and Girard, *France since 1800*, 36.

[44] De Grandmaison, *Un Curé de Paris*, 13.

[45] Ibid., 24.

[46] A. Le Touzé, *Petite Chronique Familiale*, V: 70.

[47] Nevin, *Thérèse of Lisieux*, 77.

[48] Ibid., 76.

[49] A. Le Touzé, *Petite Chronique Familiale*, V: 42–43.

[50] Ibid., 66–67.

[51] Ibid., 67.

[52] Ibid., 109.

[53] Ibid., 69.

[54] Ibid., 70.

[55] Ibid., 71.

[56] Cf. Lanzetta, *Radical Wisdom*, 66–77.

[57] Boutle, *Journal Spirituel*, 282–83; Poulain, *Journal Spirituel*, 187.

Chapter Two: A Woman of Her Times, 1865–1873

[1] A. Le Touzé, *Petite Chronique Familiale*, V: 73.

[2] Ibid., 67.

[3] Ibid., 85.

[4] Parry and Girard, *France since 1800*, 62.

[5] Strayer et al., *The Mainstream of Civilization*, 599–600.

[6] Ibid., 600.

[7] Ibid., 599.

[8] Price, *A Social History of Nineteenth Century France*, 418–19, 422.

[9] Horne, *Seven Ages of Paris*, 248.

[10] Ibid., 249.

[11] Ibid., 250.

[12] Jonas, *France and the Cult of the Sacred Heart*, 148.

[13] Horne, *Seven Ages of Paris*, 252–53.

[14] De Grandmaison, *Un Curé de Paris*, 66.

[15] Horne, *Seven Ages of Paris*, 254.

[16] Ibid., 255–56.

[17] De Grandmaison, *Un Curé de Paris*, 66–67.

[18] Ibid., 67.

[19] Horne, *Seven Ages of Paris*, 262–63.

[20] De Grandmaison, *Un Curé de Paris*, 68.

[21] Poulain, *Journal Spirituel*, 27.

[22] Horne, *Seven Ages of Paris*, 258.

[23] Ibid., 264–65.

[24] Ibid.

[25] Ibid., 266–67.

[26] De Grandmaison, *Un Curé de Paris*, 72–73.

[27] Horne, *Seven Ages of Paris*, 270–73.

[28] Ibid., 269–75; Parry and Girard, *France since 1800*, 69–70.

[29] Strayer et al., *The Mainstream of Civilization*, 612–13.

[30] Ibid., 617.

[31] McManners, *Church and State in France*, 21.

[32] Strayer et al., *The Mainstream of Civilization*, 655.

[33] Ibid., 611; Parry and Girard, *France since 1800*, 71.

[34] Poulain, *Journal Spirituel*, 32.

[35] Ibid., 26.

[36] Ibid., 25.

[37] Ibid., 26–33.

[38] A. Le Touzé, *Petite Chronique Familiale*, V: 79.

[39] Poulain, *Journal Spirituel*, 32.

[40] Ibid., 30–31.

[41] Ibid., 28–29.

[42] Ibid., 33.

[43] Teresa of Avila, *The Interior Castle*, 4. 2. 3, 323; 4. 2. 4, 324. Cf. Lanzetta, *Radical Wisdom*, 111.

[44] Poulain, *Journal Spirituel*, 33.

[45] Sr. Linda Julian Dowler, O.S.H., email to Astrid O'Brien, 2009.

[46] Poulain, *Journal Spirituel*, 26.

Chapter Three: A New Life, 1873–1879

[1] Thomas à Kempis, *The Imitation of Christ*.

[2] Poulain, *Journal Spirituel*, 35.

[3] Ibid., 35–36.

[4] Ibid., 12, 36.

[5] Petroff, *Body and Soul*, 6.

[6] Poulain, *Journal Spirituel*, 36.

[7] Price, *A Social History of Nineteenth-Century France*, 302–3.

[8] Poulain, *Journal Spirituel*, 37–38.

[9] Ibid.

[10] A. Le Touzé, *Petite Chronique Familiale*, V: 79.

[11] Ibid., 80.

[12] Poulain, *Journal Spirituel*, 38.

[13] Ibid.

[14] Ibid., 38–39.

[15] Ibid., 39.

[16] Ibid.

[17] Ibid., 40.
[18] Ibid., 40–41.
[19] Ibid., 41.
[20] Ibid., 211–12.
[21] Ibid., 212.
[22] Ibid., 42.
[23] Ibid., 14.
[24] Ibid., 50.
[25] Ibid., 42.
[26] Ibid., 43–44.
[27] Ibid., 45.
[28] Ibid., 184–91.
[29] Ibid., 44–45.
[30] Ibid., 45.
[31] Ibid., 145.
[32] Ibid., 45–46.
[33] Ibid., 46–47.
[34] Ibid., 47.
[35] Ibid., 394.
[36] Ibid., 48.
[37] Ibid.
[38] Ibid., 51.
[39] Boutle, *Journal Spirituel*, 38–39.
[40] Ibid., 51; cf. chapter five, below.
[41] Poulain, *Journal Spirituel*, 51–52.
[42] Ibid., 52.

Chapter Four: A Wise Guide, 1879

[1] McManners, *Church and State in France*, 21–22.
[2] Poulain, *Journal Spirituel*, 49.
[3] Ibid.
[4] Ibid., 50.
[5] Ibid.
[6] Ibid.
[7] Wright, *Heart Speaks to Heart*, 25–26.
[8] Ibid., 30.
[9] Ibid., 31.
[10] Ibid., 37.
[11] Thompson, *Bérulle and the French School*, 9–19.

[12] Cochois, *Bèrulle et l'École Française*, 146; DeVille, *The French School of Spirituality*, 10.

[13] Dupre, introduction, "Jansenism and Quietism," *Christian Spirituality III*, 122–23.

[14] Ibid., 126.

[15] Ibid., 127.

[16] O'Connell, *Blaise Pascal*, 86–87.

[17] Ibid., 95–97.

[18] Dupre, "Jansenism and Quietism," 130.

[19] Ibid.

[20] G. N. Alford, O.C.D.S., email to Astrid O'Brien, 2009.

[21] Ibid.

[22] Sheldrake, *A Brief History of Spirituality*, 126–27.

[23] Wright, *Heart Speaks to Heart*, 111–12, 194, n. 4.

[24] Ibid., 111.

[25] Ibid, 194, n. 4

[26] Ibid.

[27] Ibid., 112.

[28] Sr. Catherine-Marie, Diocese d'Evreux, pers. comm., 2008.

[29] Wright, *Heart Speaks to Heart*, 85–86.

[30] Ryan and Rybolt, *Vincent de Paul and Louise de Marillac*, 21; cf. Wright, *Heart Speaks to Heart*, 87.

[31] Sr. Catherine-Marie, Diocese d'Evreux, pers. comm., 2008.

[32] Wright, *Heart Speaks to Heart*, 85.

[33] Lemoyne, *The Biographical Memoirs of Saint John Bosco*, 518; cf. Wright, *Heart Speaks to Heart*, 120.

[34] Wright, *Heart Speaks to Heart*, 111.

[35] Ibid., 172–78.

[36] *Semaine Religieuse du diocese d'Evreux*, 173.

[37] Ibid., 173–76.

[38] Ibid., 177.

[39] Poulain, *Journal Spirituel*, 23.

[40] Ibid., 53.

[41] Gibson, *A Social History of French Catholicism*, 123.

[42] Cf. letter, chapter 5 below.

[43] Poulain, *Journal Spirituel*, 59.

[44] Boutle, *Journal Spirituel*, 1417.

[45] Poulain, *Journal Spirituel*, 53–54.

[46] Ibid., 54–55.

47 Ibid., 55.

48 Ibid., 56.

49 Ibid., 55.

50 Nevin, *Thérèse of Lisieux*, 82–83.

51 Gibson, *A Social History of French Catholicism*, 119.

52 J. Maritain, *Notebooks*, 220.

53 R. Maritain, *Raïssa's Journal*, 163.

54 J. Maritain, *Notebooks*, 162.

55 Ibid., 163.

56 Ibid., 122.

57 Cf. O'Brien, "Contemplation along the Roads of the World," *Lay Sanctity, Medieval and Modern*, 156.

58 J. Maritain, *Notebooks*, 251.

59 Poulain, *Jouirnal Spirituel*, 56–57.

60 Gibson, *A Social History of French Catholicism*, 255.

61 Poulain, *Journal Spirituel*, 57–58.

62 A. Le Touzé, *Petite Chronique Familiale*, V: 81–82.

63 Poulain, *Journal Spirituel*, 58–59.

64 Ibid., 61–62.

65 Ibid., 62–63.

66 Ibid., 63.

67 Ibid., 63–64.

68 Ibid., 64–65.

69 Ibid., 65.

70 Ibid., 66–67.

71 Ibid., 68–69.

72 Ibid., 69.

Chapter Five: Adoration Réparatrice, Founded in 1854

1 *A People for Worship*, Introduction.

2 King and Rabil, *The Other Voice in Early Modern Europe*, xviii.

3 J. Ruffing, R.S.M., email to Astrid O'Brien.

4 Cf. Gibson, *A Social History of French Catholicism*, 187.

5 Polart, *L'adoration au cœur de la ville*, 23–25.

6 Sr. Cecilia, personal comm.; cf. Polart, *L'adoration au cœur de la ville*, 27.

7 Polart, *L'adoration au cœur de la ville*, 25.

8 Grace, *Adoration and Reparation*, 3.

9 Dubouché, *A People for Worship*, 31.

[10] Grace, *Adoration and Reparation*, 3–4.

[11] Ibid., 2–3.

[12] Ayral-Clause, *Camille Claudel*.

[13] Ibid., 221.

[14] Ibid.

[15] Polart, *L'adoration au cœur de la ville*, 34.

[16] Ibid.

[17] Ibid., 34–35.

[18] Grace, *Adoration and Reparation*, 7.

[19] Polart, *L'adoration au cœur de la ville*, 37.

[20] Ibid., 38.

[21] Leconte, *Souvenirs d'une Amie*, II: 79; trans. Sr. Cecilia, A.R., email to Astrid O'Brien, 2009.

[22] Leconte, *Souvenirs d'une Amie*, II: 79, V: 115; trans. Sr. Cecilia, A.R., email to Astrid O'Brien, 2010.

[23] Grace, *Adoration and Reparation*, 7.

[24] Ibid., 9.

[25] Devèze, *A Brief Guide to French History*, 66.

[26] Polart, *L'adoration au cœur de la ville*, 9–10.

[27] Ibid., 10–11.

[28] Grace, 11–12.

[29] Ibid., 12–14.

[30] Dubouché, *A People for Worship*, 10

[31] Ibid., 15.

[32] For a definitive description of the organization, see D'Hulst, *Vie de la Vénérable Marie Térèse du Coeur de Jésus*.

[33] Dubouché, *A People for Worship*, 29.

[34] Ibid., 31.

[35] Ibid., 23.

[36] Ibid.

[37] Ibid., 33.

[38] T. Dubouché (Mother Marie Thérèse), letter, 21.

[39] Grace, *Adoration and Reparation*, 17.

[40] Ibid., 24–25.

[41] Ibid., 27–29.

[42] Sr. Cecilia, A.R., pers. comm., 2002.

[43] Sr. Cecilia, A.R., pers. comm., 2002.

[44] Savigny-Vesco, *Lucie-Christine*.

Chapter Six: Divine Education, 1881–1882

[1] Poulain, *Journal Spirituel*, 81.

[2] Boutle, *Journal Spirituel*, 38–39; Poulain, *Journal Spirituel*, 51–52.

[3] Poulain, *Journal Spirituel*, 69.

[4] Ibid., 70–71.

[5] Ibid., 78–79.

[6] Ibid., 73–74.

[7] Ibid., 74–75.

[8] Ibid., 75–76.

[9] Ibid., 76.

[10] Cf. Vanauken, *A Severe Mercy*.

[11] Poulain, *Journal Spirituel*, 75–76.

[12] Ibid., 79–80.

[13] Ibid., 80.

[14] Ibid., 80–81.

[15] Ibid., 90.

[16] Ibid., 85–86.

[17] Ibid., 86; Poulain, *The Graces of Interior Prayer*, 220.

[18] Poulain, *Journal Spirituel*, 86.

[19] Ibid., 86–87.

[20] Ibid., 87.

[21] Ibid., 89.

[22] Ibid., 82.

[23] Ibid.

[24] Ibid., 83.

[25] Ibid., 83–84.

[26] Ibid., 84.

[27] Ibid., 84–85.

[28] Ibid., 90.

[29] Ibid., 89–90.

[30] Ibid., 90.

[31] Ibid., 90–92

[32] Ibid., 92–93.

[33] Ibid., 95.

[34] Ibid., 96.

[35] Ibid., 96–97.

[36] Ibid., 97.

[37] Ibid., 98.

[38] Ibid., 99–100.

[39] Ibid., 100–101.

[40] Ibid., 101–3.

[41] Ibid., 103.

[42] Ibid., 104.

[43] Poulain, *The Graces of Interior Prayer*, 301.

[44] Poulain, *Journal Spirituel*, 170.

[45] Ibid., 105–6.

[46] Ibid., 106–7.

[47] Ibid., 108–9.

[48] Ibid., 110–12.

[49] Ibid., 113–14.

[50] Ibid., 114–15.

[51] Ibid., 117.

[52] Ibid., 126–27.

[53] Ibid., 118–19

[54] Ibid., 119–120.

[55] Ibid., 121.

[56] Ibid., 121.

[57] Boutle, *Journal Spirituel*, 145.

[58] Poulain, *Journal Spirituel*, 122–23.

[58] Strayer et al., *The Mainstream of Civilization*, 618; Price, *A Social History of Nineteenth-Century France*, 303.

[59] McManners, *Church and State in France*, 21–22.

[60] Ibid., 40, 52.

[61] Cf. Ibid., 45–54.

[62] Poulain, *Journal Spirituel*, 124; Boutle, *Journal Spirituel*, 133.

[63] McManners, *Church and State in France*, 167–68.

[64] Ibid., 125–26.

[65] Ibid., 127.

[66] Ibid., 127–29.

[67] Ibid., 131.

[68] Ibid., 138.

[69] Ibid., 137.

[70] A. Le Touzé, *Petite Chronique Familiale*, V: 83.

[71] Ibid., 84.

[72] Ibid., 85.

[73] Boutle, *Journal Spirituel*, 126; cf. A. Le Touzé, *Petite Chronique Familiale*, V: 85–86.

Chapter Seven: A Veiled Ostensorium, 1882–1884

[1] Poulain, *Journal Spirituel*, 138–39; Boutle, *Journal Spirituel*, 167–68.

[2] Poulain, *Journal Spirituel*, 142.

[3] Ibid., 143–45.

[4] Poulain, *The Graces of Interior Prayer*, 288–89.

[5] Boutle, *Journal Spirituel*, 183; Poulain, *Journal Spirituel*, 148.

[6] Cf. Poulain, *Journal Spirituel*, 145–48.

[7] Poulain, *Journal Spirituel*, 149–50.

[8] Ibid., 152.

[9] Ibid., 153–55.

[10] Ibid., 156–57; Boutle, *Journal Spirituel*, 202–5.

[11] J. Maritain, *Notebooks*, 251.

[12] Poulain, *Journal Spirituel*, 158–59.

[13] Ibid., 161–62.

[14] Boutle, *Journal Spirituel*, 214–15.

[15] Poulain, *Journal Spirituel*, 161–62.

[16] Cf. Ibid., 174.

[17] Boutle, *Journal Spirituel*, 245.

[18] Poulain, *Journal Spirituel*, 174; Boutle, *Journal Spirituel*, 246.

[19] Boutle, *Journal Spirituel*, 247–48.

[20] Poulain, *Journal Spirituel*, 160.

[21] Ibid., 163; Boutle, *Journal Spirituel*, 217.

[22] Poulain, *Journal Spirituel*, 164.

[23] Boutle, *Journal Spirituel*, 228–30; cf. 134.

[24] Poulain, *Journal Spirituel*, 165–66.

[25] Ibid., 166–70.

[26] Poulain, *The Graces of Interior Prayer*, 301.

[27] Poulain, *Journal Spirituel*, 175.

[28] Ibid., 137.

[29] Boutle, *Journal Spirituel*, 340–41.

[30] Ibid., 238.

[31] Stevens, *The One Year Book of Saints*, 81.

[32] Poulain, *Journal Spirituel*, 169–71.

[33] Boutle, *Journal Spirituel*, 232; cf. 241.

[34] Poulain, *Journal Spirituel*, 171–74.

[35] Poulain, *Journal Spirituel*, 172–73; cf. Boutle, *Journal Spirituel*, 258.

[36] Poulain, *Journal Spirituel*, 178–79.

[37] Ibid., 180–81.

[38] Ibid., 181–82.

[39] Ibid., 184–85.

[40] Boutle, *Journal Spirituel*, 294.

[41] Gibson, *A Social History of French Catholicism*, 9, 230–31; cf. 174–81.

[42] Poulain, *Journal Spirituel*, 195–96.

[43] Ibid., 199.

[44] Ibid., 198–99.

[45] A. Le Touzé, *Petite Chronique Familiale*, V: 88.

[46] Boutle, *Journal Spirituel*, 312–13.

[47] Poulain, *Journal Spirituel*, 201–2.

[48] Boutle, *Journal Spirituel*, 319–23.

[49] Ibid., 324–27.

[50] Ibid., 327–29.

[51] A. Le Touzé, *Petite Chronique Familiale*, V: 89

[52] Boutle, *Journal Spirituel*, 334–35.

[53] Ibid., 336–37.

[54] Ibid., 338.

[55] Poulain, *Journal Spirituel*, 204–5.

[56] Boutle, *Journal Spirituel*, 339–40.

[57] Poulain, *Journal Spirituel*, 205–6.

[58] Boutle, *Journal Spirituel*, 345.

[59] Poulain, *Journal Spirituel*, 206–7.

[60] Boutle, *Journal Spirituel*, 348.

[61] Boutle, *Journal Spirituel*, 349; Poulain, *Journal Spirituel*, 207.

[62] Poulain, *Journal Spirituel*, 207.

[63] Ibid., 208.

[64] Boutle, *Journal Spirituel*, 355–56.

[65] Poulain, *Journal Spirituel*, 210.

[66] Ibid., 214–15.

[67] Boutle, *Journal Spirituel*, 371.

[68] Poulain, *Journal Spirituel*, 20.

[69] Ibid., 211.

[70] Ibid., 216–17.

[71] Ibid., 217–18.

[72] Ibid., 212–14.

[73] Boutle, *Journal Spirituel*, 409–10; Poulain, *Journal Spirituel*, 226–27.

[74] Nevin, *Thérèse of Lisieux*, 80.

[75] Boutle, *Journal Spirituel*, 411–14.
[76] Poulain, *Journal Spirituel*, 228–30.
[77] Ibid.
[78] Ibid., 231–32.
[79] Nevin, *Thérèse of Lisieux*,105.
[80] Boutle, *Journal Spirituel*, 434.
[81] Poulain, *Journal Spirituel*,234, 238; cf. note, 238.
[82] Boutle, *Journal Spirituel*, 429.
[83] Ibid., 455–56.
[84] Ibid., 459–60.
[85] Poulain, *Journal Spirituel*, 240–41.
[86] Ibid., 241–42.
[87] Boutle, *Journal Spirituel*, 463.
[88] Ibid., 465, 467–68.
[89] Poulain, *Journal Spirituel*, 244.
[90] Cf. Boutle, *Journal Spirituel*, 339–40.
[91] Poulain, *Journal Spirituel*, 244.
[92] Boutle, *Journal Spirituel*,481
[93] Poulain, *Journal Spirituel*, 247–48.
[94] Ibid., 248–49.
[95] Boutle, *Journal Spirituel*, 504–5.
[96] Ibid., 468–69.
[97] Poulain, *Journal Spirituel*, 252.
[98] Boutle, *Journal Spirituel*, 509.
[99] Poulain, *Journal Spirituel*, 252.
[100] Boutle, *Journal Spirituel*, 529.
[101] A. Le Touzé, *Petite Chronique Familiale*, V: 82.
[102] Ibid., 82, 90.
[103] Ibid., 90.
[104] Ibid., 92.
[105] Poulain, *Journal Spirituel*, 254.
[106] Ibid., 254–55.
[107] Ibid.

Chapter Eight: A Battered Wife, 1885

[1] Boutle, *Journal Spirituel*, 547.
[2] Ibid.
[3] Ibid., 551.
[4] Kerns, *Treatise on the Love of God*, 249–50; cf. Boutle, *Jour-*

nal Spirituel, 552.

⁵ Boutle, *Journal Spirituel*, 553.

⁶ Ibid., 554; cf. Poulain, *Journal Spirituel*, 255.

⁷ V. Frankl, *Man's Search for Meaning*.

⁸ Boutle, *Journal Spirituel*, 554.

⁹ Poulain, *Journal Spirituel*, 256

¹⁰ Ibid., 256–57.

¹¹ Boutle, *Journal Spirituel*, 556.

¹² A. Le Touzé, *Petite Chronique Familiale*, V: 92–93; cf. Boutle, *Journal Spirituel*, 561–62.

¹³ A. Le Touzé, *Petite Chronique Familiale*, V: 92–93; cf. Boutle, *Journal Spirituel*, 561–62.

¹⁴ Boutle, *Journal Spirituel*, 562–69.

¹⁵ Poulain, *Journal Spirituel*, 258.

¹⁶ Ibid., 260.

¹⁷ A. Le Touzé, *Petite Chronique Familiale*, V: 93; Boutle, *Journal Spirituel*, 574.

¹⁸ Poulain, *Journal Spirituel*, 261.

¹⁹ Short, "Answers about Alcohol," *University of Alabama at Birmingham Magazine*, 21:2.

²⁰ A. Le Touzé, *Petite Chronique Familiale*, V: 94.

²¹ Boutle, *Journal Spirituel*, 582.

²² Ibid., 590–91; Poulain, *Journal Spirituel*, 262–63; cf. A. Le Touzé, *Petite Chronique Familiale*, V: 94.

²³ Poulain, *Journal Spirituel*, 263–64.

²⁴ Ibid., 264.

²⁵ Boutle, *Journal Spirituel*, 600–01.

²⁶ Poulain, *Journal Spirituel*, 265.

²⁷ Boutle, *Journal Spirituel*, 605, 608.

²⁸ Poulain, *Journal Spirituel*, 266.

²⁹ Boutle, *Journal Spirituel*, 619–20; cf. Poulain, *Journal Spirituel*, 268.

³⁰ Boutle, *Journal Spirituel*, 621–24; Poulain, *Journal Spirituel*, 269.

³¹ Boutle, *Journal Spirituel*, 625–27.

³² Poulain, *Journal Spirituel*, 269–71.

³³ Ibid., 271–72.

³⁴ Boutle, *Journal Spirituel*, 620–21.

³⁵ Poulain, *Journal Spirituel*, 272–73.

³⁶ Boutle, *Journal Spirituel*, 650–51; cf. A. Le Touzé, *Petite Chronique*

Familiale, V: 94.

[37] Boutle, *Journal Spirituel*, 653; Poulain, *Journal Spirituel*, 274.

[38] A. Le Touzé, *Petite Chronique Familiale*, V: 95

[39] Ibid., 96.

[40] Ibid., 96–97.

[41] Ibid., 97–98.

[42] Poulain, *Journal Spirituel*, 275.

[43] Ibid., 277–78.

[44] A. Le Touzé, *Petite Chronique Familiale*, V: 98–99.

[45] Poulain, *Journal Spirituel*, 278–79.

[46] A. Le Touzé, *Petite Chronique Familiale*, V: 99–100

[47] Ibid., 98–99.

[48] Poulain, *Journal Spirituel*, 279–80.

[49] Ibid., 279–80; Boutle, *Journal Spirituel*, 674–75.

[50] Poulain, *Journal Spirituel*, 282; cf. A. Le Touzé, *Petite Chronique Familiale*, V: 101.

[51] Lanier, *Absinthe*, 10–11.

[52] Ibid., 12.

Chapter Nine: Illness and Death of Thomas, 1885–1887

[1] A. Le Touzé, *Petite Chronique Familiale*, V: 102.

[2] Boutle, *Journal Spirituel*, 689.

[3] Ibid., 691.

[4] Poulain, *Journal Spirituel*, 284–85.

[5] Ibid., 286.

[6] Ibid., 285–86.

[7] Ibid., 286–87.

[8] Ibid., 287–88.

[9] Boutle, 709–10.

[10] Ibid.

[11] Ibid., 714.

[12] Ibid., 715; Poulain, *Journal Spirituel*, 291.

[13] Boutle, *Journal Spirituel*, 718; Poulain, *Journal Spirituel*, 292.

[14] A. Le Touzé, *Petite Chronique Familiale*, V: 108.

[15] W. G. Morgan, email to Astrid O'Brien, 2009.

[16] Boutle, *Journal Spirituel*, 720.

[17] McManners, *Church and State in France*, xix.

[18] Boutle, *Journal Spirituel*, 722.

[19] Poulain, *Journal Spirituel*, 293.

[20] Boutle, *Journal Spirituel*, 731.

[21] Ibid., 735.

[22] Ibid., 735–36.

[23] Ibid., 737–38.

[24] Ibid., 744–45.

[25] Ibid., 745–46.

[26] Ibid., 746.

[27] Poulain, *Journal Spirituel*, 294–95.

[28] Boutle, *Journal Spirituel,* 749.

[29] Ibid., 753.

[30] Ibid., 758–59.

[31] Ibid., 762.

[32] Ibid.

[33] A. Le Touzé, *Petite Chronique Familiale*, V: 104.

[34] Boutle, *Journal Spirituel*, 779.

[35] Ibid., 780.

[36] Ibid., 781–82.

[37] Ibid., 794.

[38] Ibid., 845.

[39] Ibid., 794–95.

[40] Ibid., 795–96.

[41] Ibid.

[42] Ibid., 796–99.

[43] Ibid., 799.

[44] Ibid., 801.

[45] A. Le Touzé, *Petite Chronique Familiale*, V: 106.

[46] Boutle, *Journal Spirituel*, 803.

[47] Poulain, *Journal Spirituel*, 297–98.

[48] Ibid., 298–99.

[49] Boutle, *Journal Spirituel*, 812.

[50] Ibid., 816.

[51] Ibid., 819.

[52] Ibid., 820.

[53] Ibid., 820–22.

[54] Ibid., 829–30.

[55] Ibid., 833.

[56] Ibid., 834–36; cf. Poulain, *Journal Spirituel*, 301.

[57] Boutle, *Journal Spirituel*, 841–42.

[58] Ibid., 842–43.

[59] Ibid., 843.

[60] Ibid., 843–44.

[61] Poulain, *Journal Spirituel*, 302.

[62] Boutle, *Journal Spirituel*, 845.

[63] Boutle, *Journal Spirituel*, 846–48; cf. Poulain, *Journal Spirituel*, 303.

[64] Boutle, *Journal Spirituel*, 857.

[65] Ibid., 858–60.

[66] Ibid., 869–70; cf. Poulain, *Journal Spirituel*, 306.

[67] A. Le Touzé, *Petite Chronique Familiale*, V: 106; Boutle, *Journal Spirituel*, 876–77.

[68] Boutle, *Journal Spirituel*, 877–78.

[69] Ibid., 879.

[70] A. Le Touzé, *Petite Chronique Familiale*, V: 109.

[71] Ibid.

[72] Boutle, *Journal Spirituel*, 885–86.

[73] Ibid., 887; cf. Poulain, *Journal Spirituel*, 307.

[74] Boutle, *Journal Spirituel*, 891

[75] Ibid., 893–94.

[76] Ibid., 894–95.

[77] Ibid., 902–3.

[78] Ibid., 907.

[79] Poulain, *Journal Spirituel*, 230–32, 311–13.

[80] Boutle, *Journal Spirituel*, 909–12.

[81] Ibid., 912.

[82] Ibid., 915–16.

[83] Ibid., 917–19.

[84] Ibid., 922–24.

[85] Ibid., 930–33.

[86] Ibid., 941–42.

[87] Ibid., 942–43.

[88] Ibid., 945–46.

[89] Dansette, *Religious History of Modern France*, I: 313.

[90] Ibid., II: 37.

[91] Ibid., I: 345.

[92] Ibid., 346–47.

[93] Ibid., II: 37.

[94] Boutle, *Journal Spirituel*, 953.

[95] Ibid., 954–55.

[96] Ibid., 957–59.

[97] Ibid., 963.

[98] Ibid., 965.

[99] Ibid., 966.

[100] Johnson, *Quest for the Living God*, 44–47.

[101] Boutle, *Journal Spirituel*, 969; Poulain, *Journal Spirituel*, 317.

[102] Boutle, *Journal Spirituel*, 970.

[103] Ibid., 983.

[104] Ibid., 985–86; cf. A. Le Touzé, *Petite Chronique Familiale*, V: 114.

[105] Poulain, *Journal Spirituel*, 318–19.

[106] Ibid.

[107] Burrows, *The Essence of Prayer*, 107–18.

[108] Ibid., 7.

[109] Boutle, *Journal Spirituel*, 996.

[110] Ibid., 999.

[111] Ibid., 1000.

[112] Ibid., 1001–2.

[113] Ibid., 1005–6.

[114] Ibid., 1007–8.

[115] Ibid., 109–10; Poulain, *Journal Spirituel*, 322–24.

[116] Boutle, *Journal Spirituel*, 1014.

[117] Ibid., 1019.

[118] Ibid., 1020.

[119] Poulain, *Journal Spirituel*, 323–24.

[120] Ibid., 324.

[121] Boutle, *Journal Spirituel*, 1021.

[122] Poulain, *Journal Spirituel*, 242, 324.

[123] Boutle, *Journal Spirituel*, 1021.

[124] Ibid., 1022.

[125] Ibid., 1022–23.

[126] Poulain, *Journal Spirituel*, 324–25.

[127] Boutle, *Journal Spirituel*, 1024.

[128] Ibid., 1025.

[129] Poulain, *Journal Spirituel*, 325–26.

[130] Boutle, *Journal Spirituel*, 1028; Poulain, *Journal Spirituel,* 327.

[131] Poulain, *Journal Spirituel,* 327–28.

[132] Cf. Nevin, *Thérèse of Lisieux*, 76.

[133] A. Le Touzé, *Petite Chronique Familiale*, V: 109.

Chapter Ten: The Harvest Years, 1888–1894

[1] Boutle, *Journal Spirituel*, 1036.

[2] Ruysbroeck, *The Adornment of Spiritual Marriage*, 1293–1381.

[3] Boutle, *Journal Spirituel*, 1036–37.

[4] Ibid., 1031.

[5] Ibid., 1039.

[6] Ibid., 1048.

[7] American Psychiatric Association, *Diagnostic and Statistical Manual of Mental Disorders*, 428–29; B. Musgrave, email to Astrid O'Brien, 2009.

[8] Poulain, *Journal Spirituel*, 330.

[9] Romans 8:28.

[10] A. Le Touzé, *Petite Chronique Familiale*, V: 119, 121.

[11] Boutle, *Journal Spirituel*, 1056.

[12] Ibid., 1045.

[13] Ibid., 1046–47.

[14] Ibid., 1051.

[15] Ibid., 1052.

[16] Ibid., 1054–55.

[17] Ibid., 1068.

[18] Poulain, *Journal Spirituel*, 333.

[19] Boutle, *Journal Spirituel*, 1070.

[20] Ibid., 1070–71.

[21] Ibid., 1077–78.

[22] Ibid., 1081–82.

[23] Daniel 9:3–10.

[24] Hardon, *Modern Catholic Dictionary*, 562.

[25] Boutle, *Journal Spirituel*, 1107.

[26] Ibid., 1082–83.

[27] Boutle, *Journal Spirituel*, 1084–85; Poulain, *Journal Spirituel*, 335.

[28] Boutle, *Journal Spirituel*, 1098; Poulain, *Journal Spirituel*, 337.

[29] Boutle, *Journal Spirituel*, 1104.

[30] Ibid., 1114.

[31] A. Le Touzé, *Petite Chronique Familiale*, V: 121–22.

[32] Boutle, *Journal Spirituel*, 1108.

[33] A. Le Touzé, *Petite Chronique Familiale*, V: 123.

[34] Boutle, *Journal Spirituel*, 1124.

[35] Ibid., 1125–26; A. Le Touzé, *Petite Chronique Familiale*, V: 122.

[36] Boutle, *Journal Spirituel*, 1124.

[37] Ibid., 1143.

[38] A. Le Touzé, *Petite Chronique Familiale*, V: 123.

[39] Boutle, *Journal Spirituel*, 1160.

[40] A. Le Touzé, *Petite Chronique Familiale*, V: 123–24.

[41] Boutle, *Journal Spirituel*, 1162.

[42] Ibid., 1170.

[43] Ibid., 1177; Poulain, *Journal Spirituel*, 347.

[44] Boutle, *Journal Spirituel*, 1189–91; cf. Poulain, *Journal Spirituel*, 348–49.

[45] Boutle, *Journal Spirituel*, 1208–9.

[46] Ibid., 1231–32; cf. 1309; Poulain, *Journal Spirituel*, 357–58.

[47] Boutle, *Journal Spirituel*, 1234; cf. Poulain, *Journal Spirituel*, 352.

[48] Boutle, *Journal Spirituel*, 1252.

[49] Ibid., 1221.

[50] Ibid., 1248, 1250.

[51] Ibid., 1258; Poulain, *Journal Spirituel*, 352.

[52] Boutle, *Journal Spirituel*, 1283.

[53] Ibid., cf. 1280–82, 1298–1302.

[54] Ibid., 1333.

[55] Ibid., 1337.

[56] Ibid., 1291; Poulain, *Journal Spirituel*, 355–56.

[57] Boutle, *Journal Spirituel*, 1316–19.

[58] Ibid., 1331.

[59] Jonas, *France and the Cult of the Sacred Heart*, 149.

[60] Ibid., 150.

[61] Ibid., cf. 153–57.

[62] Ibid., 176 ff.

[63] Boutle, *Journal Spirituel*, 1332.

[64] Jonas, *France and the Cult of the Sacred Heart*, 205.

[65] Boutle, *Journal Spirituel*, 1354–55.

[66] Ibid., 1377; Poulain, *Journal Spirituel*, 363.

[67] Boutle, *Journal Spirituel*, 1356; A. Le Touzé, *Petite Chronique Familiale*, V: 125.

[68] Boutle, *Journal Spirituel*, 1377–78.

[69] Ibid., 1357–58.

[70] Ibid., 1889, 1380.

[71] Horne, *Seven Ages of Paris*, 286–87.

[72] Boutle, *Journal Spirituel*, 1384–87; Poulain, *Journal Spirituel*, 363–65.

73 Boutle, *Journal Spirituel*, 1399.

74 Ibid., 1403–4; Poulain, *Journal Spirituel*, 367; cf. A. Le Touzé, *Petite Chronique Familiale*, VI: 61.

75 Boutle, *Journal Spirituel*, 1396–98; Poulain, *Journal Spirituel*, 366.

76 Boutle, *Journal Spirituel*, 1413.

77 Ibid., note in her own hand taped between 1420 and 1421 in Marguerite's copy; Poulain, *Journal Spirituel*, 367–69; A. Le Touzé, *Petite Chronique Familiale*, V: 127.

78 Boutle, *Journal Spirituel*, 1415–16.

79 Ibid., 1420.

80 Ibid., 1428–29.

81 Ibid., 1431–32; Poulain, *Journal Spirituel*, 370.

82 Boutle, *Journal Spirituel*, 1432–33; Poulain, *Journal Spirituel*, 370–71.

83 Boutle, *Journal Spirituel*, 1433–34; Poulain, *Journal Spirituel*, 371–72.

84 Boutle, *Journal Spirituel*, 1435.

85 Ibid., 1436.

86 Ibid., 1440.

87 Ibid., 1281, 1443–45; Poulain, *Journal Spirituel*, 373–74.

88 Boutle, *Journal Spirituel*, 1445–46.

89 Ibid., 1448; Poulain, *Journal Spirituel*, 374.

90 Boutle, *Journal Spirituel*, 1448.

91 Ibid., 1456–57; Poulain, *Journal Spirituel*, 377–78.

92 Boutle, *Journal Spirituel*, 1458.

93 Ibid., cf. 1459.

94 Ibid., 1460.

95 Ibid., 1462.

96 Ibid., 1465–67; Poulain, *Journal Spirituel*, 379–80.

97 Boutle, *Journal Spirituel*, 1467–68.

98 Ibid., 1469.

99 Ibid., 1481; Poulain, *Journal Spirituel*, 380.

100 Boutle, *Journal Spirituel*, 1475–80, 1503–4.

101 Ibid., 1509.

102 A. Le Touzé, *Petite Chronique Familiale*, V: 130.

103 Boutle, *Journal Spirituel*, 1504–5.

104 A. Le Touzé, *Petite Chronique Familiale*, V : 39.

105 Ibid., V : 129–30, VI: 40.

106 Boutle, *Journal Spirituel*, 1508.

107 A. Le Touzé, *Petite Chronique Familiale*, V: 131–35.

108 Ibid., VI: 2–3.

109 Boutle, *Journal Spirituel*, 1519.

110 Ibid., 1613.

111 Ibid., 1615.

112 Ibid., 1616.

113 Poulain, *Journal Spirituel*, 207, 393–94.

114 Dupre and Wiseman, *Light from Light*, 25.

115 Ibid.

116 Boutle, *Journal Spirituel*, 1520.

117 Ibid., 1747; Poulain, *Journal Spirituel*, 404–5.

118 Boutle, *Journal Spirituel*, 1534–36,

119 Ibid., 1537.

120 Ibid., 1572–73, 1584; cf. Poulain, *Journal Spirituel*, 389–90.

121 Boutle, *Journal Spirituel*, 1622–23); Poulain, *Journal Spirituel*, 394–95.

122 Boutle, *Journal Spirituel*, 1599; Poulain, *Journal Spirituel*, 392.

123 Boutle, *Journal Spirituel*, 1615, 1622.

124 Cf. Poulain, *Journal Spirituel*, 394.

125 Boutle, *Journal Spirituel*, 1622; Poulain, *Journal Spirituel*, 394.

126 A. Le Touzé, *Petite Chronique Familiale*, VI: 10–11.

127 Ibid., 11.

128 Boutle, *Journal Spirituel*, 1673.

129 Ibid., 1826; Poulain, *Journal Spirituel*, 411.

130 Boutle, *Journal Spirituel*, 1897–98; Poulain, *Journal Spirituel*, 417).

131 Boutle, *Journal Spirituel*, 1674.

132 Ibid., 1683–84.

133 Ibid., 1709.

134 Ibid., 1694; Poulain, *Journal Spirituel*, 400.

135 Boutle, *Journal Spirituel*, 1727; Poulain, *Journal Spirituel*, 403.

136 Boutle, *Journal Spirituel*, 1729–35.

137 Ibid., 1737.

138 A. Le Touzé, *Petite Chronique Familiale*, VI: 17.

139 Boutle, *Journal Spirituel*, 1817–18; Poulain, *Journal Spirituel*, 411.

140 A. Le Touzé, *Petite Chronique Familiale*, VI: 18–20; Boutle, *Journal Spirituel*, 1823.

141 Boutle, *Journal Spiriteul*, 1829–30.

142 A. Le Touzé, pers. comm.

143 A. Le Touzé, *Petite Chronique Familiale*, death notices in VI, facing

p. 42; in VIII, facing p. 62.

[144] A. Le Touzé, *Petite Chronique Familiale*, VI: 18; Boutle, *Journal Spirituel*, 1827, 1832.

[145] Boutle, *Journal Spirituel*, 1858.

[146] Ibid., 1881–82.

[147] Ibid., 1884, 1886.

[148] Ibid., 1884–85; Poulain, *Journal Spirituel*, 314, 415.

[149] Boutle, *Journal Spirituel*, 1896.

[150] Ibid., 1908–9.

[151] A. Le Touzé, *Petite Chronique Familiale*, VI: 20–21.

[152] Boutle, *Journal Spirituel*, 1909; Poulain, *Journal Spirituel*, 417.

[153] A. Le Touzé, *Petite Chronique Familiale*, VI: 21–27.

[154] Ibid., 28–39.

[155] Boutle, *Journal Spirituel*, 1920.

[156] Ibid., 1917; Poulain, *Journal Spirituel*, 418.

[157] Boutle, *Journal Spirituel*, 1922.

[158] Ibid.

[159] A. Le Touzé, *Petite Chronique Familiale*, VI: 40.

[160] Boutle, *Journal Spirituel*, 1925; A. Le Touzé, *Petite Chronique Familiale*, VI: 25.

[161] Boutle, *Journal Spirituel*, 1948–49; cf. A. Le Touzé, *Petite Chronique Familiale*, VI: 41–42.

[162] Boutle, *Journal Spirituel*, 1949; Poulain, *Journal Spirituel*, 420–21.

[163] Boutle, *Journal Spirituel*, 2010.

Chapter Eleven: From Darkness to Light, 1894–1908

[1] Boutle, *Journal Spirituel*, 2018–33.

[2] Ibid., 2045; Poulain, *Journal Spirituel*, 428.

[3] Boutle, *Journal Spirituel*, 2039–40; Poulain, *Journal Spirituel*, 428.

[4] Cf. Boutle, *Journal Spirituel*, 2098.

[5] Poulain, *Journal Spirituel*, 433.

[6] Boutle, *Journal Spirituel*, 2046–47; Poulain, *Journal Spirituel*, 429.

[7] Boutle, *Journal Spirituel*, 2093–94.

[8] Ibid., 2134–35; cf. A. Le Touzé, *Petite Chronique Familiale*, VI: 43–44.

[9] Boutle, *Journal Spirituel*, 2135.

[10] A. Le Touzé, *Petite Chronique Familiale*, VI: 44.

[11] Boutle, *Journal Spirituel*, 2134–35.

[12] A. Le Touzé, *Petite Chronique Familiale*, VI: 44.

[13] Boutle, *Journal Spirituel*, 2040–42.

[14] Ibid., 2143.

[15] Ibid., 2160.

[16] Ibid., 2162.

[17] Ibid., 2170–71; cf. Poulain, *Journal Spirituel*, 437.

[18] A. Le Touzé, *Petite Chronique Familiale*, VI: 45.

[19] Boutle, *Journal Spirituel*, 2172–73.

[20] Ibid., 2212–13.

[21] Ibid., 2214.

[22] Ibid., 2219.

[23] Ibid., 2226–27.

[24] Ibid., 2230; Poulain, *Journal Spirituel*, 446.

[25] Boutle, *Journal Spirituel*, 2231

[26] Ibid.; Cf. chapter 4 above.

[27] A. Le Touzé, *Petite Chronique Familiale*, VI: 45–48

[28] Poulain, *Journal Spirituel*, 446.

[29] Boutle, *Journal Spirituel*, 1900.

[30] Ibid., 2243–44, 2250–51; cf. Poulain, *Journal Spirituel*, 446.

[31] Boutle, *Journal Spirituel*, 2251–52; Poulain, *Journal Spirituel*, 447–48.

[32] Boutle, *Journal Spirituel*, 2259–60.

[33] Ibid., 1590–91; Poulain, *Journal Spirituel*, 391.

[34] Boutle, *Journal Spirituel*, 2261; Poulain, *Journal Spirituel*, 448.

[35] Boutle, *Journal Spirituel*, 2263; Poulain, *Journal Spirituel*, 448.

[36] Gibson, *A Social History of French Catholicism*, 230–31; Boutle, *Journal Spirituel*, 230–31.

[37] Boutle, *Journal Spirituel*, 2281–83.

[38] A. Le Touzé, *Petite Chronique Familiale*, VI: 65; Boutle, *Journal Spirituel*, 2261–62.

[39] Boutle, *Journal Spirituel*, 2263.

[40] Ibid., 2285, 2287; cf. Poulain, *Journal Spirituel*, 452.

[41] Boutle, *Journal Spirituel*, 2292–93; Poulain, *Journal Spirituel*, 452–53.

[42] Boutle, *Journal Spirituel*, 2295; cf. Poulain, *Journal Spirituel*,, 454.

[43] Boutle, *Journal Spirituel*, 2296.

[44] Ibid., 2302.

[45] Ibid., 2303–4; Poulain, *Journal Spirituel*, 455–56.

[46] Boutle, *Journal Spirituel*, 2308–9.

[47] Ibid., 2309–11.

[48] Boutle, *Journal Spirituel*, 2314–16; Poulain, *Journal Spirituel*, 457–58.

[49] Boutle, *Journal Spirituel*, 2326–27; cf. *Semaine Religieuse du diocese d'Evreux*, 175.

[50] Boutle, *Journal Spirituel*, 2336–37; Poulain, *Journal Spirituel*, 458–59.

[51] Boutle, *Journal Spirituel*, 2338–39; Poulain, *Journal Spirituel*, 459–60.

[52] McManners, *Church and State in France*, xxi.

[53] Gibson, *A Social History of French Catholicism*, 129.

[54] Boutle, *Journal Spirituel*, 2341; Poulain, *Journal Spirituel*, 460.

[55] Boutle, *Journal Spirituel*, 2364; Poulain, *Journal Spirituel*, 463.

[56] Boutle, *Journal Spirituel*, 2342; Poulain, *Journal Spirituel*, 460.

[57] Boutle, *Journal Spirituel*, 2344–45.

[58] Ibid., 2346–48; Poulain, *Journal Spirituel*, 461.

[59] Boutle, *Journal Spirituel*, 2355.

[60] Poulain, *Journal Spirituel*, 35.

[61] Ibid., 461.

[62] Boutle, *Journal Spirituel*, 2360.

[63] Ibid., 2362; Poulain, *Journal Spirituel*, 461–62.

[64] McManners, *Church and State in France*, xxii.

[65] Boutle, *Journal Spirituel*, 2368–69; Poulain, *Journal Spirituel*, 464.

[66] Cf. A. Le Touzé, *Petite Chronique Familiale*, VI: 65.

[67] Boutle, *Journal Spirituel*, 2370; Poulain, *Journal Spirituel*, 464.

[68] Boutle, *Journal Spirituel*, 2371–72; cf. Poulain, *Journal Spirituel*, 464.

[69] Boutle, *Journal Spirituel*, 2378.

[70] Ibid., 2377–2378.

[71] Ibid., 2381; Poulain, *Journal Spirituel*, 466.

[72] Boutle, *Journal Spirituel*, 2383–84.

[73] Ibid., 2385; Poulain, *Journal Spirituel*, 467.

[74] Boutle, *Journal Spirituel*, 2885–86; Poulain, *Journal Spirituel*, 467.

[75] Poulain, *Journal Spirituel*, 469.

[76] A. Le Touzé, *Petite Chronique Familiale*, VI: 75–76.

[77] Boutle, *Journal Spirituel*, 2388.

[78] Ibid., 2390.

[79] Ibid., 2390–91; Poulain, *Journal Spirituel*, 469.

[80] A. Le Touzé, *Petite Chronique Familiale*, VI: 76–79.

[81] Boutle, *Journal Spirituel*, 2391–92.

[82] Ibid., 2393; Poulain, *Journal Spirituel*, 470.

[83] Boutle, *Journal Spirituel*, 2393; Poulain, *Journal Spirituel*, 471.

[84] Boutle, *Journal Spirituel*, 2393–94.

[85] Ibid., 2394; Poulain, *Journal Spirituel*, 471.

[86] Boutle, *Journal Spirituel*, 2395.

[87] Ibid., 2395; Poulain, *Journal Spirituel*, 471.

[88] Poulain, *Journal Spirituel*, 15–16.

[89] A. Le Touzé, *Petite Chronique Familiale*, VI: 76–77.

[90] Poulain, *Journal Spirituel*, 297; A. Le Touzé, *Petite Chronique Familiale*, V: 106.

[91] Boutle, *Journal Spirituel*, 800.

[92] Ibid., 2217; cf. Poulain, *Journal Spirituel*, 451.

[93] Savigny-Vesco, *Lucie-Christine*, 49.

[94] Poulain, *Journal Spirituel*, 367; cf. O'Brien, preface, in Poulain, 9.

[95] Savigny-Vesco, *Lucie-Christine*, 49.

Afterword

[1] Underhill, *Mystics of the Church*, 244.

[2] Wenner, "Lucie Christine," in *Dictionnaire*, 9: Columns 1129–30.

[3] Sr. Marie-Jacques, S.G., letter to Reverend Philip Sandstrom, 1988.

[4] Windeatt, *The Book of Margery Kempe*.

[5] Guardini, *Lucie Christine, Geistliches Tagebuch*, introduction.

[6] Zahn, "Review of *Lucie Christine, Geistliches Tagebuch*," *Theologische Revue* 3/4, 44–45.

[7] A. Le Touzé, *Petite Chronique Familiale*, V: 77–78.

BIBLIOGRAPHY

American Psychiatric Association. *Diagnostic and Statistical Manual of Mental Disorders* (4th ed). Washington, DC: American Psychiatric Association, 2000.

Ayral-Clause, O. *Camille Claudel: A Life*. New York: Harry N. Abrams, 2002.

Bougaud, Msgr. *St. Chantal and the Foundation of the Visitation*. New York: Benziger Brothers, 1895.

Boutle, M. *Journal Spirituel*. Unpublished spiritual journal. Archives Adoration Réparatrice, 1870–1908.

Burrows, R. *Essence of Prayer*. Mahwah, NJ: Hidden Spring, 2006.

Charle, C. *The Social History of France in the Nineteenth Century*. Providence, RI: Berg, 1994.

Cochois, P. *Bérulle et l'École Française*. Paris: Seuil, 1963.

Dansette, A. *Religious History of Modern France*. Vols. 1 and 2. New York: Herder & Herder, 1961.

De Grandmaison, G. *Un Curé de Paris: Monsieur de Cabanoux*. Paris: La

Société Bibliographique, 1927.

Demolombe, C. *Traité de l'adoption et de la Tutelle officieuse de la Puissance Paternelle* (4th ed). Paris: Auguste Durand and L. Hachette, 1869.

Devèze, L. *A Brief Guide to French History*. Carcassonne, France: G. Caste. 1984.

DeVille, R. *The French School of Spirituality*. Trans. A. Cunningham. Pittsburg, PA: Duquesne, 1994.

D'Hulst, M. *Vie de la Vénérable Marie-Térèse du Coeur de Jésus*. Paris: J. de Gigord, 1935.

Dubouché, T., (Mother Marie Thérèse). *A People for Worship in Spirit and in Truth*. Paris: Adoration Réparatrice, 1851–60.

———.*Walk on the Waters: Letters on Self-Abandonment*. Trans. C. Maddalena. Antrim, Ireland: Bethlehem Abbey Press, no date.

Dupre, L. K. "Jansenism and Quietism." Pp. 121–42 in Dupre, L. K., and D. E. Saliers, ed., *Christian Spirituality III: Post-Reformation and Modern*. New York: Crossroads. 1996.

———, and J. A. Wiseman, ed. *Light from Light: An Anthology of Christian Mysticism*. Mahwah, NJ: Paulist Press, 1988.

Frankl, V. *Man's Search for Meaning*. Trans. I. Lasch. Boston: Beacon, 2006.

Garrigou-Lagrange, R. *The Three Ages of Interior Life: Prelude of Eternal Life*. Rockford, IL: Tan Books, 1989.

Gibson, R. *A Social History of French Catholicism, 1789–1914*. London: Routledge, 1989.

Grace, M. M. *Adoration & Reparation: Life of Mother Marie-Thérèse, Foundress of the Family of Adoration*. Antrim, Ireland: Bethlehem

Abbey Press, no date.

Grom, B. "Ich sprach zu dir, ohn' alle worte": die mystikerin Lucie Christine (1844–1908). *Geist und Leben* 81 (March–April 2008): 112–24.

Guardini, R., trans. *Lucie Christine, Geistliches Tagebuch*. Dusseldorf, Germany: Schwann, 1921.

Hardon, J., ed. *Modern Catholic Dictionary*. Bardstown, KY: Eternal Life, 1999.

Horne, A. *Seven Ages of Paris*. New York: Vintage, 2004.

Johnson, E. A. *Quest for the Living God*. New York: Continuum, 2007.

Jonas, R. *France and the Cult of the Sacred Heart*. Berkeley: University of California Press, 2000.

Kerns, V., trans. Francis de Sales, *Treatise on the Love of God*. Westminster, MD: Newman Press, 1962.

King, M. L., and A. Rabil Jr., series eds. In Pascal, J. *A Rule for Children and Other Writings*. Ed. and trans. John J. Conley. Chicago: University of Chicago Press, 2003.

Kselman, T. A. *Miracles and Prophecies in Nineteenth-Century France*. New Brunswick, NJ: Rutgers University Press, 1983.

Lanier, D. *Absinthe: The Cocaine of the Nineteenth Century*. Jefferson, NC: McFarland, 1995.

Lanzetta, B. *Radical Wisdom: A Feminist Mystical Theology*. Minneapolis, MN: Fortress, 2005.

Leconte, L.-C. *Souvenirs d'une Amie*. Paris: René Haton, 1891.

Lemoyne, G. B. *The Biographical Memoirs of Saint John Bosco*, vol. 1. Trans. D. Borgatello,. New Rochelle, NY: Salesiana Publications,

1966.

Le Touzé, A. *Petite Chronique Familiale*. Volumes V, VI, and VIII. Unpublished family history, 1990–2000.

Le Touzé, Y. Letter in Archives of Adoration Réparatrice Mother House, Paris, no date.

Maritain, J. *Notebooks*. Trans. J. Evans. Albany, NY: Magi, 1984.

Maritain, R. *Raïssa's Journal*. Albany, NY: Magi, 1947.

Matthew, I. *The Impact of God: Soundings from John of the Cross*. London: Hodder & Stoughton, 1995.

McManners, J. *Church and State in France, 1870–1914*. New York: Harper & Row, 1973.

Nevin, T. R. *Thérèse of Lisieux: God's Gentle Warrior*. New York: Oxford University Press, 2006.

O'Brien, A. "Contemplation along the Roads of the World." In A. W. Astell, ed., *Lay Sanctity, Medieval and Modern: A Search for Models*. Notre Dame, IN: University of Notre Dame Press: 2000, 147–60.

————. "Lucie Christine: Nineteenth-Century Wife, Mother, and Mystic." In Sister Paula Jean Miller, ed. *Mapping the Catholic Cultural Landscape*. New York, Rowman & Littlefield: 2004, 145–56.

————. "Preface." In Poulain, A., ed., *Journal Spirituel de Lucie Christine*. Paris: Téqui, 1999.

O'Connell, M. R. *Blaise Pascal: Reasons of the Heart*. Grand Rapis, MI: Eerdmans 1997.

Parry, D. L. L., and P. Girard. *France since 1800: Squaring the Hexagon*. New York: Oxford University Press, 2002.

Petroff, E. A. *Body and Soul: Essays on Medieval Women and Mysticism.* New York: Oxford University Press, 1994.

Polart, M.-M. *L'Adoration au coeur de la ville.* Paris: Médiaspaul, 1988.

Poulain, A. *The Graces of Interior Prayer.* Trans. L. L. Yorke-Smith. London: Routledge & Kegan Paul, 1950.

———. *Revelations and Visions: Discerning the True and the Certain from the False or the Doubtful.* New York: Alba House, 1998.

———. ed. *Journal Spirituel de Lucie Christine, 1870–1908.* Paris: Téqui, 1999.

———. *The Spiritual Journal of Lucie Christine.* St. Louis, MO: B. Herder, 1920.

Price, R. *A Social History of Nineteenth-Century France.* New York: Holms & Meier, 1987.

Ruysbroeck, St. Jean of. *The Adornment of Spiritual Marriage.* 1293–1381. Retrieved 30 June 2009 from http://www.ccel.org/ccel/ruysbroeck/adornment.html.

Ryan, F., and J. E. Rybolt, eds. *Vincent de Paul and Louise de Marillac: Rules, Conferences, and Writings.* Mahwah, NJ: Paulist Press, 1995.

Savigny-Vesco, M. *Lucie-Christine: L'Ostensoir sous le Voile.* Paris: Tournai, 1948.

Semaine Religieuse du diocese d'Evreux. 1908.

Sheldrake, P. *A Brief History of Spirituality.* Malden, MA: Blackwell, 2007.

Short, D. "Answers about Alcohol: Poison or Panacea." *University of Alabama at Birmingham Magazine* 21 (2001):1.

Stevens, C. *The One Year Book of Saints.* Huntington, IN: Our Sunday Visitor, 1989.

Strayer, J., et al. *The Mainstream of Civilization*. New York: Harcourt, Brace, 1969.

Teresa of Avila, *The Interior Castle*. K. Kavanaugh and O. Rodriguez, trans. New York:Paulist Press, 1979.

Thomas à Kempis. *The Imitation of Christ.* New York: Random House, 1998.

Thompson, W. M., ed. *Bérulle and the French School: Selected Writings.* Trans. Lowell M. Glendon. Mahwah, NJ: Paulist Press, 1989.

Underhill, E. *Mysticism*. New York: E. P. Dutton, 1911.

———. *Mystics of the Church*. New York: Schocken, 1964.

Une Mère Chrétienne. Lyon: Eugène Mercier, no date.

Vanauken, S. *A Severe Mercy*. New York: Harper & Row, 1977.

Wenner, F. "Lucie Christine." In *Dictionnaire de spiritualité ascétique et mystique. Doctrine et histoire*. Ed. M. Viller, et al. Paris: Beauchesne, 1976.

Windeatt, B., trans. Kempe, M. *The Book of Margery Kempe*. London: Penguin, 1994.

Wright, W. M. *Heart Speaks to Heart*. New York: Orbis, 2004.

Zahn, J. "Review of *Lucie Christine, Geistliches Tagebuch*." *Theologische Revue* 3:4 (1923): 44–45.